lectionary worship workbook

PLANNING IDEAS AND RESOURCES FOR THE ENTIRE CHURCH YEAR
CYCLE C GOSPEL TEXTS

wayne h. keller

HOW TO MAKE SEASONAL WORSHIP BANNERS
AN APPENDIX BY WARREN S. SATTERLEE II

C.S.S. Publishing Co., Inc.
Lima, Ohio

Dedication

*To all who have celebrated
the Good News with me.*

*You are my inspiration
for this book.*

LECTIONARY WORSHIP WORKBOOK C

Copyright © 1988 by
The C.S.S. Publishing Company, Inc.
Lima, Ohio

You may copy the material in this publication if you are the original purchaser, for use as it was intended (worship material for worship use; educational material for classroom use; dramatic material for staging and production). No additional permission is required from the publisher for such copying by the original purchaser only. Inquiries should be addressed to: The C.S.S. Publishing Company, Inc., 628 South Main Street, Lima, Ohio 45804.

Library of Congress Cataloging-in-Publication Data

Keller, Wayne H., 1930-
   Lectionary worship workbook.

   Appendix: how to make worship banners / Warren S. Satterlee II.
   Contents: — C. A planning resource for use with common, Lutheran, and Roman Catholic lectionaries.
   1. Public worship — Handbooks, manuals, etc. 2. Church pennants. I. Satterlee, Warren S., 1946- II. Title.
BV25.K44 1988   264   88-14536

ISBN: 978-1-55673-066-5   PRINTED IN U.S.A.

Table of Contents

Editor's Introduction 5
A Word About Lectionaries 6
Acknowledgments 7
Why I Created This Worship Resource (A word from the author) 8
Preface 9
Foreword 10
About the Author 11

The Season of Advent 13
    Advent 1 17
    Advent 2 21
    Advent 3 25
    Advent 4 28

The Season of Christmas 33
    The Nativity of Our Lord 35
    Christmas 1 39
    Christmas 2 43

The Season of Epiphany (Ordinary Time) 47
    The Epiphany of Our Lord (January 6) 50
    The Baptism of Our Lord (Epiphany 1) 53
    Epiphany 2 • Ordinary Time 2 56
    Epiphany 3 • Ordinary Time 3 60
    Epiphany 4 • Ordinary Time 4 64
    Epiphany 5 • Ordinary Time 5 67
    Epiphany 6 • Ordinary Time 6 70
    Epiphany 7 • Ordinary Time 7 74
    Epiphany 8 • Ordinary Time 8 78
    The Transfiguration of Our Lord 82

The Season of Lent 87
    Ash Wednesday 89
    Lent 1 90
    Lent 2 94
    Lent 3 97
    Lent 4 101
    Lent 5 104
    Sunday of the Passion (Palm Sunday) 109
    Palm Sunday (Sunday of the Passion) 113
    Maundy Thursday 116
    Good Friday 121

The Season of Easter 125
    The Resurrection of Our Lord 127
    Easter 2 131
    Easter 3 135
    Easter 4 138
    Easter 5 141
    Easter 6 145
    The Ascension of Our Lord 149
    Easter 7 152
    The Day of Pentecost 155

The Sundays after Pentecost

Part I. *How We Are Called to New Life in Christ* 161
    The Holy Trinity 164
    Understanding the Lectionary 167
    Corpus Christi (Roman Catholic only) 169
    Proper 4 • Pentecost 2 • Ordinary Time 9 171
    Proper 5 • Pentecost 3 • Ordinary Time 10 174
    Proper 6 • Pentecost 4 • Ordinary Time 11 177
    Proper 7 • Pentecost 5 • Ordinary Time 12 180

Part II. *Living in Our New Life in Christ* 185
    Proper 8 • Pentecost 6 • Ordinary Time 13 187
    Proper 9 • Pentecost 7 • Ordinary Time 14 190
    Proper 10 • Pentecost 8 • Ordinary Time 15 193
    Proper 11 • Pentecost 9 • Ordinary Time 16 197
    Proper 12 • Pentecost 10 • Ordinary Time 17 200
    Proper 13 • Pentecost 11 • Ordinary Time 18 203
    Proper 14 • Pentecost 12 • Ordinary Time 19 206

Part III. *Sharing Christ's Love With Others* 209
    Proper 15 • Pentecost 13 • Ordinary Time 20 211
    Proper 16 • Pentecost 14 • Ordinary Time 21 214
    Proper 17 • Pentecost 15 • Ordinary Time 22 218
    Proper 18 • Pentecost 16 • Ordinary Time 23 222
    Proper 19 • Pentecost 17 • Ordinary Time 24 226
    Proper 20 • Pentecost 18 • Ordinary Time 25 230
    Proper 21 • Pentecost 19 • Ordinary Time 26 233

Part IV. *Preparing for Christ's Return and the Judgment* 237
    Proper 22 • Pentecost 20 • Ordinary Time 27 239
    Proper 23 • Pentecost 21 • Ordinary Time 28 242
    Proper 24 • Pentecost 22 • Ordinary Time 29 246
    Proper 25 • Pentecost 23 • Ordinary Time 30 250
    Proper 26 • Pentecost 24 • Ordinary Time 31 253
    Proper 27 • Pentecost 25 • Ordinary Time 32 256
    Proper 28 • Pentecost 26 • Ordinary Time 33 259
    Pentecost 27 (Lutheran only) 262
    Christ the King 266
    Reformation Sunday (Lutheran only) 269
    All Saints' Day / All Saints' Sunday 272
    Thanksgiving Eve / Thanksgiving Day 276

Appendix — *How to Make Worship Banners* 279
    Warren S. Satterlee II

Editor's Introduction

The material in this workbook was assembled by a Christian pastor and worship planner. He happens to be Presbyterian, but his prods, suggestions, fresh beginnings and new directions will prove salutary for Christians of all backgrounds.

Your own parish may follow a fixed and formal liturgy. If this is the case, you will find in this resource ideas for enriching that liturgical experience, particularly at points where you and your worship planning team begin to sense that worshipers are "going to sleep with their eyes open." On occasion you may decide to depart from the formal liturgy altogether and plan the day's experience around suggestions in this workbook, adapted appropriately to your own needs.

If your worship tradition is one which already assumes a free style, this book will prove a gold mine of new and workable ideas. Use as many or as few of them as seem helpful to you at any time. Use the material in this book sparingly in one season and generously in another. Or, make this resource your guidebook for every-Sunday planning.

The themes in this resource are based on the three-year lectionary. While Lutherans, Roman Catholics, and Protestants follow variations of this three-year A-B-C cycle, the Gospel readings for each Sunday are almost identical across all three lectionaries. It is this series of Gospel pericopes which have been used as anchors here, to provide Sunday-to-Sunday unity and continuity.

The present volume resources material for Sundays in Cycle C. Companion volumes for Cycles A and B will appear in subsequent years.

One final note: this *Lectionary Worship Workbook* does not provide more than rudimentary suggestions for lectionary preaching. For help in this area we suggest you consult any or all of three series of the *Lectionary Preaching Workbook,* all available from C.S.S. Publishing Company. The authors of those three series are (by chronology of issue) Dr. John R. Brokhoff, Dr. Perry H. Biddle Jr., and Dr. George M. Bass.

A Word About Lectionaries

This planning resource is designed for use with any of three popular Christian lectionaries, namely the Lutheran, Common, and Roman Catholic. While First Lesson, Psalm, and Second Lesson texts may vary among the three lectionaries, sometimes significantly, the Gospel texts are virtually identical. There are, however, some peculiarities to which the user of this *Workbook* will want to be alert.

1. The short Christmas Season is followed by the longer Epiphany Season, the first day of which, The Epiphany of Our Lord, is celebrated only on 6 January (or, in congregations where worship only occurs on a Sunday, only when 6 January falls on a Sunday). When 6 January occurs on a week day, Epiphany 1 will always be observed on the next Sunday following this day.

2. The seven Sundays following Epiphany 1 are designated, for Lutheran and Common lectionary users, as "Epiphany 2-8." The identical Sundays are designated "Sundays in Ordinary Time 2-8" in the Roman Catholic lectionary. Roman Catholics do not observe the Transfiguration of Our Lord as the last Sunday in the Epiphany Season, as do users of the Lutheran and Common lectionaries.

3. The Thursday before Easter 7 may be observed as Ascension Day. For congregations in which worship only occurs on Sundays, Easter 7 may instead be observed as Ascension Sunday.

4. The Sunday following The Holy Trinity (the beginning of the "Sundays after Pentecost") is observed as Pentecost 2 in the Lutheran and Common lectionaries. The Gospel reading for that and following Sundays may not be identical, however, for these two lectionaries. A table on page 167 explains how the texts are assigned during the second half of the church year. In the Roman Catholic lectionary this Sunday following The Holy Trinity is observed as Corpus Christi.

5. For users of the Lutheran lectionary, the last Sunday in October may be observed as Reformation Sunday. When this occurs, the Pentecost text for the Sunday that would otherwise have been observed on that day is dropped.

6. The first Sunday in November may be observed in the Lutheran and Common lectionaries as All Saints' Sunday. When this occurs, the Pentecost text for the Sunday that would otherwise have occurred on that day is dropped. In the Roman Catholic lectionary, All Saints' Day is only observed when 1 November falls on a Sunday, in which case the texts for the Sunday in Ordinary Time that would otherwise have been used on the first Sunday in November are dropped.

7. Unlike Advent, Christmas, Lent, and Easter, the season of Epiphany and the Sundays after Pentecost vary in length from year to year. There may be as many as eight Sundays after the Epiphany, but ordinarily there are fewer. The longer the Epiphany Season in any church year, the correspondingly fewer Sundays there will be after Pentecost. Conversely, when Epiphany shrinks, the number of Sundays after Pentecost expand. The determination as to which season expands and which contracts is made by the assignment of Easter (which then fixes the day for Ash Wednesday and, therefore, the length of the Epiphany Season).

Acknowledgments

For over thirty years I have collected worship material from a multitude of sources. Though I have created many of the resources in this *Workbook,* I have also included stimulating ideas, suggestions, quotations — some original, some revised — the creators of many of which I no longer know.

Where material appears which deserves a credit, but for which I no longer know (or have never discovered) the source, I have indicated "author or source unknown" (or "a.u."). I do not wish to receive credit for the originality of others, even though I cannot identify them. For that reason I wish to apologize at the outset to those who may recognize their material here, but who do not find a suitable credit line included.

Because the publisher anticipates a long shelf-life for this three-year resource, I invite purchasers of this *Workbook* to write to me and indicate sources which they may recognize, which I may fail to credit, so that in future printings we may give credit where it is due.

The following sources are quoted in the *Workbook* with permission:

Seasons and Symbols: A Handbook on the Church Year, by Robert Wetzler and Helen Huntington, 1962, Augsburg Publishing House, Box 1209, Minneapolis, Minnesota 55440.

Presbyterian Worship, by Donald MacLeod 1980 edition, revised, John Knox Press, 341 Ponce de Leon Avenue NE, Atlanta, Georgia 30356. [This volume is now out of print.]

Excerpts from *The Cotton Patch Version of Paul's Epistles* (1968), *The Cotton Patch Version of Luke and Acts* (1969), *The Cotton Patch Version of Matthew and John* (1970), and *The Cotton Patch Version of Hebrews and the General Epistles* (1973), all by Clarence Jordan, are reprinted with permission of the publisher, New Century Publishers, Piscataway, New Jersey. Copyright for the first two in the series is assigned to Clarence Jordan, the last two in the series to Florence Jordan.

Wayne H. Keller

Why I Created This Worship Resource

Several years ago, *Life Magazine,* and others, referred to 11:00 a.m. Sunday morning worship as the most segregated hour of the week. For many, however, Sunday worship has become the most *boring* hour of the week. And why not! Many view worship as a spectator sport, in which congregations compete for members who pick and choose what suits their fancy. Much worship has become I-centered. "What can I get from it for me and my family? And if my church doesn't produce what I want, I'll go elsewhere."

We should allow no spectators in worship. God calls the congregation to celebrate — sometimes silently, sometimes loudly, sometimes casually, sometimes formally — with heart, spirit, strength, and mind. Worship, as celebration, leads to life as celebration, amidst joy, sadness, fear, confusion, anger. Celebration involves comforting and confronting. I consider the liturgy as the work — and the play — of the people. Worship, at its best, celebrates every dimension of life, every aspect of existence.

Wayne H. Keller

Preface

Here is a book for the busy pastor! It is both practical and stimulating. The material can be used just as it is presented. There are enough down-to-earth suggestions to last a long time. However, it has a value beyond its immediate use. It will stimulate thought, get the creative juices flowing. When one considers all the possibilities that Wayne Keller has presented here, he or she will not be content just to use them. They practically demand that we begin to give the same kind of imaginative thought to the ordering of worship. This is a keeper!

> Don Keller
> Pastor, First Presbyterian Church
> Aberdeen, Washington

Foreword

The Lectionary Worship Workbook by Wayne Keller is a very good thing to own. Every page has some exciting and stimulating and interesting and fun things for those planning or thinking about worship. There are a number of really nice surprises, for example, the congregational quizzes and litanies. For those who try his ideas it is essential to have pencils and possibly paper in the pews — and that's not a bad idea in itself. We do it for the children; now we have a reason for doing it for adults.

                                                Donald S. Marsh
                                                Richard Avery
                                                Proclamation Productions, Inc.
                                                Port Jervis, New York

About the Author

A church officer in the Presbyterian Church once introduced me as a person who has led "a checkered life." After checking the dictionary, I agree with him.

I'm fortunate to exist. My mother weighed two pounds at birth; her parents kept her alive by placing her in a cigar box which they put in the oven of the old wood stove. During my first twenty years, I rattled between atheism and agnosticism. After a variety of dramatic experiences, I became a Christian at age twenty, and decided to enter seminary at the same time.

From my earliest seminary days, I had a particular interest in worship as celebration, drama, play. I have seen people bored to death in worship, seemingly because they come to worship as spectators, not as participants. Soren Kierkegaard's analogy of worship as drama has guided my thinking and planning. Dick Avery, Don Marsh, and Doug Adams have prepared the way for me through their stimulating approach to worship. My son, when a teenager, said that even though he didn't always agree with me, he was never bored in worship. My interest has opened opportunities for me to lead workshops and seminars in the states of Washington and Oregon.

My life took on new dimensions when I served for two and one-half years as director of a halfway house for chronically mentally ill adults and a year and a half in a private counseling practice, before returning to the pastorate in an interim ministry. During my four-year absence from parish ministry, I worked mostly with people outside of the institutional church — and discovered their reasons for avoiding the body of Christ.

I believe that my approach to the liturgy — which I define as the work and play of the people — invites and encourages people who have been turned off to much worship to give it another try.

In my present pastorate, I have developed an exciting, innovative, challenging order of worship which centers around Isaiah 6:1-8, the call of Isaiah. I take seriously every part of the worship, including the quotations at the beginning and at the end of the order of worship; and I give people the freedom to speak during any part of the worship experience in order to keep the lines of communication open, and to keep misunderstanding at a minimum.

I like what I do and am grateful for the opportunity to share these ideas, some borrowed, some original, with others.

Wayne H. Keller

THE SEASON OF ADVENT

Advent, the Season of Expectancy

The church regulates its church year, not by the civil or astronomical calendar, but by the events in the life of Jesus the Christ, the Son of Righteousness and Salvation. The church year, therefore, begins with Advent, the season of preparation for the celebration of the Incarnation of the Son of God. Since the seventh century, the Western church has begun Advent on the Sunday closest to the Feast of Saint Andrew, ending it on the Sunday before Christmas Day, a period of four weeks.

Blue is the color for Advent. It is the color of royalty, suggesting the righteous rule of Christ as King of kings and Lord of lords. In the endless cycle of the year, Advent is both the beginning and the ending — directing Christian meditation and worship toward the appearance of God among people in the person of Jesus of Nazareth; but following the Sundays after Pentecost, it also points persons to that future coming of Christ at the end of time when his righteous rule will encompass the world.

The custom of the Advent wreath, with its four candles, comes to us from Europe, and gains in popularity each year. It may be included in worship, the church school, the youth fellowship, or most fittingly, as a family activity around the dinner table. It is good to encourage such activity in our homes, for we are surrounded on all sides by the commercialization of the holiday season, and need positive help to regain or retain its biblical meaning.

THE SUNDAYS IN ADVENT

Familiarity breeds contempt. We've heard the Advent message so often, we may no longer hear it. To get worshipers to listen, hear, and respond to the Good News requires solid, innovative planning, without making innovation for innovation's sake a new god. Advent is no exception. What do people expect, what do people need, when they come to another Advent?

The Bulletin

Suggestion:

A. Use the bulletin, including the cover, symbols, and colors, as an educational tool. Make every aspect of it a creative adventure. Include a symbol to identify each Sunday's theme, as for example, the Sundays of Advent in Cycle C, as follows: (1) Readiness, (2) Promise, (3) Wonder, (4) Fulfilment. Use an Advent wreath to emphasize the same themes.

B. Use the bulletin, also, to open the congregation to the world-wide Body of Christ. Many bulletins focus only on the local congregation, and have no universal outreach. Present an introductory statement which includes all the people as a world-wide community of faith, hope, and love, as for example:

The Church of Jesus Christ
Meets Occasionally at (this address)
And Scatters Usually around the County, State, Nation, World.
We Celebrate the Season of Expectancy
Even Though We Already Know the Outcome.

The Advent Wreath

Consider this:

Ask different families to light the wreath and review the theme. Do not limit yourself to biological families. Put widows with someone else's children. Put a divorcee with a family with children. Ask the youth fellowship as a group. Include a family of father, mother, children.

Be sure to have them use the microphone; they will think that the congregation hears when it does not.

To prepare for, and to reinforce, what happens on Sunday, develop an Advent booklet for home use. Perhaps a group within the congregation would be willing to produce one.

Various Parts of the Order of Worship

Try this:

Vary the headings for the parts of the worship for each season of the church year. For Advent, consider these:

```
WORSHIP THROUGH SOLITUDE
WORSHIP THROUGH ADORATION
WORSHIP THROUGH INTROSPECTION
         CONFESSION
         FORGIVENESS
WORSHIP THROUGH INSPIRATION
WORSHIP THROUGH MEDITATION
WORSHIP THROUGH CONSECRATION
```

1. Include a statement at the beginning and end of the order of worship which focuses on, and summarizes, the theme for the day.

2. Include the Scriptures for the following Sunday. Ask the people to read them, and to pray for the hearing and the doing of the Word.

THE SEASON OF EXPECTANCY

ADVENT 1

Liturgical Color: Purple/Blue

Gospel: Luke 21:25-36

Theme: Judgment — "We do not break God's Law; we only break ourselves on God's Law."

Pastoral Invitation to the Celebration: *Getting the People's Attention*

Planning Notes

Suggestion: Avery and Marsh's "Hey, Hey, Anybody Listening?" (copyright 1967, *The Avery and Marsh Songbook*) will get people to sit up and take notice, maybe even startle a few. Use this all four Sundays of Advent, adding additional voices and instruments each week.

Hymns of Advent

Try this:

1. A visual display of the back of Mary and Joseph, to emphasize Advent rather than Christmas.

2. Be aware that some people will complain. However, usually by Christmas Day, we've heard the Christmas carols *ad infinitum*. Use the carols during Christmastide and Epiphany. Many of them are usable both seasons.

Confession *(Recognizing Who We Are)* and Forgiveness *(Receiving New Life)*

Consider this: Deal with the theme of waiting — our impatience with others and our expectation that others will remain patient with us — and the value-judgments we place on others while excusing ourselves. Use several people from the congregation to do this without words.

Ask: "What do you suppose would happen if we waited on God in meditation and prayer, and then took the initiative to go to those from whom we are alienated, including those sitting in the sanctuary with us today, even as God took the initiative to pursue us while we were still alienated"?

Try this: Give a 3" by 5" card that folds over, with a seal. People write the name of someone who has hurt them, or whom they have hurt, seal the card, put their own name on outside. Cards are kept at church, to be returned each week and reopened. Person makes out a new card if becoming reconciled. If not reconciled, use same person the next week.

Message to the Children of All Ages

Consider this: Include and invite the "child" in the adults also to participate, by

Planning Notes

coming forward to sit with the younger children. Focus both on Advent as "coming" and what it means in the children's lives. For example: "Come here! Come along! Hurry up!"; and upon judgment, both in its harsh interpretation and in the biblical sense of teaching.

Compare harsh punishment with sensitive correcting. Consider the statement, in child's language, "We never break God's law; we only break ourselves on God's law." The law stands no matter what we do with it.

Responding to What We Believe

One congregation does this:

1. Focus on announcements as opportunities. Consider this: Use this printed statement in the bulletin; "The Church in the World: Life, Work, Ministry of this Congregation."

2. Stewardship thought. Use humor often. For example:
You've heard the injunction, "Give 'til it hurts." That's not biblical. You may have heard the remark, "Give 'til it heals." That's a little closer to the biblical idea. You may not have heard, "Give until you enjoy it!" That's biblical. God loves a cheerful giver. The biblical word is "hilarious." I invite us to give hilariously; because that's how God gives to us.

THE SCATTERING

Charge to the Congregation

Try this: Bring together the whole worship experience into one succinct statement. For example: Judgment does not mean that God hates us. God disciplines (teaches) because of love. We rejoice that God loves so much that we cannot break God's law. We rejoice that God loves us enough to take the judgment in order to reconcile us and to bring us wholeness.

One Congregation does this every week:

The pastor prints a meditation at the end of the order of worship which captures the worship theme in one statement, which reminds people of worship throughout the week. Some people will save the statements for their own notebook.

For example: "God's love (agape) never changes. Against all who oppose God, God expresses love in wrath and judgment. In this same love, God took upon Self, judgment and death in Jesus Christ to bring us to repentance, liberation, and new life." (a.u., revised)

Planning for Your Congregation

Suggestions   Your Situation

I. Other Scriptures   *Lay readers:*

- Psalm 25:1-10, 14
- Jeremiah 33:14-16
- 1 Thessalonians 3:9—4:2

II. Hymn Possibilities   *Hymn selections:*

(Use Advent hymns, not Christmas carols)
"Come, Thou Long-Expected Jesus"
   (Advent hymn of the month)
"O Come, O Come, Emmanuel"
   (soloist, sing first stanza; congregation, sing others)

III. Other Music Possibilities   *Music selections:*

Choral Invitation:
   "Hey, Hey, Anybody Listening?"   Avery and Marsh
   (Proclamation Productions, Inc., Orange Square,
   Port Jarvis, New York 12771)
Response after Act of Forgiveness
   "You Are the Lord, Giver of Mercy"
   (Applachian Folk Melody)
Offertory
   "In Questa Tomba Obscura"   Beethoven
   "Good Friend, For Jesus' Sake Forsaken"

IV. Bulletin Cover   *Bulletin design ideas:*

V. Bulletin Symbols

VI. Lighting of the Advent Candles   *Family or person:*

VII. Miscellaneous Details *(Assignments):* _____

- Ushers
- Banners
- Flowers
- Assistant(s) at Holy Communion

- Greeters
- Candlelighters
- Soloists
- Other

THE SEASON OF EXPECTANCY

ADVENT 2

Liturgical Color: Purple/Blue

Gospel: Luke 3:1-6

Theme: Anticipation — Well, what are you waiting for? Our restlessness; God's initiative.

Confession *(Recognizing Our Humanness)*
and Forgiveness *(Receiving New Life)*

Planning Notes

Consider this: Develop some questions around several of our life-time anticipations. For example:

1. A young woman, anticipates that tonight her favorite beau will pop the question.

2. A child excitedly waits for Christmas morning.

3. A man waits for the results of his job interview.

Keep these focused on your own people's anticipations — birth, baptism, school, graduation, job, mate, parenthood, grandparenthood, retirement, death.

Give plenty of time, three minutes of silence, to think and pray.

Message to the Children of All Ages

Try this: Develop the theme around the children's anticipation about Christmas. The mass media and much of the church's program emphasizes a legalistic approach, "Obey your parents . . . you'd better be good . . . you'd better not cry." Distinguish between doing in order to be accepted, and God's gift of unconditional acceptance. Involve them in the conversation about how they see the difference.

Scripture Readings

Consider this: Use different versions, occasionally reading the same passage from several versions. Always distinguish between a translation, a paraphrase, and a transliteration. If you use lay readers, practice with them.

Proclamation of the Word

Try this: Following the sermon, ask the people to sit quietly and to jot down any thoughts, questions, affirmations, or disagreements. Ask them to bring their ideas to God and to discuss them with you.

Planning Notes

Stewardship Challenge

Consider using this quote:

"We've heard about the rich, young ruler and his obviously wrong choice. However, no matter how much wealth he had, he could not ride in a car, have surgery, turn on a light, buy penicillin, wash dishes in running water, fly in a plane, sleep on an innerspring mattress, or talk on the phone. If he was rich, what am I?"

Charge to the Congregation

One paster did this:

The charge was developed around the brief conversation in Samuel Beckett's drama, *Waiting for Godot,* the scene between Vladimar and Estrogen, who sit around waiting for Godot to come, and all the while Godot is present, and they don't know it.

Meditation at the End of the Order of Worship

Consider this: "If someone were to ask us, 'What is your greatest expectation?' how would we answer?" Or, write your own thought and sign your name after it. You may even get quoted at a future worship service.

Planning for Your Congregation

Suggestions | Your Situation

I. Other Scriptures   *Lay readers:*

- Psalm 126
- Malachi 3:1-4
- Baruch 5:1-9
- Philippians 1:3-11

(Perhaps the choir can find music for one of the Scriptures.)

II. Hymn Possibilities   *Hymn selections:*

"Come, Thou Long-Expected Jesus"
Charles Wesley, 1744
Try this: Use the above hymn of the month; Provide brief history each week, something additional each time.

"Lift Up Your Heads, You Mighty Gates"
Georg Weissel, 1642. Translated by Catherine Winkworth, 1855; altered.
Point out the qualities of prayer and commitment suggested in the hymn.

III. Other Music Possibilities   *Music selections:*

Prelude (Music for Preparation)
 "Come Now Redeemer"   J. S. Bach
Invitation to the Celebration:
 "Hey, Hey, Anybody Listening?"
 The Avery and Marsh Songbook, Proclamation Productions, Inc., Orange Square, Port Jarvis, New York 12771
Response to the Old Testament
 "This Is the Good News"
 Based on Dakota Indian Melody
 (*The Worshipbook,* Westminster Press).
Postlude (Music for Dismissal)
 Advent Hymns

IV. Bulletin Cover   *Bulletin design ideas:*

V. Bulletin Symbols

VI. Lighting the Advent Candles   *Family or person:*
With brief summary of last week, and brief statement about this week.

VII. Miscellaneous Details *(Assignments):* _____

- Ushers
- Banners
- Flowers
- Assistant(s) at Holy Communion

- Greeters
- Candlelighters
- Soloists
- Other

THE SEASON OF EXPECTANCY

ADVENT 3

Liturgical Color: Purple/Blue

Gospel: Luke 3:7-18

Theme: Yearning — We believe, yet we scarcely dare to believe.

Call to Worship *(Declaration of Joyful Expectation)*

Planning Notes

One congregation used this one (identifying the congregation as ministers — the priesthood of all believers):

Leader: There's a yearning in us too deep for words. There's much we don't understand or even perceive.
People: **There's a yearning to touch the holy in life, to stand for a moment on "holy ground."**
Leader: As we gather in worship this Advent season, we yearn to believe that the universe is held together at the center.
People: **We yearn to believe that there is in the whirling galaxies somewhere to hang our hats and pin our hopes;**
Leader: A yearning that will not rest . . .
People: **A yearning amidst the rat race to be and to stand,**
Leader: A yearning to break through all the walls that divide,
People: **A yearning to shake hands with life and love,**
Leader: A yearning to sing, even amidst tragedy, the praise of life.
People: **We yearn in this Advent season for our sighs to burst into song, cascading through creation, richocheting off of the stars, echoing in human hearts, with joyful amens — to our Creator, Liberator, Sustainer!** (a.u.)

Musical Responses Throughout Worship

Consider this: Integrate the anthem where it, and all music, best fits in the order of worship. There is no such thing as "special music" in corporate worship.

Proclamation of the Word

Consider this:

1. Distinguish between anticipation and yearning.

2. Ask three or four members, in advance, to identify a time in their lives when the results of their yearning were too good *not* to be true.

Planning Notes

Stewardship Challenge

Try this: "Some people who give the Lord credit are reluctant to give him cash." (Jack Herbert)

Suggestion: Occasionally, print the prayers of dedication in the bulletin, so people will have a reminder during the week.

Meditation

Paul Scherer *(Love Is A Spendthrift)* traces the wrod "Hope" through the Scripture. Study how it shines forth in the Psalms, and how it (the noun) does not appear in the Gospel (because there is no need for it).

Planning for Your Congregation

Suggestions   Your Situation

I. **Other Scriptures**

- Isaiah 12:2-6
- Zephaniah 3:14-20
- Philippians 4:4-13

Lay readers:

II. **Hymn Possibilities**

"Come, Thou Long-Expected Jesus"
"Watchman, Tell Us of the Night"
   (substitute "get" for "hie" in line 3, stanza 3)

Hymn selections:

III. **Other Music Possibilities**
Music for Preparation
   "In Dulce Jubilo"   Karg-Elert
Choral Invitation "Hey, Hey, Anybody Listening?"
   (add a few more instruments, including hand instruments for the choir)
Offertory
   "In Dulce Jubilo"   Dupre
Music for Dismissal   Advent Hymns

Music selections:

IV. **Bulletin Cover**

Bulletin design ideas:

V. **Bulletin Symbols**

VI. **Lighting the Advent Candles**
(Summary of last two; statement about this week.)

Family or person:

VII. **Miscellaneous Details** *(Assignments):* _____

- Ushers
- Greeters
- Banners
- Candlelighters
- Flowers
- Soloists
- Assistant(s) at Holy Communion
- Other

THE SEASON OF EXPECTANCY
ADVENT 4

Liturgical Color: Purple/Blue

Gospel: Luke 1:39-55

Theme: Fulfilment — What God has done to recreate Christmas: Christmas without the Cross is not Christmas.

Planning Notes

Recognizing Who We Are

One congregation used this poem by Claire Whitaker Soule as the confession of sin:

[1 = First Reader; 2 = Second Reader]

1. "Now, it came to pass in those days, there went out a decree . . .
2. *"Look at what we offer you this year! A doll that cries real tears.*
1. Wrapped in swaddling clothes and lying in a . . .
2. *Six room doll house with colonial furniture and satin drapes,*
1. Because there was no room for them in the inn . . .
2. *And a quick-trigger gun so you can outshoot your friends . . .*
1. And on earth, peace among humans . . .
2. *Don't let your child be disappointed . . .*
1. And they were sore afraid . . .
2. *Hundreds of children were on hand to greet Santa when he arrived by helicopter today . . .*
1. And they fell down and worshiped him . . .
2. *Parents! Make Christmas a day to be remembered by giving your children . . .*
1. Good tidings of great joy . . .
2. *Don't wait! The supply is limited . . .*
1. And they said to one another, let us now go even to . . .
2. *The big toy department. Only $29.95.*
1. And they offered gifts, gold and frankincense . . .
2. *And stuff and nonsense . . .*
1. And all that heard it wondered at the things which were spoken to them by the
2. *Hucksters."*

Claire Whitaker Soule
(Used by permission from *The Christian Century.*)

Message to the Children of All Ages

Try this: Bring some beautifully wrapped presents and then enact the typical Christmas morning scene. Tear off the ribbons, rip open the packages, toss the paper in every direction. And then ask, with much disappointment, "Is that all there is?" Talk about God's gift that keeps on giving, even when we forget or ignore it.

(*Preparation for next Sunday:* Ask each child to bring one of their new Christmas presents to worship with them.)

Proclamation of the Word

Consider this idea:
What have we done to abuse Christmas? Make this more than an harangue about advertising. Get underneath the ads to focus on how we, the church, reflect the culture. Then, deal with the theme about what God has done to re-create Christmas. We easily remember the stable; we dare not forget the Cross.

Stewardship Challenge

A suggested thought-provoker:
"What kind of a gift would we put in the offering plate if we didn't give money?"

Meditation

"Christmas destroys, once and for all time, the notion that God is a mere onlooker of history." (Ernest T. Campbell)

Planning Notes

Planning for Your Congregation

Suggestions	Your Situation

I. Other Scriptures

- Psalm 80:1-7, 15-16, 18-19
- Micah 5:2-5a
- Hebrews 10:5-10

Lay readers:

II. Hymn Possibilities

"Come, Thou Long-Expected Jesus"
    (Advent hymn of the month; *continue telling its history*)
Response to the Sermon
    "Born in the Night, Mary's Child"
                        Geoffrey Ainger, 1964
Response to the Old Testament
    "Lo, a Voice to Heaven Sounding"   Bortiansky
Response of Commitment
    "Once in Royal David's City"
                  Cecil Frances Alexander, 1848, altered

Hymn selections:

III. Other Music Possibilities

Music for Preparation
    "How Beautiful the Morning Star"   Pachelbel
Choral Invitation
    "Hey, Hey, Anybody Listening?" Avery and Marsh

Consider this idea: Choir members give hand instruments to some members of the congregation as they arrive, with brief instruction about how and where to use them. Use as many instruments as possible to let the world hear the announcement of the Savior's birth.

Hymn of Adoration
    "Come, Thou Long-Expected Jesus"
Choral response after Assurance of Pardon
    "Lord, Have Mercy Upon Me"
                          Lutheran Service, 1528
Response to the Old Covenant
    "Lo, A Voice to Heaven Sounding"   Bortiansky
Response to the Sermon
    "Born in the Night, Mary's Child"
Hymn of Commitment
    "Once in Royal David's City"

    Again, a caution: Because of the congregation's pressure, our temptation is to sing Christmas hymns during Advent. To change peoples' thinking and demands requires patience and perseverance. The carols can be used on Christmas Eve and the twelve days of Christmas; many of them are also Epiphany hymns.

Music for Dismissal
    "From Heaven to Earth I Come"   Pachelbel

Music selections:

Suggestions	Your Situation

IV. Bulletin Cover   *Bulletin design ideas:*

V. Bulletin Sumbols

VI. Lighting of the Advent Candles   *Family or person:*
    (With brief summary and statement)

VII. Miscellaneous Details *(Assignments):* _____

- Ushers
- Banners
- Flowers
- Assistant(s) at Holy Communion
- Greeters
- Candlelighters
- Soloists
- Other

THE SEASON OF

CHRISTMAS

Christmastide, the Season of the Nativity

"Who has seen me has seen the Father..." (John 14:9)

The most popular of all the Christian festivals is the season of Christmas. Its removal would create a tremendous vacuum in our religious and cultural life. The name itself, a contraction of the phrase, "Christ Mass," did not become general until the twelfth century, although other earlier designations, such as the Feast of the Nativity, did appear.

It may contain either one or two Sundays, depending on the day of the week upon which Christmas falls. Its message focuses on the word "Incarnation," which comes from the Latin *care* (flesh) and of *Immanuel* (God with us).

As a specific festival, Christmas was unknown in the church for the first two centuries of the Christian era. This occurred because during the spread of Christianity, the church emphasized the ministry and mission of Christ climaxed by his death and resurrection. In addition, during those early years, Christians regarded birthday celebrations as pagan. Actually, Christmas developed from a pagan festival celebrating the birth of the sun-god. On the first day of winter, the shortest day of the year, the sun-god is said to have had a "rebirth." From that day on, the length of the sun's appearance increases each day. In our times, the day falls on December 21. However, in the fourth century, it occurred on December 25. At that time, Julius I (Bishop of Rome, A.D. 337-352) was Pope. Saint Chrysostom reported that Julius was probably responsible for establishing December 25 as Christ's birthday.

We need to celebrate the birth of Jesus along with his death and resurrection, so that we do not sentimentalize the Christmas season.

(Consider using this information for the weekly bulletin during Christmastide; our people need to recall and to remember their history.)

THE SEASON OF THE NATIVITY

THE NATIVITY OF OUR LORD

Liturgical Color: White

Gospel: John 1:1-18

Theme: Birth of the world's savior; a theme which anticipates Jesus' crucifixion and resurrection.

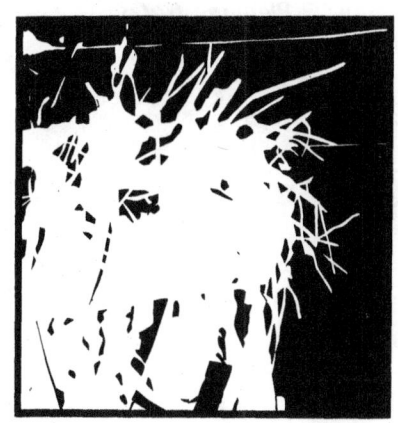

Pastoral Invitation to the Celebration

Consider this: Begin with a summary of Advent; themes shared when lighting the Advent Candles. *(Include the theme of each in the bulletin.)*

Choral Invitation to the Celebration

Try this: Before the choir sings the invitation, ask the people to reflect about how the Christ has come, is coming, and will come to them through this service and beyond.

Second Pastoral Invitation

Suggestion: Invite the congregation to share in this birthday party by greeting one another.

Prayer of Praise

One pastor* wrote this prayer:

Well, God, it's happening again — another Christmas, and we bring to you a jumble of thoughts and feelings . . .

. . . *memories* caught on film or in the heart — the squeals of children, the glance that speaks more than thanks, the warmth that cannot be attributed to the fireplace alone;

. . . *relief* — it was a lot of work for some of us, so much that deep down there is a bit of gladness that we made it through to today in one piece;

. . . *surprise* — that we still have some capacity for wonder, surprise that we made it here [tonight/today];

. . . *gratitude* for the gifts — most especially for the gifts that are wrapped up and all too often concealed in those around us;

. . . *regret* — for the feelings and words that didn't get out, for some that did, for some that we wish hadn't been there in the first place;

. . . *apprehension* — that the winds and routine of January are not far off, that the lovely interlude will be over soon.

Lord, we use this time to sort these feelings and thoughts out, to gift them, to clear away the jumble and see what this Christmas business is all about.

. . . You've come again to be born in us.

Planning Notes

Planning Notes

. . . Forgive us if there hasn't been much room.

. . . Forgive us to let your love into the main house, to open all the doors, and find our common life, even without tinsel and greens . . . something to celebrate. Amen

*John Lynn Carr, address unknown

A Celebration of Scriptures and Carols
(revise for your personal use)

(Section IV on the planning page provides resources for this section.)

Meditation

Consider this theme: "The Christmas Question"

One pastor always includes the themes of crucifixion and resurrection. Here is one idea:

    I. the joys of a birth
    II. the pain of a death
    III. the victory of a tomb

The great Christmas question is not so much what we think about the little baby in Bethlehem's manger, but rather, what that strange and noble figure outside of Jerusalem thinks about us.

Ceremony of Candlelighting

Suggested Procedure: (Caution — Check with state and local authorities about lighting individual candles.)

1. Pastor — describes the mechanics of candlelighting.
2. Anthem as candles are lit: "No Candle Was There or No Fire" Lehmann
3. Silence for one minute after candles are lit.
4. Pastoral Prayer — Bring together the expectancy of Advent,
   the joy of Christmas,
   the pain of Good Friday,
   the victory of Easter,
   the power of Pentecost,
       in order to avoid sentimentalizing the season, and to present the whole gospel, in order to challenge the body of Christ.

Charge to the Congregation

One pastor did this:

Comments centered on the remarks, "If only I had been there . . . How quick I would have been to help the baby . . . We can do it now. We have Christ in our neighbor." *(Idea stimulated by Martin Luther.)*

Planning for Your Congregation

Suggestions	Your Situation
I. Other Scriptures	*Lay readers:*

- Psalm 97
- Psalm 98
- Isaiah 52:7-10
- Hebrews 1:1-12

Try this: Ask someone to develop his/her own tune for the Psalm(s) if it is your custom to sing them.

II. Carol Possibilities   *Carol selections:*

Processional Music —
"O Come, All You Faithful,"
Latin, eighteenth century

Suggestion: If the congregation has banners, let them precede the choir into the sanctuary. If you have none, invite some people, perhaps retired folk, to make them. See appendix for some ideas.

Recessional Music —
"Joy to the World"
Choir and banner-bearers recess to narthex.

III. Other Music Possibilities   *Music selections:*

Music for Preparation
"The Trumpet Tune"   Purcell
Choral Invitation
"O Come, O Come, Emmanuel"
Latin, twelfth century
Choral Response after Benediction
"Seven-Fold Amen"
Music for Dismissal
"Swiss Noel"   Daquin

IV. A Celebration of Scriptures and Carols
(revise as appropriate for your use)

Scripture	Isaiah 40:1-5
Carol	"Watchman, Tell Us of the Night"
	Stanzas 1, 2
Scripture	Micah 5:2-4
Violin-Cello Duet	"He Shall Feed His Flock"
	Handel
Scripture	Luke 2:15
Carol	"O Little Town of Bethlehem"
	Stanzas 1, 2
Scripture	Luke 2:1-5
Anthem	"Go, Tell It On the Mountain"
	George Lynn

Suggestions

Your Situation

Scripture	Luke 2:6-7
Children's Carol	"Away in the Manger"
Scripture	Luke 2:8-9
Anthem	"While Shepherds Were Watching"
	David Williams
Scripture	Luke 2:10-14
Carol	"Angels from the Realms of Glory"
	All
Scripture	Luke 2:15-20
Anthem	"The Shepherd's Carol"
	William Billings
Scripture	Selected from Matthew 2
Carol	"We Three Kings of Orient Are"
	Stanzas 1, 2, 3

V. Bulletin Cover *Bulletin design ideas:*

VI. Bulletin Symbols

VII. Lighting the Advent candles and Christ candle *Family or person:*

VIII. Miscellaneous Details *(Assignments):*

- Ushers
- Banners
- Flowers
- Assistant(s) at Holy Communion

- Greeters
- Candlelighters
- Soloists
- Other

THE SEASON OF THE NATIVITY

CHRISTMAS 1

Liturgical Color: White

Gospel: Luke 2:41-52

Theme: The Humanity of Jesus. "If you want to know what God is like, take a snapshot of Jesus Christ." (a.u.)

Bulletin Heading

Suggestion: Revise the heading to reflect the particular season of the church year, as for example,

> The Church of Jesus Christ
> Gathers at this Address,
> occasionally,
> To Celebrate Corporately the Birth of Christ
> as we learn how to receive Christ's love
> and to share his love
> with the world which God loves unconditionally.

Pastoral Invitation

Consider this: One pastor developed the invitation around the idea that if Christmas is now over, then it never really began.

Invitation to the Celebration

Suggestion: The Scripture tells us that every congregation has many ministers, the priesthood of all believers, and usually one, two, or three pastors. Encourage the people to see themselves as ministers, rather than as pastor's helper. In printed responses, write P for pastor and M for ministers (the people).

Hymns for the Christmas Season

Consider this:

1. Instead of always using "Hymn of Praise or Adoration," change the wording to fit the season. Never use the words "opening or closing hymn." (That's obvious.)

2. Vary the singing procedure occasionally.
    All — sing stanza 1 (not "verse," verse is used with poetry.)
    Men, stanza 2
    Women, stanza 3
    All, stanza 4
        Invite the people to read the words when not singing.

Planning Notes

Planning Notes

Confession *(Recognizing Who We Are)*

Try this for Reflection:

1. Bring as much of the world as possible into the sanctuary, in order to help people to be "in but not of the world."

2. Popular songs are useful because they express the human condition clearly and concisely. Select one whose words speak meaningfully for this moment in this service.

Assurance *(Receiving New Life)*

Follow up from Confession:
Remind the congregation of the truth that we have more similarities than differences as humans. Christ came for all. Christ calls us to minister to all, beginning with those in our own homes.

Message to the Children of All Ages

Try this: Ask the children *(see note last week)* to bring something they received for Christmas. Talk about how important it was, how he/she anticipated, yearned about, wanted it. Ask them to think about how long they thought and talked about wanting it. Compare the peoples' immediate response to Jesus with their later response. They got what they thought they wanted more than anything else in the world; but when they got it, they didn't like it. And no matter how the people of Jesus' day, or we, respond, God keeps giving God's favorite gift, the gift of love.

Stewardship Challenge

Suggestion: Develop idea about this: If God loves the world and calls the church to minister to the world, what part of the world will we think about and pray about this coming week? Invite the people to do some reading about that part of the world.

Next week, during worship, ask for some feedback.

Meditation

The Christmas good news is a part *of* life, (all of it), not apart *from* life.

Planning for Your Congregation

Suggestions | Your Situation

I. Other Scriptures *Lay readers:*

- Psalm 111
- Psalm 128:1-5
- 1 Samuel 2:18-20, 26
- Jeremiah 31:10-13
- Sirach 3:2-6, 12-14
- Colossians 3:12-21
- Hebrews 2:10-13

II. Hymn Possibilities *Hymn selections:*

Hymn for Christmas Season
  "Joy to the World"
            Isaac Watts, 1719 (with trumpets)
Response to the Good News
  "Where Cross the Crowded Ways of Life"
       Frank Mason North, 1903, alterted 1972
       (replace the sexist language as you ask the people to consider Jesus' humanity)
Hymn of Commitment
  "Angels from the Realms of Glory"

III. Other Music Possibilities *Music selections:*

Choral Invitation
  "Break Forth, O Beauteous Heavenly Light"
                                              Bach
Music for Preparation
  "Sinfonia to the Christmas Oratorio"   Bach
Recognizing Who We Are
  "Within You, Without You"
       George Harrison (Beatles), copyright 1967, Northern Songs, Ltd., 71-75 New Oxford St., London W. C. 1, England
Choral Response after Benediction
  "O God, Who By a Star Did Guide"
                       John Mason Neale, 1842
Music for Dismissal
  "In Dulci Jubilo"   Dupre

IV. Bulletin Cover *Bulletin design ideas:*

V. Bulletin Symbols

VI. Trumpeteers

VII. Miscellaneous Details *(Assignments):* _____

- Ushers
- Banners
- Flowers
- Assistant(s) at Holy Communion

- Greeters
- Candlelighters
- Soloists
- Other

THE SEASON OF THE NATIVITY

CHRISTMAS 2

Liturgical Color: White

Gospel: Luke 2:15-21, John 1:1-18

Theme: Christmas is not merely for children. Christmas is not so much about a baby in a manger, but about the God-man on earth, on a cross.

Invitation to the Celebration of the Christmas Message

Planning Notes

Suggested: (Ministers respond with "Alleluia" after each statement by the pastor. Vary the loudness and tempo.)

Pastor: Christ is born!
Pastor: Christ is alive!
Pastor: Gladness is mine!
Pastor: Gladness is yours!
Pastor: Gladness is ours!
Pastor: Shout to the Lord with thanks!
Pastor: Sing to the Lord with joy!
Pastor: Speak to the Lord with hope!
Pastor: Glorious things God has done for us, and to us, and with us, and through us!

Act of Confession and Forgiveness
(Recognizing Who We Are)

If you haven't done this try it:
  "Where Have All the Flowers Gone"
    Pete Seeger (copyright 1961, Fall River Music, Inc.)
  Soloist: sing moderately slowly, with dignity.

Act of Receiving New Life *(pardon)*

Follow the confession with this:
  "Pass it On"
    Words/Music by Kurt Kaiser (copyright 1969, Lexicon Music, Inc.)
  Congregation/choir sing with much enthusiasm

The pastor needs to introduce the theme and purpose of this music as illustrative of the human condition and the divine response.

Message to the Children of All Ages

Consider this: Put or keep a Christmas tree in the chancel and talk about the twelve days of Christmas. God's gift keeps giving year after year. Ask: what are some ways that you can keep giving God's gift to others?

Planning Notes

Proclamation of the Word

Try this: To stimulate dialog, use as your theme that Christmas is not merely for children. Christmas is not so much about a baby in a manger, but about the God-man on earth, on a cross.

Perhaps you will want to use this outline:

    I. Everyone wondered
   II. Mary pondered
  III. Jesus grew

Invite the people to write down questions and concerns about the message; or, invite verbal responses during the sermon; or, have a discussion following the benediction.

Stewardship Challenge

Try this: Include a page from your denomination's mission yearbook in each bulletin. Ask the congregation to read it during the offering. Then, ask two or three people to give a thirty-second synopsis of what they read.

Meditation

"On the basis of the eternal will of God, we have to think of every human being, even the oddest, most villainous or miserable, as one to whom Jesus Christ is a Brother and God is Father [Mother]; and we have to deal with him [her] on that assumption." Karl Barth (source unknown/bracketed material inserted by WHK).

Planning for Your Congregation

Suggestions   Your Situation

I. Other Scriptures   *Lay readers:*

- Psalm 8
- Psalm 67
- Numbers 6:22-27
- Philippians 2:9-13
- Galatians 4:2-3, 4-6, 8

II. Hymn Possibilities   *Hymn selections:*

"Angels, We Have Heard on High"   French Carol
(Use trumpets and piano)
"O Sing a Song of Bethlehem"   Louis Benson
(Before singing, ask the people how they will sing the song of Bethlehem during the week.)

III. Other Music Possibilities   *Music selections:*

Music for Preparation
    Medley of Christmastide Carols
Choral Invitation
    "There's a Song in the Air"   Josiah P. Holland
Response to the Old Testament
    "Break Thou the Bread of Life"   Stanza 2
Choral Response to the Benediction
    "Joy to the World
Music for Dismissal
    "All Glory Be to God on High"   Bach

IV. Bulletin Cover   *Bulletin design ideas:*

V. Bulletin Symbols

VI. Miscellaneous Details *(Assignments):* _____

- Ushers
- Banners
- Flowers
- Assistant(s) at Holy Communion

- Greeters
- Candlelighters
- Soloists
- Other

THE SEASON OF

THE EPIPHANY

Epiphany, the Season of the Evangel

January 6, the beginning of Epiphany, is followed by a season which varies in length, depending on the date of Easter, and continues to Ash Wednesday. The difference, created in the length of the year, is compensated for during the Sundays after Pentecost.

Epiphany, the oldest festival of the church year, originally a pagan festival to the sun-god, was taken over by the Christian Church and packed with new meaning. This pagan festival celebrated the birth of Aeon in the night between January 5 and 6. From that day, the sun appeared longer each day. Eventually, due to errors in measuring time, the first day of winter shifted to an earlier date; but January 6 was retained as the date for this festival.

By the fourth century B.C., the first day of winter occurred on December 25, and a new pagan sun-festival was instituted. Christmas later replaced this latter festival. Both Christmas and Epiphany thus originated from a sun-festival held on the first day of winter. The first day of winter now normally occurs on December 21, but the festivals emerging from previous winter solstices remain as they were.

The word "epiphany" means "to show." In its root form, the word often was used to describe the dawn and the appearances of the gods to people. The word "manifestation" also describes the meaning of Epiphany, which refers to the demonstration of the Glory of God in sending Christ into the world. Until the institution of Christmas in the fourth century A.D., both the birth and baptism of Jesus were commemorated on Epiphany. With the celebration of Christ's birth at Christmas, the Eastern Church (Byzantine) restricted Epiphany to the celebration of Christ's baptism. In the Western Church (Rome), however, Epiphany became associated with the coming of the Wise Men. Because the Wise Men were not Jews, Epiphany's message deals with the manifestation of Christ to the Gentiles. Therefore, the Epiphany season has become a time for emphasis on the church's missionary task.

Two symbols which focus on Epiphany are the Cross and the Crown. The Crown represents the wise men who came to Jesus and his father and mother; and also the Crown proclaims the fact that Christ is the King, not only of Israel, but of all people who put their trust in him for new and eternal life.

The Sundays of Epiphany

During the Epiphany Season, consider a variation on the bulletin heading. Here is one possibility:

The Church of Jesus Christ
meets occasionally at this address
to celebrate
the season of Epiphany
as we learn
to share the Good News of Christ's love
with the world
of
education, recreation, economics,
politics, family, neighborhood,
and all the rest.

Throughout the Sundays of Epiphany, continue to educate the people about the meaning of this season. People know much more about Advent, and Lent than the other extended seasons. Each is unique in its own right and contributes to the wholeness of the Christian life.

Include in the bulletin each week a different symbol of the season, and a brief statement in the bulletin about what it means. As one alternative, consider using the symbols which accompany every Sunday in this *Workbook*. They may be copied and reproduced by the original purchaser of this planning resource, without securing specific prior permission from the publisher. We clergy and worship planners take much for granted about what we think that people know concerning the faith.

THE SEASON OF THE EVANGEL

THE EPIPHANY OF OUR LORD

(January 6)

Liturgical Color: White

Gospel: Matthew 2:1-12

Theme: Discipleship

Planning Notes

Pastoral Invitation to the Celebration

Consider this: In the October, 1980 issue of *In the Worship Workshop,* (published by C.S.S.), Richard Avery and Don Marsh suggest the following emphases for Epiphany:

Mission   Story   Discipleship

For Cycle C, begin with discipleship.

In the pastoral invitation, begin with God's commitment to us in nature, in the history of the Israelites, in the prophets, in the person of Jesus of Nazareth, in the body of Christ from the Resurrection-Pentecost event.

Show the faithfulness of God to us, even when we were not faithful to God.

Act of Recognizing our Humanness and Act of Receiving New Life

Try this: Ask several people, prior to today's worship, to bring some signs to worship, which identify our lack of discipleship: for example, laziness, greed, gossip, misdirected anger, self-righteousness, pouting, etc. Give the congregation sufficient time to look at the signs. Then, ask those holding the signs to offer a sentence prayer of confession for that particular sin.

Following the act of confession, have a soloist sing "Agnus Dei" by Herbert G. Draesel, Jr. Have him/her sing it through once, and ask the people to identify their "favorite" sin. Then, have the soloist sing it again with the people, and ask them to insert their "favorite" sin, in place of the word "sins."

Allow one minute of silence following the song.

Proclamation of the Word

You may want to consider these ideas:

1. Charles Schulz, in his delightful cartoon book, *Young Pillars,* shows a couple teenagers talking about a third, and how the church involved the third one in just about everything going on in the institution, until the congregation "involved him right out of the church."

Many avoid the church for this reason, and of course, blame the church, instead of their unwillingness to say "no."

2. *The Saturday Evening Post,* many years ago, ran a cartoon, in which one primitive man, observing an impressive pagan religious ceremony, says to his friend, "It's impressive, but I find dial-a-prayer more convenient." So do some Christians.
3. You may want to focus, then, on the life of discipleship which includes the following:
    a. living an ordered, not scattered, life.
    b. living a sober, not sour, life.
    c. living a prayerful, not wishful, life.

Stewardship Challenge

Try this: Remind the congregation that it's relatively easy for most of us to give money. Ask: "What would you give today if you didn't give money? How will you live out Christ's discipleship through you this next week?"

Charge to the Congregation

Suggested: Develop the charge around the statement, "To be a Christian is to be in Christ." This means, simply, yet profoundly, to be involved in Christ's continuing work and presence on this earth. This means that we take no detours around anything. To be a Christian involves an ordered, sober, prayerful life. It won't, it can't happen by osmosis, by seepage, by insinuation, by environment, by heredity. It *does* happen by commitment, obedience, dedication to the highest, to the Lord Christ in every sphere of life.

Planning Notes

Planning for Your Congregation

          Suggestions   Your Situation

I. Other Scriptures   *Lay readers:*

- Psalm 72
- Isaiah 60:1-6
- Ephesians 3:1-12

II. Hymn Possibilities   *Hymn selections:*

"O God, Who By a Star Did Guide"
    John Mason Neale, 1842; altered 1972
"O Lord, Whose Gracious Presence Shone"
    Stanzas 1, 2, 4, Marion Franklin Ham, 1912; altered 1972
    Stanza 3, Dalton E. McDonald, 1972
"Without a Star to Follow," and/or "Follow the Star"
    Songs for All Seasons, Richard Avery/Don Marsh, Proclamation Productions, Inc., Port Jervis, New York 12771

III. Other Music Possibilities   *Music selections:*

Music for Preparation   Medley of Epiphany hymns
(Select all music from your hymnbook's selection of Epiphany hymns)
Music for Dismissal   Medley of Epiphany hymns

IV. To encourage alertness at worship, consider not using a bulletin for this worship service.

V. Miscellaneous Details *(Assignments):* _____

- Ushers
- Greeters

- Banners
- Candlelighters

- Flowers
- Soloists

- Assistant(s) at Holy Communion
- Other

THE SEASON OF THE EVANGEL

THE BAPTISM OF OUR LORD

(Epiphany 1)

Liturgical Color: White

Gospel: Luke 3:15-17, 21-22

Theme: The baptism of Jesus as his ordination to mission: our baptism in his name as our ordination to missions.

Epiphany Hymns During Epiphany

Planning Notes

Most will recognize these as Christmas carols. Perhaps if people hear these hymns beyond Advent and Christmas Eve, they will begin to appreciate their being used during the proper church season.

Pastoral Invitation

Try this semi-bold approach:

We have survived the madness, the craziness of Christmas. Perhaps we vowed never to get that busy again. Now that the mass-media and our own internalized messages have toned down a bit, we will take time to integrate who this Christ is, and what kind of people we have become and can become and will become. Let's do that!

Act of Recognizing Our Humanness and Act of Receiving New Life

One pastor/congregation did this:

Think about the people who were missionaries, witnesses to you — those people who helped break down the barriers, those who pulled back the curtains, to reveal the Christ to you. Write down the names of those people. Remember how they reached out to you, even when you didn't seem to care, even when you said "no" and put them to the test, even when you insisted, "I prefer to run my own life without you, without God." (Give several minutes for people to do this.) Then, during the week, send these people a thank-you letter. Sometimes, a letter is better than a phone call, because they have something to see.

Receiving New Life *(Pardon)*

Try this as a follow-up to the confession:

Give the people an opportunity to offer verbal prayers of thanks for the witnesses they have identified.

Planning Notes

Message to the Children of All Ages

(If possible, coordinate this Sunday with the baptism of infants.)

Suggested: Invite the children to sit in the chancel before the parents and infants came forward, in order to show them the baptismal font, and discuss their own baptism. Talk about your denomination's understanding. Emphasize the difference between sacrament and dedication.

If children leave the sanctuary after the message to the children, use Avery and Marsh's "Passed Thru the Waters," (copyright 1971, *The Avery and Marsh Songbook).*

Proclamation of the Word

Possible Approach: Call attention to the sacrament as God's taking the initiative and our responding with thanks.

Response to the Proclamation

Try this: Repeat "Passed Thru the Waters." Perhaps it will have greater significance the second time.

Church in the World

One Congregation Does This:

Routine announcements are referred to as "opportunities for the week and month." Never read the printed words, word for word. (Some worship leaders have taken ten to fifteen minutes for this part of the worship service!)

Charge to the Congregation

Suggested: If we have been ordained (baptized), we share Christ's message, whether we want to or not, whether we are conscious of our witness or not. People see us and make their value-judgment, rightly or wrongly, about the faith.

Meditation

The heart of Christianity is not concern for the soul, but concern for the world. (John 3:16)

Planning for Your Congregation

Suggestions　　　　　　　　　　　　　　**Your Situation**

I. Other Scriptures　　　　　　　　　　*Lay readers:*

- Psalm 29
- Psalm 45:7-9
- Isaiah 42:1-7; 61:1-4
- Acts 8:14-17; 10:34-38

II. Hymn Possibilities　　　　　　　　　*Hymn selections:*

"Angels from the Realm of Glory"
　　　　　　　　　　James Montgomery
　(Epiphany Hymn of the Month)
　Use a variety of instruments
"Go, Tell It On the Mountain"　　Negro Spiritual

　　　　　　　　　　　　　　　　　　　　Music selections:

III. Other Music Possibilities

Music for Preparation
　Medley of Epiphany hymns
Choral Invitation
　"O God, Who By a Star Did Guide"
　　　　　　　　　John Mason Neale
Response to the Old Testament
　"Come, O Thou God of Grace,"　Stanza 3
　　　　　　　　William E. Evans, 1886
Choral Response to the Benediction
　Chorus only, "Go, Tell It on the Mountain"

　　　　　　　　　　　　　　　　　　　Bulletin design ideas:

IV. Bulletin Cover

V. Bulletin Symbols

VI. Miscellaneous Details *(Assignments):* _____

• Ushers	• Banners	• Flowers	• Assistant(s) at Holy Communion
• Greeters	• Candlelighters	• Soloists	• Other

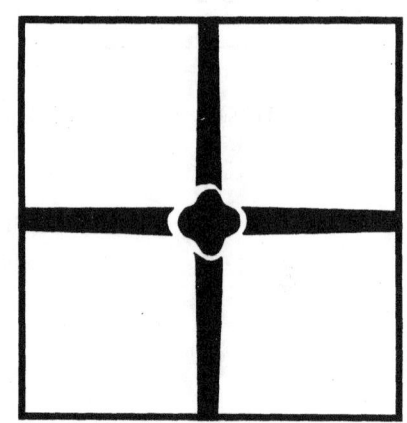

THE SEASON OF THE EVANGEL

EPIPHANY 2
(Common, Lutheran)

ORDINARY TIME 2
(Roman Catholic)

Liturgical Color: Green/White

Gospel: John 2:1-12

Theme: Miracle or Magic — Jesus was no David Copperfield. "Miracles are not in contradiction to nature. They are only in contradiction with what we know about nature." (Saint Augustine, 354-430)

Planning Notes

Pastoral Invitation

Suggestion: Develop the call around the question, "Why do we celebrate corporately?" and then, offer the response, "To let the life of the Spirit and of each other strengthen us, and to let the rest of the world know who we are."

Hymns of Epiphany

Consider this: Use hymns from the Epiphany section of the hymn book. If Epiphany hymns are not listed as such, check out another hymn book. For example, *The Worshipbook,* published by Westminster Press.

Recognizing our Humanness *(Confession)*

Consider the use of "I" rather than "we" for the prayer of confession. For example, "O God, I remember my broken vows, my selfish ambitions, and some of my failures in the life of the Spirit. According to your grace, remember me. Pardon my offenses, the following in particular [*silent prayer of confession*]. And now, inspire me to do justly, and love mercy, and walk humbly with You.

Pastor: God, grant us your grace.
People: Lord, Give us your peace.

Children's Message for the Children of All Ages

Try this: Distinguish between magic and miracle. Check to see if they know the difference between the magic of TV, as for example, the Road Runner or The Transformers, and the miracle of breathing, seeing, hearing. Perhaps, use a magician to perform several magical tricks, and the reason for doing so. (Maybe he/she would divulge the secret of one.) Then talk about the reason that Jesus performed miracles — not to entertain, but to heal.

Proclamation of the Word

Consider this: Following the pattern of the children's message, distinguish between miracle and magic.

    I. Describe the ways in which people have looked at miracles —
1. as proof of revelation;
2. that all are explainable by natural law;
3. as developments in psychosomatic medicine;
4. that there are no "absolute" laws, only statistical probabilities.

    II. Distinguish between "proofs" and "signs."
Jesus mighty acts and God's mighty acts in the Old Testament are called "signs." In the Bible, a "sign" is any event which points people to God.

Meditation
(To be printed after the order of worship)

"If you try to annihilate their gods, they'll kill you."
(The Big Valley TV Program)

Planning for Your Congregation

Suggestions

I. Other Scriptures

- Psalm 36:5-10
- Psalm 96:1-3, 7-10
- Isaiah 62:1-5
- 1 Corinthians 12:1-11

II. Hymn Possibilities

"Angels from the Realms of Glory"
James Montgomery

(Epiphany hymn for the first half of Epiphany)
"All My Heart Today Rejoices"
Johann Ebeling, 1666

(Point out Jesus as the greatest miracle before the congregation sings.)

III. Other Music Possibilities

Processional and Recessional Music
   Epiphany hymns
   (Continue to educate the people to the fact that many hymns sung during Advent are actually Christmas and Epiphany hymns.)
Response to the Proclamation
   "Good News"   Jane Marshall
   (Focus again on the miracle of Jesus' birth)
Offertory
   "The Hour of Utmost Need"   Bach
Choral Response to the Benediction   Chorus Only
   "Go, Tell it on the Mountain"

IV. Bulletin Cover

V. Bulletin Symbols

Your Situation

Lay readers:

Hymn selections:

Music selections:

Bulletin design ideas:

VI. Miscellaneous Details *(Assignments):* _____

- Ushers
- Banners
- Flowers
- Assistant(s) at Holy Communion

- Greeters
- Candlelighters
- Soloists
- Other

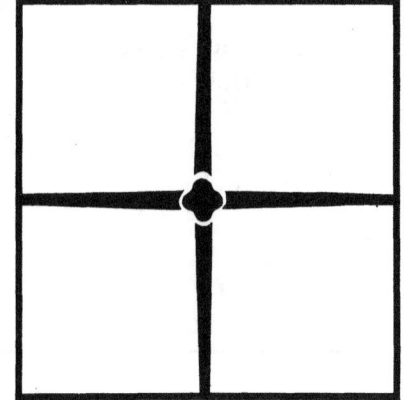

THE SEASON OF THE EVANGEL

EPIPHANY 3
ORDINARY TIME 3

Liturgical Color: Green/White

Gospel: Luke 1:1-4; 4:14-21

Theme: The mission of Jesus and the church's mission; for his mission is ours.

Planning Notes

Choral Invitation to the Celebration

(Choir and Congregation sing acapella — make up the tune as you proceed; or have the choir sing and congregation read)

Try this:

Choir: Come, come with open hearts and lives.
Congregation: O Lord, we come.
Choir: Come into community, communion with one another and with God.
Congregation: O Lord, we come.
Choir: Come then, awake, aware hearts and hopes waiting.
Congregation: O Lord, we come.
Choir: Come to meet the reality of today and the vision of tomorrow.
Congregation: O Lord, we come.

(author unknown, revised)

Continue this as a follow-up:

Ask: What are we doing here today? What do we expect to happen because we have come, because we have responded to God's invitation? Are we expecting a one-dimensional response — that is, "What can I get out of this celebration?"; or a multi-dimensional response — that is, "Not only what will I receive, but will I have the courage to share what I will receive?" Worship is always a two-way street — what we receive and what we give.

Recognizing Who We Are and Whose We Are

Pastor's invitation (consider this introduction):

Christ never stops coming to us, for Christ comes to us in the events and experiences of our daily lives.
- Are we on the lookout for him, or, are we primarily looking out for ourselves?
- Are we ready to respond to the Christ where we are and with whom we are?

Possible follow up to the confession: *Planning Notes*

[P = Pastor; M = Ministers]

P. If we forget that you, O God, created the earth and all that is in it,
M. Forgive us, O Lord. *Choir: Amen*
P. If through carelessness, selfishness, or ignorance, we waste precious resources,
M. Forgive us, O Lord. *Choir: Amen*
P. If we seek from the earth only personal gain and material wealth,
M. Forgive us, O Lord. *Choir: Amen*
P. If we fail to declare with our lips and our lives that all thanks belong to you,
M. Forgive us, O Lord, and make us grateful for your merciful goodness.
 Choir: Amen
P. O God, in your presence, we believe that your forgiveness has been granted to us. We thank you for the prospect of the harvest of love, joy, faith, and peace in our hearts, because of your forgiveness to us, and because of our forgiveness of each other. *Choir: Amen*

(a.u., revised)

Message to the Children of All Ages

Try This: Bring a doghouse into the chancel. Ask the children to talk about "doghouse," both for a dog, and for someone in the home that feels as though he/she deserves to be "in the doghouse." Sometimes, father says, "I'm in the doghouse with your mother." For children, the doghouse is sometimes their own bedroom when mother says, "Go to your room!" Review Robert Short's book, *The Parables of Peanuts,* which suggests that the church/tabernacle is a doghouse, a gathering of people, including children, who don't always feel good about themselves, and who get into trouble, who are mixed up and scared and even get angry. We may find ourselves "in the doghouse," only to discover that we've really found a home. God and God's people love us even when we're not loveable.

Proclamation of the Word

Suggested Development:

Theme: The mission of Jesus.
 I. Describe Jesus' struggle to discover his mission, his fear in the struggle, and his power having discovered his mission.
 II. Compare our struggle with Jesus' struggle, and the necessity of leaving our own secure Egypt for the necessity of our own Exodus.

Consider this (as a follow-up for the sermon):

In silence, ask the people to consider their mission, how they live it out, and how they back off from it. Review the Scripture. Ask people to make a silent commitment to discover and fulfil Christ's ministry through them as individuals and as members of a congregation. Possibly conclude with this prayer: "Forgive us, Lord, for our cowardliness; Empower us for your ministry."

Planning Notes

Stewardship Challenge

Highlight a specific ministry of the local congregation, and of the denomination in another country.

Here is a Suggestion:

Prayer of Dedication

"Thank You for sending Your missionaries to us; send us out of here as Your missionaries to others. Amen"

Charge to the Congregation

Suggestion: "The early Christians were persecuted, not because of what they believed, but because of what they actually practiced." (a.u.)

We have received God's power to transform the status-quo, interpersonal relationships, the abuses of life. So let's be about God's business.

Printed meditation

For the bulletin:
"The most radical and urgent task of our time is to prepare people for eventual refusals to obey."

(Father Regamy, French Roman Catholic Priest)

Planning for Your Congregation

Suggestions

I. Other Scriptures

- Psalm 19:7-15; 113
- Nehemiah 8:1-4a, 5-6, 8-10
- Isaiah 61:1-6
- 1 Corinthians 12:12-30

II. Hymn Possibilities

"Angels from the Realms of Glory"
                                          James Montgomery
   (Epiphany hymn for the first half)
"Clap Your Hands"   Ray Repp
   (Text and music copyright 1966 by F. E. L. Church Pub., Ltd. *The original text has been updated to eliminate sexist language.*)

III. Other Music Possibilities

Music for Preparation
    "Pastorale"   Milhaud
Response to the Old Testament   Choir
   "Songs of Immortal Praise"   Theron Kirk
Offertory
   "How Brightly Shines the Morning Star" Pachelbel
Choral Response following Benediction Chorus only
   "Go, Tell it on the Mountain"
Music for Dismissal   Epiphany Hymns

IV. Bulletin Cover

V. Bulletin Symbols

VI. Miscellaneous Details *(Assignments):* _____

- Ushers
- Banners
- Flowers
- Assistant(s) at Holy Communion

- Greeters
- Candlelighters
- Soloists
- Other

Your Situation

Lay readers:

Hymn selections:

Music selections:

Bulletin design ideas:

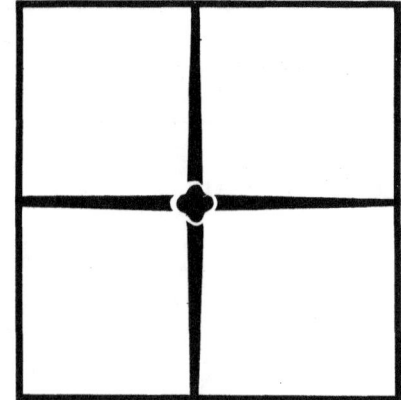

THE SEASON OF THE EVANGEL

EPIPHANY 4
ORDINARY TIME 4

Liturgical Color: Green/White

Gospel: Luke 4:21-30

Theme: The clash between Jesus' and the peoples' understanding of his mission.

Planning Notes

Choral Invitation to the Celebration

Try this: Use Luke 4:18-19. Have the choir choose its own tune; make certain that the congregation knows that what is sung represents the words of Jesus.

Follow with this: "Did you hear the words of the choral invitation? What did you hear? What do they mean to you in your daily walk? How do they make a difference in your celebration of the presence of God? Now, listen once more to the choral invitation. (Have the choir sing it again.)

Recognizing Who We Are and Whose We Are
(confession and assurance)

Consider developing this segment around the hymn, *"There's a Wideness in God's Mercy"*

Introduce the confession with silence.

Leader: Yours, God, is the greatness and the power and the glory and the beauty. Yours is the loveliness of this new day. You are the One certainty amidst all the changes and chances of life. You are the vital, throbbing reality — towering above the false and faltering dreams *we* try to grasp.
(Moments of silence, so that our thoughts may expand to a greater awareness of the majesty and might of God — even as a telescope is adjusted to vaster skies.)

Response: *(Leader speaks sentence; congregation repeats)*
We celebrate your presence. We bless you. We lift our lives in gratitude to you.

Leader: You who made the mighty cluster of stars have also made our hearts to seek you. You who rule over the destiny of nations and empires rule also over the tenderest hopes and destinies of our inmost aspirations.
(silence)

Response: *(repeat after leader)* **We seek You. We still our thoughts that your will may be made known to us.**

Hymn: "There's a Wideness in God's Mercy." *(remain seated)* Before singing, ask the people,
  1. How would you visualize the hymn?
  2. Do so if you wish, either with your imagination or with your body.

Leader: "Those who wait upon the Lord shall renew their strength; they shall mount up with wings as eagles; they shall run and not be weary; they shall walk and not faint." (RSV)

Response: "Awake My Heart"   Adult Choir

Message to the Children of All Ages

Jesus said things that some people didn't like — at all! Part of this had to do with the fact that he grew up in the community as did the other little boys, but then went away for awhile, came back, and spoke some things people didn't want to hear. People said, "Who does this fellow think he is anyway!" Compare our going away and returning years later. People would think, "What can little Johnny or Sally teach us about life or ourselves? We remember them when they were just children." I decided not to become a pastor in my home congregation after graduating from seminary for that reason. Sometimes, even people we know (parents, relatives, friends) think that we're too young, naive, stupid, little. We feel sad when that happens. So did Jesus. Yet, he kept saying what he believed God wanted him to say.

Response to the Proclamation of the Word

One pastor does this occasionally:

Ask the congregation to sit in silence for a few minutes to jot down any of their concerns about this passage. Provide an opportunity, if possible, to discuss them following worship.

Stewardship Challenge

Try this: Develop the challenge around the question, "Do we give only when we agree with the pastor?"

Charge to the Congregation

Suggested: Summarize the worship experience (always) in one, brief, succinct statement. For example, "The purpose of life is not 'to be happy,' but to *make a difference,* even when we seem alone, forsaken by our family and friends."

Planning Notes

Planning for Your Congregation

Suggestions   Your Situation

I. Other Scriptures   *Lay readers:*

- Psalm 71:1-6, 15-17
- Jeremiah 1:4-10, 17-19
- 1 Corinthians 12:27—13:13

II. Hymn Possibilities   *Hymn selections:*

"Angels from the Realms of Glory"
    (for first half of Epiphany)
"Brightest and Best of the Sons of the Morning"
(change "sons" to "ones")
    Reginald Heber, 1811, altered 1972

III. Other Music Possibilities   *Music selections:*

Music for Preparation
    "Carillon"   Bach
Offertory
    "The Old Year Now Has Passed"   Bach
Response to the Old Testament
    "Awake My Heart"   Marshall
Choral Response following benediction
    "Christ is the World's True Light"
    George Briggs 1931, altered 1972
    (Replace the sexist language)

IV. Bulletin Cover   *Bulletin design ideas:*

V. Bulletin symbols

VI. Miscellaneous Details *(Assignments):* _____

• Ushers	• Banners	• Flowers	• Assistant(s) at Holy Communion
• Greeters	• Candlelighters	• Soloists	• Other

THE SEASON OF THE EVANGEL

EPIPHANY 5
ORDINARY TIME 5

Liturgical Color: White/Green

Gospel: Luke 5:1-11

Theme: Learning How to Fish

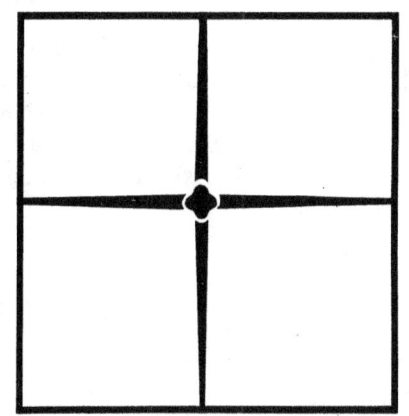

Planning Notes

Pastoral Invitation

Reminder: Keep the birth and life of Christ before the people during the Epiphany season. And also, tie it in with Lent, in which we explore Christ's pain and death. "Let's celebrate the wholeness of life — from birth to death!"

Invitation to Worship

Pastor: We have come because the living God has invited us to come.
Ministers: *We have come to affirm who we are, whose we are, what we do, where we go in the power of the living Christ.*
Pastor: We affirm our life, all of it, in the presence of the Holy Spirit, for the world's sake.
Ministers: *Be it so! Amen!*

Recognizing Who We Are and Whose We Are

Try this: Make sure that the confession hits people where they are today, rather than praying in generalities. Introduce printed or spoken questions for consideration, such as these:

1. Do I harbor memories which disquiet and disturb?
2. Do I set high standards for myself and others?
3. Do I find it difficult to accept human frailty?
4. Am I filled with judgmentalism?
5. Do I overtax my strength and schedules?
6. Do I plan, do, spend, more than I have?
7. Do I give in to pressure and live in anxiety?
8. Do I worship and serve "tomorrow"?
9. Do I love things and use people?
10. Do I strain relationships and break communication with those I love and need most?

Follow with this: Let the pastor bring together his/her thoughts based on these concerns, and then, lead into a written prayer imparting the assurance of pardon.

Message to the Children of All Ages

Bring fishing equipment. Develop message around fishing. Mention impatience when fish don't bite, and excitement when they do. Jesus' disciples had similar experiences. Tie in with Jesus' invitation to love and care about people, both when we're impatient and when we're excited. He asks us to follow him when it's easy and fun, but also when it isn't. Ask children when and how they can follow him during easy and hard times.

Proclamation of the Word

Suggested development:

Theme — Learning how to fish.
  I. Selecting the proper bait.
 II. Possessing patience/perseverance.
III. Learning to think as a fish.
    (Think about that for a few minutes.)

Response to the Proclamation

Consider this approach:

1. Ask what methods people use in order to witness in daily life to the Good News — both verbally and non-verbally.
2. Develop a prayer which seeks God's courage and strength for our witnessing.

Stewardship Challenge

Suggested follow-up for the sermon:

> Ask, "What is a specific way that you will deliberately decide to witness to a neighbor, friend, relative, both verbally and non-verbally this week? The fact is that we witness every moment, in either positive or negative ways."

Prayer of Commitment

Suggestion: "Lord, it's relatively easy to give money. It's not so easy to give our attention. Grant that your spirit shall interpret to us the urgency of both. Amen."

Charge to the Congregation

Consider this: Review today's worship experience and challenge the people. You may find the following useful.

> "The disciples left everything and followed him." What do we need to leave to follow the Christ? Some time in front of the TV? A job that demands a seventy-hour week? An unhealthy liason? An attitude that insists, "I'm always right!" A demand for more leisure time? What do we need to change in our lives in order to become the people Christ calls us to be?

Meditation at the End of Worship

"A Christian is one who recognizes that he/she lives on Holy Ground." (a.u.)

Planning for Your Congregation

Suggestions	Your Situation

I. Other Scriptures   *Lay readers:*

- Psalm 85:8-13
- Psalm 138
- Isaiah 6:1-8 (9-13)
- 1 Corinthians 14:12b-20; 15:1-11

II. Hymn Possibilities   *Hymn selections:*

"God of our Life, Through all the Circling Years"
    Hugh T. Kerr, 1916, altered 1928, 1972
    (Hymn of the month for the remainder of Epiphany)
"O God, our Help in Ages Past"
    Isaac Watts, 1719, altered
    (In stanza 4, change "its sons" to "the ones")

III. Other Music Possibilities   *Music selections:*

Music for preparation
    "Prelude, Fugue and Variations"   Franck
Response to the Old Testament
    "Blessed are You"   Emma Lou Diemer
Offertory
    "Lord, Be With Us Now"   Bach
Choral Response after Benediction   Choral Amen
    "Lilies of the Field Amen Chorus"
    (repeat with greater power)
Music for dismissal
    Medley of Epiphany Hymns

IV. Bulletin Cover   *Bulletin design ideas:*

V. Bulletin symbols

VI. Miscellaneous Details *(Assignments):*

- Ushers
- Banners
- Flowers
- Assistant(s) at Holy Communion

- Greeters
- Candlelighters
- Soloists
- Other

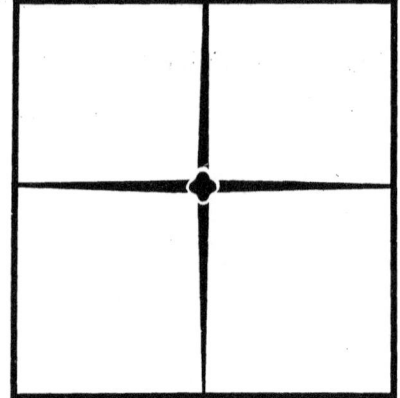

THE SEASON OF THE EVANGEL

EPIPHANY 6
ORDINARY TIME 6

Liturgical Color: White/Green

Gospel: Luke 6:17-26

Theme: Praying for persecution — being in the world but not of it.

Planning Notes

Pastoral Invitation

Suggested: We celebrate the presence of God now, because we celebrate the presence of God wherever we are. We celebrate God's love and justice, as we seek to discover God's will — for God is alive and well and living in and through us. Indeed! Amen!

Recognizing Who and Whose We Are

Consider this idea:

The pastor invites the people to pray only those parts of the following prayer which they believe pertain to them specifically.

The pastor may tailor this, or a similar prayer, to the concerns to his/her particular congregation:

> Our loving and holy God, we confess that we have done those things which we had no business doing, and now, cannot understand why we did and why we keep doing them over and over.
> We continue to dirty our love with calculation;
> We continue to powder and pamper our pride with pouts;
> We continue to permit friendships to cover cosmetic smiles;
> We continue to wear life and never live it.
>   Why, O God, why?
> Forgive us, It's not that we hate, O Lord, it's just that we don't love. Do you understand us, Lord? For we don't understand ourselves. So, we pray for forgiveness, for those things we did and did not do to further your witness this past week. Make us, Lord, through your Spirit, healthy and new persons. In the name of the Christ.

(silent meditation)

The pastor then continues: It is one thing to seek forgiveness; it is another to believe that we are forgiven, and to act differently because we *are* forgiven. How will we act differently this coming week because we know we are forgiven?

Finally, for the act of receiving new life,

1. Ask members of the congregation to write down one way each will respond differently because of God's forgiveness.
2. Invite those in the congregation (a) to share with the person sitting next to him/her; and (b) ask one or two to share with the whole congregation.

Choral Response: Congregation singing, "Born Free"
John Barry and Don Black, copyright 1966 by Screen-Gems—Columbia Music, Inc. New York.
(Remind the congregation that as Christians, we can properly recast the expression to say "re-born free.")

Planning Notes

Message to the Children of All Ages

Consider this: Build the message around the Beatitudes. "How happy (complete) you are when you're poor, hungry, sad, and when people don't like you. Rejoice and jump for joy — because your reward in heaven is great!" Ask if children have any idea what that means. If they don't, ask the adults. (Always include the adults because we all have a child within us that needs nurturing and challenging.) Compare Jesus' words with our usual approach to life and Christianity — an approach that suggests everyone is supposed to smile, love everyone else, be successful, be on top of the world. Find an example from your own ministry which illustrates this approach. Conclude with Jesus' invitation to serve him above everyone and everything.

Proclamation of the Word

Praying for Persecution: In the world, but not of it.

Consider these quotations:

1. Poster: "Involvement with people is always a very delicate thing — it requires real maturity to become involved and not get all messed up."
2. D. L. Mundy: "The tragedy is that so often our very riches blind us to the needs of the outside world. Judgment rests on our society at this point; and it could be disastrous. If we are not ready to share our riches, it may be that we shall have to share our poverty.
3. "Christ became poor that through his poverty, we might become rich."

Try this as a response to the sermon:

Make certain that the congregation clarifies any comments or questions before leaving the sanctuary. This Scripture and sermon are too easy to misunderstand.

Stewardship Challenge

One pastor does this on a regular basis:

Ask for a brief response from members of the congregation. How do the people understand their stewardship in the light of the Scripture and sermon?

Charge to the Congregation

Consider this idea:

Ask, "Do we dare to practice the belief that crucifixion is as necessary for us as it was for Christ? That is, do we know that crucifixion for us precedes resurrection? Do we believe that what was so difficult for Christ will be made easy for us? Do we dare to answer the call to be in the world, yet not of it — in the name of the Christ who is the Lord of all life, of every week, relationship, event?

Planning for Your Congregation

Suggestions

I. Other Scriptures

- Psalm 1
- Jeremiah 17:5-10
- 1 Corinthians 15:12-20

(for variation, ask the choir to sing its own tune to the Psalm)

II. Hymn Possibilities

"God of our Life, Through All the Circling Years"
                                      Hugh T. Kerr
(Hymn of the Month for the Remainder of the Epiphany)
"When I Survey the Wondrous Cross" Isaac Watts, 1707

III. Other Music Possibilities

Music for Preparation
    "Cortege and Litany"   Dupre
Choral Invitation to Worship
    "Let All Mortal Flesh Keep Silent"   Stanza 1
    (from Liturgy of Saint James, translated by Gerald Moultrie, 1864)
Choral Response to the Act of Forgiveness
    "Born Free"
    (John Barry and Don Black, copyright 1966 Screen-Gems — Columbia Music, Inc., New York)
Response to the Old Testament
    "Be Still My Soul"
Offertory
    "Praise God from Whom All Blessings Flow"
Response following Benediction
    "Now on Land and Sea Descending"
    (Chorus only: "Jubilate! Jubilate! Jubilate! Amen!" *sung with much power)*

IV. Bulletin Cover

V. Bulletin Symbols

Your Situation

Lay readers:

Hymn selections:

Music selections:

Bulletin design ideas:

VI. Miscellaneous Details *(Assignments):* _____

- Ushers
- Banners
- Flowers
- Assistant(s) at Holy Communion

- Greeters
- Candlelighters
- Soloists
- Other

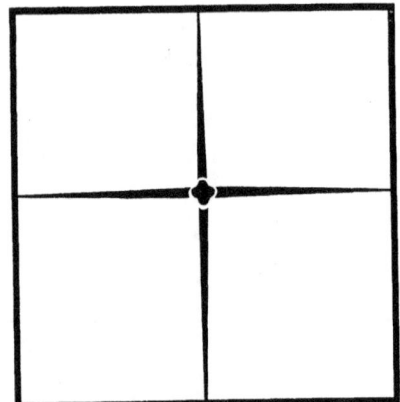

THE SEASON OF THE EVANGEL

EPIPHANY 7
ORDINARY TIME 7

Liturgical Color: White/Green

Gospel: Luke 6:27-38

Theme: The Dimensions of Forgiveness — (1) offered once and for all and continuously through the Cross of Christ; (2) offered without our being superior or self-righteous; (3) offered beginning with ourselves.

Planning Notes

Pastoral Invitation

Try this (often):

Ask, What do we expect to happen in worship today, and, as a result of worship this next week? God promises that if we expect little, we receive little; if we expect much, we receive much.

Recognizing Who and Whose We Are

If you haven't done this before,

1. Invite the congregation to think about those persons from whom they are alienated, separated, estranged. Name them (aloud?). Review how you became separated. Compare your alienations from them with your alienation from God.

2. Spend three minutes in silence (this time to think will seem like three hours). After the silence, say, "If we believe that God has forgiven us, why in God's name have we not forgiven each other or ourselves?"

3. Then, for the assurance, you may want to quote Bishop Philips Brooks: "The chief business of the Christian is the forgiveness of sin." Then, "Will we forgive without becoming self-righteous or superior?" To avoid such a response, recognize that all of us have the same need for forgiveness.

Message to the Children of All Ages

Ask a child ahead of time to share an experience about how quickly and easily most children forget and forgive disagreements and arguments. Also, ask an adult to tell how hard it is for us adults to forgive/forget what others do to us. Then, compare our usual approach as adults with Jesus' words from the cross, "Father, forgive them, for they don't know what they're doing." That wasn't easy for him to do. It's not easy for us adults either. Yet, that's what Jesus asks us to do.

Stewardship Challenge

Consider following the worship theme:

Stewardship of forgiveness — of self, of others. "Forgiveness means that I will not get even, in word, thought, or deed."

A Possible Prayer of Dedication:

"We know, Lord, that we can't buy our forgiveness; teach us, by your Spirit, how to receive it, and then share it."

Meditation
(to be printed in the bulletin)

Suggestion for a summary of worship:

"The person who cannot (will not) forgive breaks the bridge over which he (she) must pass." George Herbert

Planning Notes

Planning for Your Congregation

Suggestions

I. Other Scriptures

- Psalm 37:1-11; 103:1-13
- Genesis 45:3-11, 15
- 1 Samuel 26:2, 7-9, 12-13, 22-23
- 1 Corinthians 15:35-50

II. Hymn Possibilities

"God of our Life, Through All the Circling Years"
(Epiphany hymn of the month; in the bulletin or church newsletter include a brief history of the hymn)

"Let us with a Gladsome Mind"   Psalm 136:1, 2, 7, 25
Paraphrase by John Milton, 1624, altered
(The hymn refers to God as "Him"; at least make the congregation aware of the language, and encourage people to use "Her" through part of the hymn.)

III. Other Music Possibilities

Music for Preparation
"God Shall Nought Divide Me"   Bach
Choral Invitation
"Let the Spirit In"   Richard Blank
(copyright 1973, *Genesis Songbook,* by Agape Hope Publishing Company)
Response to the Act of Receiving New Life
"You Are the Lord, Giver of Mercy"
Based on Appalachian folk melody
(music copyright 1972, Westminster Press)
Response to Children's Message
"Let There Be Peace on Earth"
Sy Miller and Jill Jackson
(copyright 1955 by Sy Miller and Jill Jackson assigned to Jan-Lee Music)
Response to the Old Testament
"Seek and Ye Shall Find"
Kentucky-Tennessee Gospel Song, as sung by
The Temple Methodist Congregation
Response to the Sermon
Chorus only, "There is a Balm in Gilead"
Negro Spiritual
Offertory
"Chorale"   F. Zachara
Response to Benediction
"Pass it On"   Kurt Kaiser
(copyright 1969, Lexicon Music, Inc.)

Your Situation

Lay readers:

Hymn selections:

Music selections:

Suggestions

Your Situation

IV. Bulletin Cover

Bulletin design ideas:

V. Bulletin symbols

VI. Miscellaneous Details *(Assignments):* _____

- Ushers
- Banners
- Flowers
- Assistant(s) at Holy Communion

- Greeters
- Candlelighters
- Soloists
- Other

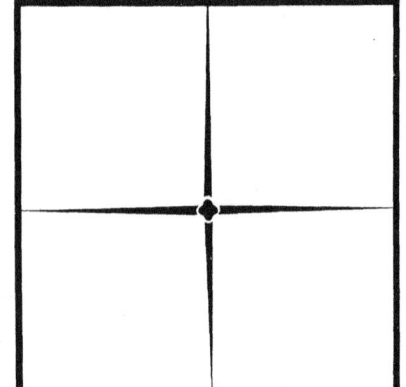

THE SEASON OF THE EVANGEL

EPIPHANY 8 ORDINARY TIME 8

Liturgical Color: White/Green

Gospel: Luke 6:39-45

Theme: You shall not take yourself too seriously.

Planning Notes

Pastoral Invitation to the Celebration

Suggested: We have journeyed through Epiphany, the Season of the Evangel, these past weeks. We have considered its roots, that is, the manifestation of Christ to the Gentiles. We continue to consider its theme, namely, the missionary task of the church. We have experienced Christ's missionaries in our lives, or we wouldn't be here today; we continue to learn of our mission to those around us, as we witness — verbally and non-verbally.

Recognizing Who and Whose We Are

One pastor used the following guided meditation (develop this idea for your congregation):

"Eyes closed; allow yourself to be open to the leading of the Spirit." (take your time with these ideas)

1. Think about how you were introduced to this congregation, or had your first contact with this congregation.
2. Review your life, relationship with and in this congregation — slowly.
3. Allow the experiences/events/relationships/people to come into your awareness. Review the joys/sadnesses/angers. Affirm all of these as a part of your growth.
4. Focus on one special experience/event.
   a. Note the environment/scene/particulars.
   b. Recall what you learned.
   c. What quality did it represent? Think about that quality.
5. You have received that quality as a gift from God.
   a. How will you pass it on?
   b. To whom will you pass it on?
   c. When will you begin?
6. Bring those decisions to this moment — and beyond.
7. If you are celebrating the sacrament of the Lord's Supper today, consider that quality as you receive the bread and cup. Consider that quality as God's gift to you, as your gift to others.

"Freely have we received, freely we give."

Message to the Children of All Ages

Suggested: Bring a log and toothpick. Tell Jesus' story about what people do.

Apply it to the children's lives, explaining how easy it is to be hard on others and easy on themselves. Conclude with a prayer of forgiveness.

Planning Notes

Proclamation of the Word

One pastor developed his sermon like this:

"We usually focus on the seriousness of these passages. When I first became a Christian, I was so serious. We need to help one another to see the twinkle in Jesus' eye as he spoke." Have in the sanctuary a painting of "The Laughing Christ" or "Christ, the Liberator."
(For the especially brave, pray a laughing prayer, or a prayer, laughing.)

Stewardship thought

Suggested follow-up to the worship theme:

The Greek New Testament says that "God loves an hilarious (cheerful) giver." We shall have arrived as a congregation when we laugh all the way through the passing of the offering plate and the singing of the doxology.

Charge to the Congregation

Try this, as a summary of worship:

"When people are up against life, and find it too much for them, one swears, one gets a headache, one prays, and one gets drunk." (And I add, "One laughs.")

J. A. Hadfield (with an addition by W. H. K.)

Meditation at the End of Worship
(printed in the bulletin):

Voltaire wrote, "O Lord, make my enemies ridiculous," and I add, "And help me to laugh at myself also."

Planning for Your Congregation

Suggestions   Your Situation

I. Other Scriptures   *Lay readers:*

- Psalm 92
- Isaiah 55:10-13
- Jeremiah 7:1-7 (8-15)
- Sirach 27:4-7
- 1 Corinthians 15:51-58

II. Hymn Possibilities   *Hymn selections:*

"Angels from the Realms of Glory"
       James Montgomery
 (Epiphany hymn of the month)
"Go, Tell it on the Mountain"
 Refrain, Negro Spiritual Stanzas, John W. Work,
 Jr. (1871-1925); altered

III. Other Music Possibilities   *Music selections:*

Music for Preparation
 Medley, Epiphany hymns
Choral Invitation
 "Christ is the World's True Light"
 George Wallace Briggs, 1931, altered 1972
 (change "man/men" to "one/we")
Response to the Old Testament
 Choral Version, Psalm 92
Offertory
 "As Torrents in Summer"   Elgar
Response to Benediction
 Chorus only, "Go, Tell It On The Mountain"
 (ask people to sing as they leave the sanctuary)

IV. Bulletin Cover   *Bulletin design ideas:*

V. Bulletin Symbols

VI. Miscellaneous Details *(Assignments):* _____

- Ushers
- Banners
- Flowers
- Assistant(s) at Holy Communion

- Greeters
- Candlelighters
- Soloists
- Other

THE SEASON OF THE EVANGEL

THE TRANSFIGURATION OF OUR LORD

Liturgical Color: White

Gospel: Luke 9:28-36

Theme: The Return to Routine — Because most of life is routine, we need to allow the Spirit of God to make our routine significant.

Planning Notes

Pastoral Invitation to the Celebration

Consider this: "Welcome to this celebration of the routine. Granted, God breaks through our routine and surprises us. However, today, most of life is routine, let us identify some of that routine, as we begin worship."

Recognizing Who and Whose We Are

Try this: Invite the people to examine their daily schedule. Allow sufficient time to permit them to get in contact with the routine

Then, invite them to think about how we put excitement into our lives. Often, we do this by playing games, emotional games, sexual games, fun games. Someone has said, "The excitement is in the game." For example, when the game's over, and we've been married for a couple years, we think that love has ended.

(Allow silence for silent reflection.)

Now, ask the congregation how the people will allow the Spirit of God to redeem the routine. Be ready with your own suggestions. For example, we can learn to laugh for the right reasons, or to develop a life of intercessory prayer.

Message to the Children of All Ages

Suggested: Compare mountain-top experiences with the daily routine. For example, compare vacations and school, eating ice cream and mowing the lawn, playing sports and cleaning your bedroom. Make certain that life is not one big holiday, and that God is the Lord of our fun times, as well as our not-so-fun times.

Proclamation of the Word

Suggested: Title the Sermon *The Return to Routine.*

You may want to use this outline:

Planning Notes

   I. Most of life is routine.
      A. Invite people, once again, to examine their daily schedule. Take sufficient time to allow them to get in contact with their routine and their feelings.
      B. When do we break out of the routine? Give a variety of examples.

  II. Routine can become significant.
      A. We need mountain-top experiences, and we don't stay on the mountain. Our work is in the world of persons, politics, economics, neighbors, nations.
      B. We receive life as an opportunity. Compare "chronos" with "kairos" time, which means, partly, that we face life in all of its dimensions.

Stewardship Challenge

Try this: How will you allow God to redeem your routine this week? What is one specific area in which you will take some action?

Charge to the Congregation

Consider this: Christ's Spirit transforms the *merely* (or "drearly") routine to the *dearly* routine. The routine of life need not frustrate us or destroy us — not if we allow the Christ to take it, and us, to make both the routine and us responsible.

Planning for Your Congregation

Suggestions   **Your Situation**

I. Other Scriptures   *Lay readers:*

- Psalm 99
- Exodus 34:29-35
- Deuteronomy 34:1-12
- 1 Corinthians 3:12—4:6

II. Hymn Possibilities   *Hymn selections:*

"Immortal, Invisible, God Only Wise"
    Walter Chambers Smith 1867, 1884, altered
"There is a Place of Quiet Rest"
    Cleland B. McAfee, 1866-1894
"Be Thou My Vision"
    Ancient Irish, Translated by May Byrne, 1927
"I Am the Light of the World"
                                    Jim Strathdee
    copyright, Jim Strathdee and Howard Thurman.
    (revised version, minus sexist language, available)

III. Other Music Possibilities   *Music selections:*

Music for Preparation and Dismissal
    Medley of Transfiguration Hymns
Response to the Acts of Who and Whose We Are
                                    Adult Choir
    "We Thank Thee Lord"   Bortiansky
Offertory
    "Christ Our Lord to Jordan Came"   Dupre

IV. Bulletin Cover   *Bulletin design ideas:*

V. Bulletin Symbols

VI. Miscellaneous Details *(Assignments):* _____

- Ushers
- Banners
- Flowers
- Assistant(s) at Holy Communion

- Greeters
- Candlelighters
- Soloists
- Other

THE SEASON OF

LENT

Lent, the Season of Renewal

The Lenten season extends over a forty-six day period, beginning with Ash Wednesday and ending with Easter Eve. The six Sundays in Lent are not really included as a part of Lent, so the Lenten season actually consists of forty days. Sundays, weekly commemorations of the first Easter (every Sunday is another "Easter"), have always been excluded from this traditional fast season. Holy Week, the last week in Lent, begins with Palm Sunday. It serves as a review of the events of Christ's Passion. (Passion refers to the sufferings of Jesus on the Cross or after the Last Supper.)

The beginning of Lent appears to have been associated with a period of discipline, reflection, and abstinence in order to imitate Christ's self-denial, and to prepare for the celebration of Easter.

Lent developed from two sources:

1. There developed a period of fasting which preceded Easter in the early church. At first, this fasting period was held on Saturday, the day before Easter, lasting until 3:00 a.m. Easter morning, when the Lord's Supper was celebrated. This recalled that Christ was raised early in the morning. Later, this fast was extended to six days, and eventually, became separated into the events of Holy Week. Holy Week, then, is an older season than the entire Lenten season.

2. There arose the practice of the baptism of people into the faith on Easter Eve. Because the early church existed "underground," candidates were screened carefully, after a long period of preparation. The strictest part of this probationary period came just before baptism. A fasting of forty days was required — suggested by Jesus' fasting forty days in the wilderness, Moses' fasting at Mount Sinai, and Elijah's fasting on the way to the Mount of God. Eventually, this period of preparation for baptism evolved into a general period of preparation for Easter, to be observed by all Christians.

THE SEASON OF RENEWAL

ASH WEDNESDAY

Liturgical Color: Purple

Gospel: Matthew 6:1-6, 16-21

Theme: The journey inward. God calls us to self-examination.

Meditation
(written or spoken at the beginning of worship)

Planning Notes

(This is an idea suggested by Avery and Marsh:)
    Instead of *giving up* something for Lent (e.g. candy, coffee, alcohol), decide to *take on* something (visit a convalescent home, read the Gospel of Mark, participate in worship each Sunday, decide on specific persons and events to pray for, be aware that all of life belongs to God.)

Suggested Scripture

- Psalm 51:1-13; Joel 2:1-2, 12-14
- 2 Corinthians 5:20b—6:2 (3-10)
- Matthew 6:1-6, 16-21

Suggested Order of Worship

1. Sit in the sanctuary for as long as you choose in silence.
2. Come forward when ready and stand or be seated at the communion table. The pastor and elders will serve the elements to you in silence.
3. Return to the pews if you choose.
4. Leave the sanctuary in silence when ready.

Suggested for Lent beyond Ash Wednesday Worship
(Print these ideas in the bulletin)

1. Take fifteen minutes a day for prayer and meditation.
2. Do the unnecessary but kind acts that we think of at other times but "never get around to" doing.
3. Read a book a week — choose a variety. *(Pastors: include a list for your people.)*
4. Write five letters to people from whom you are alienated.
5. Review your life and how you became a Christian.
6. Witness to one person each week about who Christ is to you, and invite that person to consider Christ for his/her life.

THE SEASON OF RENEWAL

LENT 1

Liturgical Color: Purple

Gospel: Luke 4:1-13

Theme: The conquest of inner space: Jesus' temptations — Power, Prestige, Popularity.

Planning Notes

Bulletin Heading

Suggestion: Revise the heading to fit the season. For example:

> **Lent** — The Season of Renewal
> A Call to Discover
> Who We Are   Whose We Are
> What We Do   Where We Go
> in
> the power of the Risen Christ.

Pastoral Invitation

Consider this: Begin, "Good morning, church — Welcome to Christ's world." Welcome the people to Lent — the season of renewal. Begin to get them to focus on two questions:
1. Where do you want to be in your journey with God by Easter?
2. How will you allow God's Spirit to lead you into greater truth and action in the name of Jesus Christ?

Celebrating the Act of Renewal
(confession and assurance of pardon)

One pastor did this:

- Focus on the traditional approach to Lent, that is, that of "giving up something." This is often, a negative approach.
- Then, focus on a contemporary approach to Lent, that is, that of "taking on something."

Invite the congregation to respond during worship, verbally, or on paper. You could ask three or four ahead of time to share in worship how they will observe Lent. *(idea inspired by Richard Avery/Don Marsh)*

Message to the Children of All Ages

Consider this: Keep the same theme. Ask the children if they know the difference between "giving up" and "taking on." Discuss ways they could take on something new. Perhaps they could put aside ten percent of their allowance for a specific need; they could decide how to help around the house without parents nagging; they could even confront their parents when they think parents are being unfair.

Stewardship Challenge

Try this, as one pastor did:

Ask the people to consider the stewardship of filtering gossip/innuendos/insinuations/half-truths this Lenten season. Ask the questions, "Is it true? Is it necessary? Is it loving?" What's the most loving response we can give when we hear it?

Dedication Prayer

Try this prayer, as follow-up of the stewardship challenge:

"We wonder, O God, if these gifts represent what we really believe about you. Whatever our motive for giving, receive them by your grace and use them in your power."

Headings for the Parts of Worship

One pastor does this:

Change the headings to fit the season. For example:

Celebrating the Presence of God
Alleluia! Alleluia!

Celebrating the Act of Renewal
We Seek Forgiveness!

Celebrating the Word
We Are Listening!

Celebrating Our Gifts
We Are Accountable!

Celebrating Our Departure
We Leave for Ministry

Planning Notes

Planning for Your Congregation

Suggestions	Your Situation

I. Other Scriptures   *Lay readers:*

- Psalm 91:1-2, 9-16
- Deuteronomy 26:1-11
- Romans 10:8b-13

II. Hymn Possibilities   *Hymn selections:*

"God of Grace, God of Glory"
      Harry Emerson Fosdick, 1930, altered 1972
(Lenten Hymn of the Month)
(Choir sing first stanza; congregation read the second; congregation/choir hum third; all sing fourth with much enthusiasm.)
"All Praise Be Yours; for You, O King Divine"
      F. Bland Tucker, 1938, 1972
(Lenten hymn for first three Sundays in Lent)

III. Other Music Possibilities   *Music selections:*

Music for Preparation
    Medley of Lenten Hymns
Response to the Prayer of Praise
    "Praise the Lord"   Based on Negro Spiritual
(arranged and composed by Richard D. Wetzel, *The Worshipbook,* p. 253)
Response to the Act of Renewal
    "Let All That You Do"
    Based on 1 Corinthians 16:14
    Words and music by Gary Hasson, copyright 1973 in *Folk Encounter,* Hope Publishing Company.
Response to the Proclamation
    "Glory Be to God on High."
    Tune: "Michael, Row the Boat Ashore"
    Folk Encounter, page 112. Hope Publishing Company.
Response to the Old Testament reading
    "You Are the Lord, Giver of Mercy"
    (based on Appalachian folk medley, copyright 1970, 1972, Westminster Press.)
Offertory   "Cantilene"   Stravinsky
Response following the Benediction
    "Lord, Who Throughout Those Forty Days"
    Claudia F. Hernaman, 1887, altered 1972

IV. Bulletin Cover   *Bulletin design ideas:*

V. Bulletin Symbols

VI. Miscellaneous Details *(Assignments):* _____

- Ushers
- Banners
- Flowers
- Assistant(s) at Holy Communion

- Greeters
- Candlelighters
- Soloists
- Other

THE SEASON OF RENEWAL

LENT 2

Liturgical Color: Purple

Gospel: Luke 9:28-36

Theme: A word we don't want to hear —
the judgment of God.

Planning Notes

Pastoral Invitation

Suggested: Continue to focus on the congregation as ministers. Point them beyond being spectators in worship. In the call to worship, spoken, use the response of pastor and ministers.

Proclamation of the Word

Consider this: Following the sermon, which might focus on these themes:
1. Our attempt to boss Jesus — the results of such an attempt;
2. Our need to accept God's grace — our incredible reluctance to accept it: ask for congregational responses, especially around the question, "What's so difficult about our accepting God's grace?" Identify the barriers.

Then, build the prayer around giving up the barriers, also by the grace of God.

Stewardship Challenge

Try this: Use this quote from *Pilgrim's Regress*: "Why is it that when I get what I want, I'm not satisfied and I want more?"

Prayer of Commitment After the Offering

Try this following the stewardship challenge:

"God, we do enjoy complaining about what we don't have, and fail to be thankful for what we do have. Grant that your Spirit shall teach us to rearrange our value system."

Charge to the Congregation

Consider this summary of worship:

If we do not have the words of discipline and judgment as part of the biblical message, we will not understand the words of grace and forgiveness. In the parent/child relationship, discipline (which means teaching) is essential for growth and wholeness. That's also true in our relationship with God, our Parent, and us, God's children.

Meditation at the End of Worship *Planning Notes*

Suggested as a summary of today's worship:

"The greatest burden we have to carry in life is self; the most difficult thing we have to manage is self." (Hannah Whitall Smith)

Planning for Your Congregation

Suggestions   Your Situation

I. Other Scriptures   *Lay readers:*

- Psalm 127; 42:1-7, 11-15;
- Psalm 27:1, 7-9, 13-14
- Genesis 15:1-12, 17-18
- Jeremiah 26:8-15
- Philippians 3:17—4:1

II. Hymn Possibilities   *Hymn selections:*

"God of Grace, God of Glory" Harry Emerson Fosdick
    (Lenten hymn of the month)
"All Praise Be Yours; O King Divine"   F. Bland Tucker
    (Hymn for first three Sundays in Lent)

III. Other Music Possibilities   *Music selections:*

Music for Preparation
    "Like a Shepherd, God Doth Guide Us"   Bach
Response after Prayer of Praise
    'Gloria Patri"   Old Scottish
Response to the Old Testament
    "You Are the Lord, Giver of Mercy"
    based on Appalachian Folk Melody
Music for Dismissal
    Medley of Lenten Hymns

IV. Bulletin Cover   *Bulletin design ideas:*

V. Bulletin Symbols

VI. Miscellaneous Details *(Assignments):* _____

• Ushers	• Banners	• Flowers	• Assistant(s) at Holy Communion
• Greeters	• Candlelighters	• Soloists	• Other

THE SEASON OF RENEWAL
LENT 3

Liturgical Color: Purple

Gospel: Luke 13:1-9

Theme: Why Do Bad Things Happen to Good People?

Pastoral Invitation

Try this: Lent's half over this next week. How are you doing in your "taking on" of some new possibilities with God and the world? By the way, we have two choices about failing: We can flagellate ourselves and feel guilty about our failures, or we can turn them over to God for forgiveness and renewal.

Recognizing Who We Are and Whose We Are

If you haven't done this before, define the human condition by playing the record, or having the choir sing, "Games People Play" made famous by Petula Clark and Eric Berne some years ago. This is what the Bible means by sin. Give the people a couple of minutes to think about the words.

When declaring the assurance, center on "God's unconditional acceptance," the word grace which too few church members understand. Ask the congregation to repeat "thanks" or "thank you" several times, until you think the people actually hear it with their emotions.

Message to the Children of All Ages

Try this, in keeping with the theme for the day:

Bring a fruit tree into the chancel — a young tree, and some fruit. Talk about what it takes to grow fruit, and what happens if the tree doesn't produce. Be careful to point out that God's love causes us to keep growing and producing our whole lifetime. God doesn't dig us up and throw us out if we don't produce. God keeps sending us more and more people to help us grow.

Proclamation

Emphasize this: Distinguish between physical and spiritual death. Jesus' teaching emphasized that because all of us face death, we face the judgment of God unafraid only if we are clear with God. This occurs only through our acceptance of God's unconditional acceptance of us. Give the people an opportunity to clarify any concerns.

Planning Notes

Planning Notes

Stewardship Challenge

Suggested: Begin with this quote from Fulton J. Sheen: "To withhold help is to participate in the authorship of misery that we fail to review. Violence slays thousands; but supine (passive) negligence slays millions."

Try this for the prayer of commitment:

"We prefer not to think about the plight/misery of others; we prefer to take it easy, relax, and enjoy our blessings. Lord, grant that your Spirit shall hone us to live on the razor-blade edge of life."

Meditation at the End of Worship

1. *The attack:* "If at first you don't deceive, try, try again." The Devil (whatever form he/she takes) (a.u.)
2. *Our response:* "The best way for me to drive out the Devil is _____" (you decide).

Planning for Your Congregation

Suggestions   Your Situation

I. Other Scriptures

Lay readers:

- Psalm 103:1-13
- Psalm 126
- Exodus 3:1-15
- 1 Corinthians 10:1-13

II. Hymn Possibilities

Hymn selections:

"God of Grace, God of Glory"   Fosdick
    (Hymn of the month)
"All Praise Be Yours, O King Divine"   Tucker
    (for first half of Lent)

III. Other Music Possibilities

Music selections:

Music for Preparation
    "The Sun's Declining Rays"   Bruce Simonds
Response to Prayer of Praise
    "Gloria Patri"
Response to the Sermon
    "O Sacred Head Now Wounded"
    Based on Medieval Latin Poem
                    Paul Gerhardt, 1656
Offertory
    "Wondrous Love"   Dale Wood
Music for Dismissal
    "In the Cross of Christ I Glory"
                    John Bowring, 1825

IV. Bulletin Cover

Bulletin design ideas:

V. Bulletin Symbols

VI. Miscellaneous Details *(Assignments):* _____

- Ushers
- Banners
- Flowers
- Assistant(s) at Holy Communion

- Greeters
- Candlelighters
- Soloists
- Other

THE SEASON OF RENEWAL

LENT 4

Liturgical Color: Purple

Gospel: Luke 15:1-3, 11-32

Theme: The Prodigal Sons — the fleshly and spiritual sins, and what God does about them.

Planning Notes

Pastoral Invitation

Try this: Keep the focus upon why the worshipers are here, as for example, "We're here to examine why we're here — and we do so in the presence and power of God's Holy Spirit who leads us into the truth — truth about ourselves, others, the world. It's not an easy pilgrimage ; but then, it wasn't easy for Jesus of Nazareth either."

Celebrating the Act of Forgiveness

One pastor did this:

1. "It's not my fault. I was only following orders. I lived believing in God, I died believing in God." Ask the congregation who made that statement. If no one knows, inform them that Adolph Eichmann, the mastermind behind eleven million deaths in World War II, did.

2. Charlie Brown, speaking to Lucy one day, remarked, "It says here that the force of gravitation is thirteen percent less today than it was four and one-half billion years ago . . ." "Whose fault is that?" asked Lucy. "Whose fault is it? It's nobody's fault," retorted Charlie, all set for a debate. Lucy promptly settled the question. "What do you mean, nobody's fault! It has be to *somebody's* fault. *Somebody's* got to take the blame." Then, Lucy, blasting Charlie off of his feet, shouted, "Find a scapegoat!"

3. That is our response to much of life. Find a Scapegoat. Compare the Adam/Eve story to the story of our lives. "It's not my fault . . . the woman you gave to me, she gave me the fruit of the tree." (Adam) "It's not my fault; the serpent tricked me." (Eve) "It's your fault, Lord."

    Now, ask the people to sit in silence for two minutes, while each examines his/her own practice of scapegoating.

    Pastoral prayer response: Center around how easily we scapegoat.
    Congregational response: "Lord, have mercy on us"
    (many versions of this are available)

4. Pastor announces that God even forgives scapegoats — if they want forgiveness. When the one prodigal son came to his senses, he went to his father. That's what we do when we come to our senses also. So, for those who've come to their senses, we pray this prayer:

    (print in bulletin)

Planning Notes

"Our Father/Mother, we realize what we do when we find others to blame for our situation. We know that you gave us Christ to empower us to take responsibility for our own actions. We accept his gift as we seek to live responsible lives."

Message to the Children of All Ages

Suggested Approach: Continue to use the Prodigal Sons. Show to them the two kinds of sin and apply them to the children's experiences.

Response to the Message

Consider this: Invite the people to sit for silent prayer for three minutes. Ask them to write down any concerns, questions to be placed in offering plate.

Stewardship Challenge

Suggested sermon follow-up:

- Stewardship of the tongue.
- How have we used our tongue to hurt?
- How will we use it to heal?

Prayer of Commitment

Consider this: "We like to think that our placing a few dollars in the offering plate is our prime responsibility in worship. Grant that Your Holy Spirit reveal to us that we are responsible for all we do, say, think."

Charge to the Congregation

Consider this: Summarize the theme of worship, as for example,

God in Christ has taken all the risks for our reconciliation and liberation. Christ dared even to fail sincerely, rather than to succeed at the price of insincerity. He bids us to come, yes, even with all of our scapegoating, and receive forgiveness, newness.
So, we come to Christ to receive love.
We go to the world to express love.

Planning for Your Congregation

Suggestions	Your Situation

I. Other Scriptures

- Psalm 34:1-8
- Psalm 32
- Joshua 5:9-12
- Isaiah 12:1-6
- 2 Corinthians 5:16-21
- 1 Corinthians 1:18-31

(perhaps you will want to use Clarence Jordan's cassette tape of the Prodigal Son, from the Cotton Patch Version)

Lay readers:

II. Hymn Possibilities

"God of Grace and God of Glory" Fosdick
   (hymn of the month)
"When We Are Tempted to Deny Your Son"
                              David W. Romig, 1965
   (for the last three Sundays of Lent)

Hymn selections:

III. Other Music Possibilities

Music for Preparation
   "O Holy Bread of Heaven" Cesar Franck
Response to the prayer of praise
   "Almighty Father, Hear Our Prayer"
   (Arr. from Felix Mendelssohn, 1846)
Response to Children's message
   "This is the Good News" Richard D. Wetzel
The Worshipbook, page 263
Offertory
   "Jesus, Priceless Treasure" Bach
Music for Dismissal
   "Alleluia, Sing Praise" Bach

Music selections:

IV. Bulletin Cover

Bulletin design ideas:

V. Bulletin Symbols

VI. Miscellaneous Details *(Assignments):*

- Ushers
- Banners
- Flowers
- Assistant(s) at Holy Communion

- Greeters
- Candlelighters
- Soloists
- Other

THE SEASON OF RENEWAL

LENT 5

Liturgical Color: Purple

Gospel: John 12:1-8 (Common)
Luke 20:9-19 (Lutheran)
John 8:1-11 (Roman Catholic)

Themes: *John 12:1-8.* Mary's act of mercy and Judas' act of pretense. We like to believe that our external acts are more significant than internal motivation.

Luke 20:9-19. The owner's trust and the renter's revenge. We like to believe that we are the good empire and they are the evil empire.

John 8:1-11. Jesus' response as the Light, and the Pharisees' response in the dark. We like to believe that our motives are pure while those of others are impure.

Result: Those who think they are first may well be last.

Planning Notes

Pastoral Invitation to the Celebration

One pastor began this way:

Welcome to the fifth Sunday in Lent. How are you doing? Even more importantly, how are you *being*? We judge much of our Christianity on what we do/don't do. God judges us on our *being*, that is, who we are in relationship to God, each other, and our best self. God invites us to find out what that means — now! So, let's be what God wants us to be, so we can do what God wants us to do.

Celebrating the Act of Renewal

Try this: Scrutinizing our sin. When "Sin" is mentioned, most of us think about sins of the flesh. Contrast our thinking about sins of the flesh with Jesus' condemnation of the sins of the "good people such as you and I," that is, the sins of the Spirit.

Take a look at this one, suggested by Huston Smith: "You can never get enough of what you really do not want."

Or this one, described by Dietrich Bonhoefer: "The sin of respectable people is running from responsibility."

Or Jesus' idea of sin as a disposition/attitude: "What is your favorite sin (that is, attitude)? Do you want forgiveness?"

Now, state: "To become a forgiven follower of Christ means to change our attitude/disposition and to relinquish making value-judgments about others and relinquishing personal (me-first, or me-only) gain as the guiding principle of life."

Message to the Children of All Ages

Suggested:

1. *John 12:1-8.* Review the Scripture. The Bible tells us that Judas was showing off. Do you ever do that; do you know others who do? How? Contrast Mary's act of humility with Judas' act of pretending.

2. *Luke 20:9-19.* Review the Scripture. Ask the children their impressions of the renter's revenge. Ask if they see anything like that on TV. If so, what do they think about it? Tie this in with the event and result of the Cross.

3. *John 8:1-11.* Review the Scripture. Bring two light bulbs, one that works, one that doesn't. Talk about how Jesus brought new light, (new ideas, hope, love) and how the people wanted to live in darkness, and still do (the burnt-out bulb). Our response is to go around turning on lights. Help the children to see how they can do this, without making this a condition of "going to heaven." Show them how you do this.

Proclamation of the Word

Consider this:

1. *John 12:1-8.* Find some examples of this Scripture in our contemporary church life. I remember a church officer who opposed our placing a tall, steel-structured cross on our church patio (cost: $2000) because "we ought to use that money for mission." He himself was a "tithing tightwad," who fought the mission every year.

2. *Luke 20:9-19.* Reflect upon how we misunderstand, and want to misunderstand, another's action. Here is a good opportunity to deal with the essence of sin as I-centeredness, as Sigmund Freud's Pleasure Principle, "I want what I want when I want it, and never mind the consequences," as "the attempt to justify our actions." In our "accepting" theology, we often fail to deal with judgment.

3. *John 8:1-11.* Think of the things we do in the dark that we wouldn't dare to do in the light. Someone once said, "If you own a circus, you will go broke if you keep it open only during the day." One of the scariest things about our society is the increase of daylight crimes. Christ came, not only to reveal the light, but to be the light. How does Christ light up your life, even when it seems dark?

Response to the Sermon

Suggested: Incorporate into the prayer the truth that it's easy to stand back and to throw rocks at the biblical people who failed to understand and follow Jesus. We do the same, only we're more subtle (we think). We need the same forgiveness they needed.

Stewardship Challenge

Consider this: The stewardship of sleeping and waking. Louis H. Evans, in *Life's Hidden Power*, suggests that many of us sleep too well at night, because we are "maladjusted to the status quo." If we seek to be God's person, we will find ourselves in constant conflict with the world.

Planning Notes

Charge to the Congregation

Suggested: Have we ever wondered how our lives and congregations would look if we ever took our commitment seriously? Do you think we would stop killing the prophets and saints of history? Do you think we would get our own lives straight with God before we begin to judge and condemn others? How are we willingly to let God's Spirit change us, our being, thinking, doing, beginning now?

Meditation at the End of Worship

We think of our activity as Christians as directed toward God — prayer, worship, Bible study — instead of toward our fellow humans. Maybe we've turned our thinking inside out. John 3:16 tells us that "God so loved the *world* . . ." What do we give to the world as a result of our worship? (from *Please Touch,* greatly revised)

Planning for Your Congregation

Suggestions   Your Situation

I. Other Scriptures
Lay readers:

- Psalm 126
- Psalm 28:1-3, 7-11
- Isaiah 43:16-21
- Philippians 3:8-14
- John 12:1-8; 8:1-11

II. Hymn Possibilities
Hymn selections:

"God of Grace and God of Glory"   Fosdick
    (hymn of the month)
"When We Are Tempted to Deny Your Son"
                                    Romig
  (for the last three Sundays of Lent)

III. Other Music Possibilities
Music selections:

Music for Preparation
    Medley of Lenten Hymns
Response to the Prayer of Praise
    "The Lord's Prayer"   West Indies Version
Response to the Children's Message   Chorus only,
    "I Am the Light of the World"
            Jim Strathdee/Howard Thurman
    (copyright 1969 by Jim Strathdee)
Response to the Old Testament
    (put it to your music)
    "Lord, We've Heard the Words;
    Teach Us to Respond to Your Word."
Offertory
    "Bless the Lord, O My Soul"   Ivanoff
Music for Dismissal
    Medley of Lenten Hymns

IV. Bulletin Cover
Bulletin design ideas:

V. Bulletin Symbols

VI. Miscellaneous Details *(Assignments):* _____

- Ushers
  (Use Children and families)
- Banners
- Flowers
- Assistant(s) at Holy Communion

- Greeters
  (Use children and families)
- Candlelighters
- Soloists
- Other

THE SEASON OF RENEWAL

SUNDAY OF THE PASSION

(When not observed as Palm Sunday)

Liturgical Color: Purple/Scarlet

Gospel: Luke 22:1—23:56

Theme: The passion of Jesus and the violence of life —
Seeing ourselves in the crowd
and seeing our response at the Cross.

Pastoral Invitation

Planning Notes

Consider this: From the beginning of worship, bring home the theme of passion and violence. Perhaps you will use T. S. Eliot's remark, "The greatest treason is to do the right thing for the wrong reason."

We worship corporately to let the power of God and the lives of each other strengthen us, and to let the world know who God and we are, in the name of God the Creator, Liberator, Sustainer.

Celebrating the Act of Renewal

If you haven't done this before, put some flesh on this act of worship:

Select someone from the congregation to be "Jesus." Ask that person to walk slowly around the sanctuary, while a soloist sings, "Jesus Walked that Lonesome Valley." As the soloist finishes, "Jesus" stands in front of the cross; ask any or all members of the congregation to join him/her there.

(Allow several moments of silence.)

Then, invite them to affirm their reconciliation by singing to the tune, "Michael, Row the Boat, Alleluia." Perhaps someone will write new words for this particular day. For example, "Come to God with songs of praise."

Reading the Scripture

One congregation did this:

While the liturgist reads, ask the people to put themselves, their feelings, their emotions into the scene. After the reading, suggest to the people that we say what the people of Jesus' day said,

"I could never have looked upon his face without tears filling my eyes."	*But Pilate did!*
Repeat.	*But the disciples did!*
Repeat.	*But the crowd did!*

Planning Notes

Stewardship Challenge

Consider this focus on the stewardship of discipleship:

"The test of discipleship is how much we are at odds with the world, not our degree of adjustment to it." (Kenneth Clarke)

Charge to the Congregation

Consider this quotation from Roger Shinn:

"The responsibility of the moral agent (the Christ-like person) is not simply to oppose evil; it is to contribute to the formation of a society (family, community, state, nation, world) in which persons do not fear only evil choices." How will we do that beginning today?

Meditation
(Printed at the end of the worship order.)

"The peace of Christ cannot be defined, only received and experienced." (Kenneth Clarke)

Planning for Your Congregation

Suggestions	Your Situation
I. Other Scriptures	*Lay readers:*
• Psalm 31:1-5, 9-16 • Isaiah 50:4-9a • Deuteronomy 32:36-39 • Philippians 2:5-11	
II. Hymn Possibilities	*Hymn selections:*
"All Glory, Laud and Honor" 　　Melchoir Teschner, 1615 "Come to Us, Mighty King" 　　Felice de Giardini, 1769	
III. Other Music Possibilities	*Music selections:*
Music for Preparation 　"Cortege and Litany"　　Dupre Response to the Old Testament 　"The Gates of Jerusalem"　　Don McAfee Response to the Children's Message 　"Rejoice, the Lord is King" 　Words by Charles Wesley, Music by Ian Mitchell 　(Music copyright 1966, 1967, 1968 by F.E.L. Church Publications, Ltd., 1543 W. Olympic Blvd., Los Angeles, 90015) Offertory 　"The Hour of Utmost Need"　　Bach Response to the Proclamation 　"Good News"　　Jane Marshall Music for Dismissal 　Medley of Holy Week Hymns	
IV. Bulletin Cover	*Bulletin design ideas:*
V. Bulletin Symbols	

VI. Miscellaneous Details *(Assignments):* _____

- Ushers
- Banners
- Flowers
- Assistant(s) at Holy Communion

- Greeters
- Candlelighters
- Soloists
- Other

THE SEASON OF RENEWAL

PALM SUNDAY

(When not observed as Sunday of the Passion)

Liturgical Color: Purple/Scarlet

Gospel: Luke 19:28-40, Matthew 26:14-27, 66

Theme: Cheering for the Wrong Reasons — Christ's triumphal entry into Jerusalem.

Pastoral Invitation

Planning Notes

One pastor began this way:

"Welcome to Palm Sunday. Let's pretend. If Jesus opened the door to the sanctuary and walked down the center aisle, how would you greet him?" (extend silence) Then, ask the congregation to respond, verbally. "And now, for the rest of worship, we shall examine our motives for how we would greet him."

Declaration of our Joyful Expectations

One congregation followed the pastor's greeting with this response:

Pastor: We want to say that we would "stand up and cheer" if Jesus the Christ walked into this sanctuary.

Ministers: **We're not sure what we would do; for we are a mixture — of joy and sorrow; of high and low moods; of hypocrisy and honesty; of hope and despair; of sadness and gladness; of hate and love.**

Pastor: You're right. We are all of these and more.

Ministers: **What do you mean, "more"?**

Pastor: I mean that whoever we are, in whatever situation, in whatever mood we find ourselves, God is there first. No matter how we treat God, no matter how we respond, God always beats us to the draw. And because of that promise, we can know for a fact that God cares, that God has compassion and concern for each of us, for all of us, no matter how we respond.

Ministers: **Great News! God loves me! God loves the family! God loves the world!**

Pastor: Rejoice and be glad about that!

Ministers: **Indeed we shall! Indeed we do!**

(idea inspired by a lost resource)

Celebrating the Act of Renewal

Suggestion: the pastor may want to introduce the confession with this statement:

A German friend of Marcus Barth said: "God forgives but society does not." What kind of sins (Sin) do we bring for forgiveness? Anyone who questions God's forgiveness of any guilty fellow human being needs to examine [his/her] own conscience. All of us are tempted to prove our own innocence/importance by condemning others. Rejection of God's grace is a sin even greater than theft, murder, adultery, or exploitation of other human beings.

Planning Notes

(Continue the confession with this, or another, printed prayer:)

"God, we admit we talk out of both sides of our mouth. We confess by our creed and formal worship that you are Lord and Master. But we live by worshiping what we can see and feel, hold and control. We admit we cannot hold to discrimination and hold on to your love, yet we allow the brainwashing of our environment to color our values, distort our logic, and accommodate our personal comforts.

We have decried overt violence, and cooperated with its subtle brother, in structures which coerce and repress others. We have blamed you for our feelings of insignificance, when we have lost our own significance by failing to champion the significance of others. And we also admit it, it is easier to confess than to change.

We are trapped by our own circumstances. Break through, Lord God, with Your Cross, stamping us with a new birthright, and a fresh fire for justice, mercy and love — for this world's sake, and for the sake of Jesus who died for all. (a.u., revised)

(one to two minutes for silence)

Select ahead of time, three people to offer prayers of forgiveness and acceptance. (Be sure they use the microphone.)

Proclamation

Consider this: Point out the reality that the crowd "cheered for the wrong reasons." Indicate ways we do the same thing.

Follow the sermon with the prayer "Why Did You Tell Me to Love?" by Michel Quoist from his book, *Prayers,* Sheed and Ward, Inc. copyright 1963

Charge to the Congregation

Consider this: "Ovation" by Herbert Brokering, from his book, *Uncovered Feelings,* Fortress Press, Philadelphia, Pennsylvania 1929, copyright 1969 for Your Congregation

Benediction

Suggested: Use your own statement, or find one that summarizes worship. An example: "You belong to Christ, even when you don't stand up and cheer. Go into the world, and live in his power."

Planning for Your Congregation

Suggestions | Your Situation

I. Other Scriptures *Lay readers:*

- Psalm 118:19-29
- Psalm 22:8-9, 17-20, 23-24
- Isaiah 50:4-9a
- Philippians 2:5-11

II. Hymn Possibilities *Hymn selections:*

"All Glory, Laud and Honor"
   Melchoir Teschner, 1615
"Lift Up Your Heads, O Mighty Gates"
   Georg Weissel, 1642

III. Other Music Possibilities *Music selections:*

   Music for Preparation
      Medley of Palm Sunday Hymns
   Response to the Old Testament
      "Rejoice in the Lord"   Theron Kirk
   Response to the Assurance of Pardon
      "The Lord's Prayer"   West Indies Version
   Offertory
      "Our Father in Heaven"   Bach
   Music for Dismissal
      Medley, Palm Sunday Hymns

IV. Bulletin Cover *Bulletin design ideas:*

V. Bulletin Symbols

VI. Miscellaneous Details *(Assignments):*

- Ushers
- Banners
- Flowers
- Assistant(s) at Holy Communion

- Greeters
- Candlelighters
- Soloists
- Other

THE SEASON OF RENEWAL
MAUNDY THURSDAY

Liturgical Color: Purple/Scarlet

Gospel: Luke 22:7-20, John 13:1-15

Theme: Corporate worship of the community of faith to celebrate the Maundy Thursday Sacrament of the Lord's Supper.

Planning Notes

ADORATION

Pastoral Invitation

Our pastor began this way:

Our Biblical symbol	Isaiah: From "Woe to me" to "Here Am I"
Our contemporary symbol	Bible in one hand; newspaper in the other
Our Maundy Thursday symbol	Introspection: Looking Within
	Direction: Looking Without
	Both are necessary.

Prayer of Praise

One congregation used this responsive prayer:

Pastor: I invite us to open our minds to the voice of God.
Ministers: **We seek to think God's thoughts.**
Pastor: I invite us to open our hearts to God's love.
Ministers: **We seek to be channels of love to our neighbors.**
Pastor: I invite us to open our lives to the invasion of God's life.
Ministers: **We seek to share in the ministry of God's life through our lives.**

All: **Come, Holy Spirit. Open our minds; warm our hearts; enter our lives.**

The pastor then says, "Let's put our words into practice; find someone whom you do not know and introduce yourself; then, take that person and introduce him/her to someone you do not know. So, please leave your seats and discover who is here." (a.u., revised)

INTROSPECTION

Hymn of Introspection

Suggested:
"Go to Dark Gethsemane" — James Montgomery, 1820, 1825

Reading from the Traditional Word *Planning Notes*

Suggested: Choir sing Psalm 116:1-19 *(choir write the tune)*
Layperson read Luke 22:7-20 *(practice with reader)*
Pastor read John 13:1-15 *(contemporary translation)*
Choral Response   "Four Chorales from 'Crucifixion' "   Stainer

DIRECTION

Consider this non-traditional approach:

Read a contemporary word, perhaps a selection from Lawrence Ferlinghetti's *A Coney Island of the Mind.*

Present God's truth, perhaps "The Sound of Silence" Paul Simon (Simon and Garfunkle, copyright, Charing Cross Music Co.)

Prayer response: Give plenty of time for silence, with a directed meditation around the first crucifixion and our present-day crucifixions.

DEDICATION

Stewardship Challenge

One pastor did this, in keeping with the theme:

Ask the people how they contribute to today's crucifixions with their money, both with what they spend and with what they withhold.

Follow with a prayer that people will have a new idea of how they spend and withhold their money, and themselves.

COMMUNION

Receiving the Elements

If you haven't done it before, try this:

For the distribution, use Russian rye bread and point out the symbolism. Jesus identifies with and establishes our relationship with our enemy (in this case the Soviets). Ask the people to say to the person to whom they pass the bread, "[Name], the body of Christ is for you."

For the cup, use juice laced with vinegar, and explain its relationship to the drink served Jesus while on the Cross. Ask the people to say to the person to whom they pass the wine, "[Name], the blood of Christ is for you." (Serve notice to the congregation in advance that this drink will have a *bitter* taste.)

Invite the people to offer the prayers of thanksgiving.

Planning Notes

Benediction

Consider this: Ask the congregation to greet one another with the words, "[Name], the Peace and Power of Christ are yours."

Meditation at the End of Worship

Print in this bulletin:

"The way from God to a human heart is through a human heart." (Samuel Gordon)

Planning for Your Congregation

Suggestions | Your Situation

I. Other Scriptures *Lay readers:*

- Psalm 116:10-19
- Jeremiah 31:31-34
- Exodus 12:1-8, 11-14
- Hebrews 10:15-39
- 1 Corinthians 11:23-26

II. Hymn Possibilities *Hymn selections:*

"The God of Abraham Praise"
   Traditional Hebrew Melody
"Go to Dark Gethsemane"
   James Montgomery, 1820, 1825
"Be Known to Us in Breaking Bread"
   James Montgomery
   (Remain seated; think about the words)
"A Parting Hymn We Sing"
   Aaron R. Wolfe, 1858

III. Other Music Possibilities *Music selections:*

Music for Preparation
   "Have Mercy on Us"   Bach
Choral Introit
   "O Lamb of God"   Weiss
Choral Response to Our "Introspection"
   "Four Chorales from 'Crucifixion'"   Stainer
Offertory
   "In the Hour of Utmost Need"   Bach
Music for Dismissal
   "O Sacred Head"
   Ascribed to Bernard of Clairvaux (1091-1153)

IV. Bulletin Cover *Bulletin design ideas:*

V. Bulletin Symbols

VI. Miscellaneous Details *(Assignments):* _____

- Ushers
- Banners
- Flowers
- Assistant(s) at Holy Communion

- Greeters
- Candlelighters
- Soloists
- Other

THE SEASON OF RENEWAL
GOOD FRIDAY

Liturgical Color: Black
(The chancel furniture may be without color on this day)

Gospel: John 18:1—19:42

Theme: Celebrating Good Friday, which on the surface, doesn't appear good at all.

WORSHIP THROUGH QUIETNESS

Planning Notes

Invitation to Worship

One pastor used this statement:

"We are here to discover the meaning of death, so we, on Easter, will experience the joy of life."

Prayer of Praise

Consider this: Following the prayer include a printed contemporary version of the Lord's Prayer.

WORSHIP THROUGH INTROSPECTION

Confession of Sin

One pastor does this:

Pastor voices slowly, and with much feeling, the seven last words from the Cross. Off stage, have someone pound nails into a piece of wood.

Then, allow silence for three minutes.

Conclude with these, or similar, words:

If we believe that God forgives us, we also are called to forgive one another. The Lord's Prayer tells us that we are forgiven only to the extent that we forgive. Ask the people to decide how they will go about doing that with someone from whom they are alienated — *before Easter morning*. Conclude with this prayer:

> God, thanks for forgiving them;
> God, thanks for forgiving us.

Planning Notes

WORSHIP THROUGH INSPIRATION

Proclamation

Consider this: Focus on our need to experience crucifixion before we can experience resurrection. Many of us want the blessing of God without obedience to God; we want the joy of Easter without the pain of Good Friday.

WORSHIP THROUGH COMMUNION

Invitation to the Sacrament

One pastor did this:

Ask the congregation. "What do we bring to the sacrament? What do we seek to hide?"
(Allow a few moments of silence to reflect)

Hymn of Communion

Consider this: As the people sing "Go to Dark Gethsemane," ask them to put themselves in the scene during last hours of Jesus' life.

Distribution of the Elements

Try this: Ask the people to come forward to receive the elements, to spend as much time as they wish for meditation, and then, to return to their seats.

WORSHIP THROUGH CONSECRATION

Statement of Dismissal

"A candle loses nothing by lighting another candle." (a.u.)

Planning for Your Congregation

Suggestions Your Situation

I. Other Scriptures *Lay readers:*

- Psalm 22:1-23
- Psalm 31:2, 6, 12-13, 15-17, 25
- Isaiah 52:13—53:12
- Hosea 6:1-6
- Hebrews 4:14-16; 5:7-9

II. Hymn Possibilities *Hymn selections:*

"O Sacred Head Now Wounded"
   Based on Medieval Latin Poem
   Paul Gerhardt, 1656
"Go to Dark Gethsemane"
   James Montgomery, 1820
"There is a Green Hill Far Away"
   Cecil Frances Alexander, 1848

III. Other Music Possibilities *Bulletin design ideas:*

Music for Preparation and Dismissal
   Medley, Good Friday Hymns
Response from the New Testament
   "Ave Verum" Liszt

IV. Bulletin Cover

V. Bulletin Symbols

VI. Miscellaneous Details *(Assignments):* _____

• Ushers	• Banners	• Flowers	• Assistant(s) at Holy Communion
• Greeters	• Candlelighters	• Soloists	• Other

Easter, the Season of the Resurrection

Christianity focuses on, and revolves around, Easter Day (No such term as "Easter Sunday" exists.) Christianity either stands or falls on the Resurrection of Jesus Christ. If we can get rid of the Resurrection, we can get rid of the Church.

The Easter season begins on the Eve of Easter and ends on the Day of Pentecost, fifty days later. The movable days and festivals of the church year depend on the date of Easter. Easter is always the first Sunday after the full moon falling upon or after March 21, the first day of spring. If the full moon occurs on Sunday, Easter occurs on the following Sunday. Easter can occur between March 22 and April 25. This method of dating makes it coincide with the feast of the Passover, because the first Easter coincided with that feast.

Easter is the oldest festival of the church year. The period of fifty days after Easter is older than either Lent or Advent. This entire season from Easter to Pentecost was once observed as one continuous festival. Later, in the fourth century, the season was separated into the Resurrection, the Ascension, and Pentecost. In recent times, worship scholars have returned to including the Day of Pentecost at the end of Easter, rather than the beginning of a season to *follow* Easter. Some have even suggested the term "The Easter — Pentecost Season." Pentecost Day finishes what begins on Easter Day.

Ascension Day comes on the fortieth day after Easter and is always a weekday, Thursday. It is seen as the final act in God's drama of redemption, and it marks the completion of Christ's ministry on the earth. The season continues for ten days, corresponding to the length of time the disciples waited in Jerusalem for the gift of the Holy Spirit, who came at Pentecost.

The color for the Easter season, including Ascension Day, is white, signifying God's victory over the powers of evil, the perfection of God's work, and our joy. For Pentecost Day the color is red.

The symbols for Easter are the Cross and the Crown. The crown is used to signify the fact that Christ has been raised in power to be Lord of lords and King of kings. To this King, every person shall bow!

THE SEASON OF THE RESURRECTION

THE RESURRECTION OF OUR LORD

(Easter Day)

Liturgical Color: White

Gospel: John 20:1-18

Theme: "Now I've Heard Everything!"
The Disbelief of the Disciples

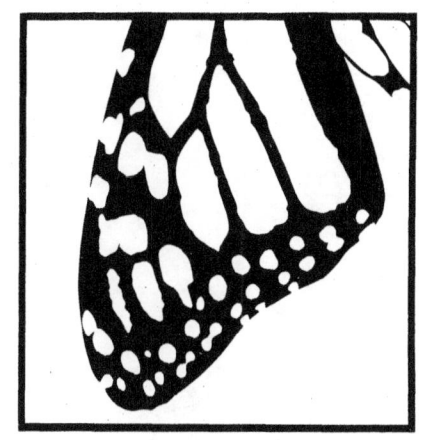

Pastoral Invitation

Planning Notes

One pastor always begins Easter with a return to Good Friday, mainly because people want the joy of resurrection without the pain of crucifixion — so, try this (if you did not do it during Holy Week):

Ask someone to sing "Jesus Walked that Lonesome Valley," while another walks around the sanctuary simulating Jesus' walk to the cross. At the end of the song, have the person either standing in front of the cross looking at it, or draped on the cross. After a few moments of silence, repeat, slowly and deliberately, the Seven Last Words from the Cross, while someone off stage pounds nails into a piece of wood. Use about ten minutes, so that the message sinks into the minds and hearts of the worshipers. Conclude with two minutes of silence.

Then, with much enthusiasm and energy, the pastor invites the people to the Easter celebration, perhaps with words similar to these:

"I assume by now that you've heard the good news — Christ lives! That ought to make a difference in our lives; and it does, even if we do not accept its reality personally. It could make more of a difference, though, if we refused to put limits on the Risen Lord in our lives — because Easter goes on, in and through us."

Celebrating the Act of Renewal

Consider this: Develop the confession around the theme of facing life with the Bible in one hand and the newspaper in the other. Read some headlines showing life as it is, and then some biblical passages showing life as it can be.

Follow with this assurance of pardon:

Pastor: Jesus declares a new humanity.
Ministers: **He accepts our lives, forgiving the past, and opening the future.**
Pastor: He calls us to face life and see it through.
Minister: **He even calls us to celebrate, in and through and with his power. Let it be!**

Choral response, from the popular song, "Let it Be."

Planning Notes

Proclamation of the Word

Consider this: One day, a pastor explained the meaning of the cross and resurrection to his young son. The pastor did a good job of telling the story, to which his son replied, "Now I've heard everything, Dad." Build on that theme.

Stewardship Challenge

Suggested: Many congregations receive the One Great Hour of Sharing offering on Easter. Develop it around the newspaper events read earlier. We get little mileage from what we spend on non-essentials. Point out how God can do much with little, which is no reason to give so little.

Prayer of Dedication

Consider this: So many of these prayers have no newness about them. Spend some time preparing this one-sentence prayer. Center on the theme suggested in the stewardship challenge.

Charge to the Congregation

Try this: Summarize in one or two sentences the theme for the day. Perhaps you will want to use this statement by E. Stanley Jones: "Religions are our search for God; the Gospel is God's search for us. There are many religions, but one Gospel." Or use this quote by Leslie Weatherhead: "The opposite of joy is not sorrow; the opposite of joy is unbelief."

Planning for Your Congregation

Suggestions	Your Situation
I. Other Scriptures	*Lay readers:*

- Psalm 118:1-2, 14-24
- Acts 10:34-43
- Exodus 15:1-11
- 1 Corinthians 15:1-11, 19-26
- Colossians 3:1-4

II. Hymn Possibilities — *Hymn selections:*

"Jesus Christ is Risen Today"　　Easter hymn
"The Strife is O'er, the Battle Done"
　　Translated by Francis Pott, 1861, altered

III. Other Music Possibilities

Music for Preparation　　　　　　*Music selections:*
　　Medley, Good Friday hymns
Response to the Old Testament
　　"Gloria Patri"
Response to the Proclamation
　　"Praise Christ, Alleluia"　　Butler
Offertory
　　"Rejoice Ye Christians"　　Bach
Response to the Benediction
　　"Lilies of the Field: Amen Chorus"
Response to the Act of New Life　　Solo
　　"Bridge Over Troubled Waters"　　Paul Simon
Response to the Prayer of Praise
　　Children/Youth Choir (if you have one)
　　"Allelu" Words and Music by Ray Repp (Copyright 1966 and 1967 by F.E.L. Publications, Ltd.)

IV. Bulletin Cover — *Bulletin design ideas:*

V. Bulletin Symbols

VI. Miscellaneous Details *(Assignments):* _____

- Ushers
- Banners
- Flowers
- Assistant(s) at Holy Communion

- Greeters
- Candlelighters
- Soloists
- Other

THE SEASON OF THE RESURRECTION

EASTER 2

Liturgical Color: White

Gospel: John 20:19-31

Theme: The necessity of doubt — (Most) Christians are first, last and always, doubters — that is, people who constantly put God to the test. As one author (unknown) has said, "Not everything that is faced can be changed, but nothing can be changed until it is faced."

Pastoral Invitation to the Celebration

Planning Notes

Consider beginning with this story:

During the pre-Easter season, a boy and man stand looking at the crucifixion scene in a store window. The boy speaks: "Them's Roman soldiers." The man remains silent. And the boy continues: "And there's Jesus; they killed him." The man starts to walk away; the boy runs after him, shouting, "Mister, I forgot to tell you the most important part! He's still alive!" (a.u.)

Suggested follow-up response:

Pastor: This is the day which the Lord has made.
Ministers: **But the days seem so full of trouble.**
Pastor: Yet God has made the heavens and the earth, and God rules over all.
Ministers: **But how can we trust God?**
Pastor: God has made Self known in Jesus Christ the Righteous One. In Christ, God has suffered all things, that our feet might be set securely on the Rock.
Ministers: **Yes, this is the day which the Lord has made, and we will rejoice and be glad in it.**

Celebrating the Act of Renewal
(Confession and Forgiveness)

Try this: Develop this act around Thomas' doubts and our own. Find a layperson, perhaps a "pillar of the church" who is willing to share his/her doubts about the faith. People will be surprised, and it is hoped, will begin to share their own doubts.

Follow this with an acknowledgment of just how much faith we express each day — when we use a bottle of medicine, or select groceries from an open shelf, or drive on the highways believing that people will stop at red lights and stop signs, or yes, even eating a hot dog without knowing its contents.

Planning Notes

Proclamation of the Word

Suggested: Focus on Thomas' doubting, "I don't believe you, Lord, unless I shove my fingers into the nail prints of your hands." Jesus didn't push him away. Deal with our legitimate reasons for doubting (that is, those rooted in moral difficulties and great sorrow, and the danger of our repressing our doubts). Then, spend some time expressing both scriptural and historical appreciation for honest doubting. Honest doubt precedes honest faith.

Stewardship Challenge

Try this as a follow-up to the doubting theme:

There is a "Stewardship of Doubting." Our doubting usually results in guilt and shame. True stewardship recognizes that we all doubt, if not in the open, then in silence, where our guilt and shame fester and where we receive no forgiveness. We are called to be honest in all things.

Prayer of Dedication

Continue this as a follow-up of the stewardship challenge:

Build the prayer around honest doubting, so that God can honestly forgive us. You may want to center on the fact that if we do not honestly doubt, we may try to buy our way into the Kingdom by what we give.

Charge to the Congregation

Suggested: Summarize today's worship experience. Perhaps you will want to build the charge around these words, borrowed from a pastor whose name eludes the author: One day a pastor visited a parishioner. The lady introduced her husband to the pastor with the words, "He's an agnostic." Pastor responded, "Aren't we all!"

The Bible says, in effect, "Appreciate your doubts. Welcome them as signs that the Holy Spirit is working in your life, compelling you to discard beliefs you need to discard. Put the Gospel to the test of your doubts. Any Gospel that won't stand up to your doubts isn't worth believing anyway. You not only have a capacity to doubt, but a duty to doubt, if you will grow into understanding of God that will meet needs of ours and the world's in this changing twentieth century. Honest doubt precedes honest faith.

Message to the Children of All Ages

Try this: Instead of always *reading* the Scriptures, this time *act* the Scriptures. Incorporate this act with the message to the children who always enjoy a story. Tie it in with their kinds of doubting, while sharing your own doubting. Fifteen years after admitting my own doubt to a faithful church member, she expressed appreciation about not having to feel guilty about her own doubts. My admission gave her permission to grow rather than to feel guilty.

Planning for Your Congregation

Suggestions	Your Situation
I. Other Scriptures	*Lay readers:*

- Psalm 2
- Psalm 149
- Psalm 118:2-4, 13-15, 22-24
- Acts 5:12-32
- Revelation 1:4-19

II. Hymn Possibilities　　　　　　　　　　　　*Hymn selections:*

"Christ the Lord is Risen Today"
    Charles Wesley, 1739, altered 1760, 1972
"The Day of Resurrection"
    John of Damascus (675?-749?)
    Translated by John Mason Neale, 1862, altered

III. Other Music Possibilities　　　　　　　　*Music selections:*

Music for Preparation
    "St. Anne Fugue"　　　　　　　　　　Bach
Response to the Act of Receiving New Life
    "Morning Has Broken"
    Popular Song made popular by Cat Stevens
Response to the New Testament　　　　　Choir
    "All Glory, Praise and Majesty"　　　　Bach
Response to the Children's Message
    "Of My Hands"　Ray Repp, Copyright 1966 by
    F.E.L. Church Publications, Ltd.
Response to the Proclamation
    Select an anthem of Joy
Offertory
    "Rejoice, Ye Christians"　　　　　　　Bach
Reponse to the Benediction
    'It Is a Great Day of Joy"　Claude Henri Vic

IV. Bulletin Cover　　　　　　　　　　　　*Bulletin design ideas:*

V. Bulletin Symbols

VI. Miscellaneous Details *(Assignments):* _____

- Ushers
- Banners
- Flowers
- Assistant(s) at Holy Communion

- Greeters
- Candlelighters
- Soloists
- Other

THE SEASON OF THE RESURRECTION

EASTER 3

Liturgical Color: White

Gospel: John 21:1-14

Theme: The sanctity of daily work;
the calling to God's work in and beyond our daily work.

Planning Notes

Pastoral Invitation to the Celebration

Suggested: Keep before the people the season of Easter, and how they see God in their daily activities. Well before worship, ask several members to write and present the call to worship by reflecting on the theme.

Celebrating the Act of Renewal

Try this: Center this part of worship around the routines of life, including that of allowing our job to be routine. Perhaps one or several members would develop a statement about their daily routines, followed with the congregational response, "God, also, is Lord of the routine!"

Follow this with a pastoral prayer which brings together the thoughts and feelings of the members' responses.

Proclamation of the Word

Suggested: Focus both on the dangers of falling into routine in everything we are and do, and of the many opportunities to redeem the routine, especially in our own homes in the ways we relate to each other. When, for example, was the last time that we told our mate and children, "I love you and I'm glad to have you as part of this family?" Then, take some time to find new ways to make the common uncommon.

Stewardship Challenge

Consider this: Continuing the same theme, the "Stewardship of the Routine," ask the people to write down one way they will allow God to bring new life to their routine schedule and to place that statement in the offering plate along with their money. Then, during the prayer of dedication, invite several to offer their prayers.

Charge to the Congregation

Consider this summary:

- A review of the worship theme;
- A challenge to redeem the routine;
- An invitation to report next week what happened (or to write a paragraph in the church newsletter), in response to the question, "How will we make Christ/love significant in all of our activities?"

Planning for Your Congregation

Suggestions

I. Other Scriptures

- Psalm 30:4-13
- Acts 9:1-20
- Acts 5:27-30, 40-41
- Revelation 5:11-14

II. Hymn Possibilities

"Christ the Lord Is Risen Again"
    Michael Weisse, 1531
    Translated by Catherine Winkworth, 1858
"Go, Labor On: Spend and Be Spent"
    Horatius Bonar, 1843

III. Other Music Possibilities

Music for Preparation and Dismissal
    Medley of Epiphany Hymns
Response to the Proclamation
    "I Walk the King's Highway"
    Evelyn Atwater Cummins
    (copyright by Zann Music, Inc. Sole Selling Agent: Edward B. Marks Music Corporation. Text used by permission of "The Church Pension Fund")
Response to the Act of Pardon
    "Of My Hands"
    Ray Repp, (Copyright 1966 by F.E.L. Church Publishing, Ltd.)

IV. Bulletin Cover

V. Bulletin Symbols

Your Situation

Lay readers:

Hymn selections:

Music selections:

Bulletin design ideas:

VI. Miscellaneous Details *(Assignments):* _____

- Ushers
- Banners
- Flowers
- Assistant(s) at Holy Communion

- Greeters
- Candlelighters
- Soloists
- Other

THE SEASON OF THE RESURRECTION

EASTER 4

Liturgical Color: White

Gospel: John 10:22-30

Theme: Refusing to believe the obvious — Believing is Seeing. We keep asking for another sign, and another, and another.

Planning Notes

Pastoral Invitation to the Celebration

Suggested: Center always on the one whom we worship and serve, upon the Christ.

You may want to use the following response:

Pastor: Jesus, called the Christ, has offered us a way of being fully human.
Ministers: **He has presented a new style of life based on love and peace and justice for all persons.**
Pastor: He has invited the church to declare this way of life.
Ministers: **Let us be the church at worship, so we can be the church in mission.**
Pastor: Let us celebrate life in Christ.
Ministers: **Let's do! Amen! Be it so!**

Celebrating the Act of Renewal

If you've never done this, try it:

Ask the people to think how they usually respond to the uniqueness of Jesus Christ. Does their thinking usually reflect a remark made by Mrs. Ed Sullivan years ago, "I have never felt that my own religion was so insufficient that I had to seek another faith. But if millions believe some other way, who am I to argue? The important thing is to believe that the world has a reason and a plan." Or consider a remark made by a Roman Catholic student from Carnegie Tech's "Panel of Americans," who said, "Even an athiest, if he is sincere in what he believes, can go to heaven." Or, the expression, "A little bit of religion can never hurt anyone."

Invite the people to think silently about those statements for a few minutes. Then, ask if they have a concern or question or clarification. Ask if they believe any of those statements. Many church members make similar remarks as casually as if they were asking for a piece of bread.

Then read some of Jesus' statements: "The Father and I are one; If you have seen me, you have seen the Father; no one comes to the Father but by me." (RSV) Ask them to meditate in silence again.

Develop the statement of pardon around our need for forgiveness to the uniqueness of the Good News wherever we are.

Proclamation of the Word

Planning Notes

Consider this: Develop the message around the theme, "Is Religion a Simple Matter of Sincerity?" Distinguish between religion and faith. Compare Christian beliefs with beliefs of other world religions. If one is true, then the other is not. For example, (1) Mohammedanism teaches that girl babies can be thrown into the garbage can if not wanted; Christianity respects every person as of equal worth. (2) Hinduism teaches that one is reincarnated into a higher or lower status depending on how one lives; Christianity teaches that salvation depends, not on what we do, but upon what God has done and is doing. (3) Buddhism teaches nothing about eternal life; Christianity teaches that eternal life begins now.

Stewardship Challenge

Consider continuing with the same theme: "The Stewardship of Belief."

It's too easy to drop our money into the offering plate without ever thinking about our motivation for giving in the first place. Drive home the need to make our Christian witness intelligent, rather than wishy-washy.

Challenge to the Congregation

One pastor always summarizes worship with a short, simple, summary. He will say, for example, "Religion is not a simple matter of sincerity. Religion is not even a matter of what we do with Christ. Faith is a matter of what we allow the Spirit of Christ to do with us. So, what difference will that make in your life this coming week?"

Planning for Your Congregation

Suggestions	Your Situation
I. Other Scriptures	*Lay readers:*

- Psalm 23
- Psalm 100:1-3, 5
- Acts 13:14-16, 26-33, 43-52
- Revelation 7:9-17

II. Hymn Possibilities   *Hymn selections:*

"All Praise to God in Highest Heaven"
   Michael Weisse, 1531
   Stanzas 1, 2, 4-6 translated by Margaret Barclay, 1950, altered 1972
   Stanza 3 by Dalton E. McDonald, 1972
"I Danced in the Morning"
   Sydney Carter, 1963
   (The Lord of the Dance)

III. Other Music Possibilities   *Music selections:*

Music for Preparation
   "Prelude and Sarabande"   Corelli
Offertory
   "Lord Christ, Be Present Now"   Boehm
Response to the Proclamation
   "Psalm 23"   *(Pick a version)*
Response to the Act of Recognizing our Humanness
                       Choir
   "Psalm 1 and Gloria"   Clokey
Music for Dismissal
   "Jesus, Lead Thou On"   Chorale

IV. Bulletin Cover   *Bulletin design ideas:*

V. Bulletin Symbols

VI. Miscellaneous Details *(Assignments):* _____

• Ushers	• Banners	• Flowers	• Assistant(s) at Holy Communion
• Greeters	• Candlelighters	• Soloists	• Other

THE SEASON OF THE RESURRECTION

EASTER 5

Liturgical Color: White

Gospel: John 13:31-35

Theme: The response of the pagan world to the new "sect," the Christians — "See how those Christians love one another."

Pastoral Invitation to the Celebration

Planning Notes

Try this: We celebrate the love of God to us and through us. Use your imagination to bring that message home, so that in worship, we not only say it and think about it, but actually do it. How do we show our love as a congregation, and how will we do so in worship?

Follow the invitation with a prayer similar to this one:

> Almighty God of love, who has created us in your own image, we praise you that you have freed us to receive your love and find our fulfilment in loving each other. Awe and wonder fill our hearts as we consider your love in Christ and acknowledge that we are the Church, the Body of Christ, a fellowship of love. Open our minds and hearts that our celebration may be a fresh encounter with your Spirit and a new experience of love for one another. (a.u.)

Celebrating the Act of Renewal

Consider this as a follow-up to the praise act of worship

You may want to have the congregation sing, "Love Divine, All Loves Excelling," to introduce the prayer of confession. Then, ask the congregation to pray this prayer silently (have it printed in the worship folder):

> "Forgive me that so little of Your love reaches others through me, and that I have borne so lightly the burden and pains of the world. Forgive me when I cherish those things that divide people, and make it hard for them to live with me, and when I have been thoughtless in my judgments, hasty in condemnation, grudging in forgiveness.

(Follow with two minutes of silence.)

For the prayer of pardon, have the congregation pray this, or a similar prayer, together:

> Convince us, God by your presence and power that the past is forgiven, that our sin is cleansed, and that our forgiveness has been bought with a price.

Possible choral response, sung by congregation or choir:

> "In your mercy hear us, Lord; in your mercy hear us Lord; We pray to you. Hear us, Lord. Amen"

141

Planning Notes

Proclamation of the Word

Suggested Theme:

"Where's the Action?" The pagan world's reaction to the first Christians' practice, "Love one another as I have loved you."

One pastor listed specific ways that the community of faith loves one another. For example:

I received a phone call from a woman who planned to attend a retreat. She had read a couple books I recommended. She called to thank me for recommending them, and to tell me how much she received from them. A call also came from a semi-retired man, who, in all of his years, had not permitted his mind to go stale, and who expressed his thanks for the sermon on sex. He said that four years previously he would probably have objected. He volunteers to take one of our ladies for cobalt treatments for twenty days. This provides an opportunity to talk about death and a person's own death.

You will find dozens of ways that people minister to each other. Secure permission in advance from individuals whose stories you would like to share at worship.

Perhaps you will want to conclude with this idea:

Someone has said, "Religion is what a person does with his/her solitude." We might better say it, "Faith is what a person does with his/her gratitude."

Stewardship Challenge

Try this: Ask several people ahead of time to share their stewardship of love. How do they respond on a daily basis as a thanks for God's love?

Perhaps they could also offer the prayers of dedication.

Challenge to the Congregation

Suggested: Give a practical challenge around the theme, "Love one another as I have loved you."

God calls us to be lovers, God's lovers, in the world. What a privilege! What pain that brings. What joy that brings.

Planning for Your Congregation

Suggestions   Your Situation

I. Other Scriptures   *Lay readers:*

- Psalm 145:1-21
- Acts 13:44-52
- Acts 14:8-27
- Revelation 21:1-6

II. Hymn Possibilities   *Hymn selections:*

"O Love That Will Not Let Me Go"
   George Matheson, 1882
"O Love, How Deep, How Broad, How High!"
   Latin, fifteenth century. Translated by Benjamin Webb, 1851, altered
"Where Cross the Crowded Ways of Life"
   Frank Mason North, 1903, altered 1972
"We Give Thee But Thine Own"
   William Walsham How, 1858

III. Other Music Possibilities   *Music selections:*

Music for Preparation
   "Meditation"   Thiman
Choral Introit
   "Hallelujah!"   (author unknown)
      "Hallelujah! Hallelujah! In His temple, God be praised; In the high and heavenly places be the sounding anthem raised."
Prayer Response
"Hear our Prayer, O Lord"
   George Whelpton, 1897
Response to the Reading of Scripture
   "Now Let the Heavens Adore Thee"   Bach
   English Text: Catherine Winkworth
Offertory
"Voluntary"   Himmel
Response following the Benediction
   "Seven-Fold Amen"
Music for Dismissal
   "Wake, Awake, for Night is Flying"   Walther
(The postlude, music for dismissal, and the response to the Scripture reading are arrangements of a melody by Philipp Nicolai from J. S. Bach's Cantata, "Sleeper's Awake.")

IV. Bulletin Cover   *Bulletin design ideas:*

V. Bulletin Symbols

VI. Miscellaneous Details *(Assignments):* _____

- Ushers
- Banners
- Flowers
- Assistant(s) at Holy Communion

- Greeters
- Candlelighters
- Soloists
- Other

THE SEASON OF THE RESURRECTION
EASTER 6

Liturgical Color: White

Gospel: John 14:23-29

Theme: Love for God, made possible by the coming of the Holy Spirit, brings us the peace of Christ, the kind of peace which the world cannot give and which the world cannot take away.

Pastoral Invitation

Planning Notes

Suggested: Keep the focus on the One whose Presence and Power we celebrate. Example: "Welcome to the corporate celebration of the Good News from the A.D. side of the Resurrection of Jesus Christ, from the A.D. side of the birth of the Christian Church. So, Rejoice!"

Follow with Moffitt's Translation of Psalm 150 *(with exuberance)*

All: **Praise the Lord! Praise the Lord! Praise the Lord!**
Right: Praise God in the sanctuary.
Left: *Praise God in the heaven of power.*
Right: Praise God for His mighty deeds.
Left: *Praise God for His sovereign strength.*
Right: Praise God with a bugle blast.
Left: *Praise God with lute and lyre.*
Right: Praise God with the drum and dance.
Left: *Praise God with strings and flute.*
Right: Praise God with resounding symbols.
Left: *Praise God with the clash of cymbals!*
All: **Let everything that breathes, praise the Lord! Praise the Lord! Praise the Lord!**
  Alleluia. Amen!

Celebrating the Act of Renewal

If you've never done this, try it:

Introduce the act of renewal by suggesting that the world and its pressures and stress are out to do us in — and we do it to others and ourselves. Ask the congregation to think silently about the following series:

"Slow to suspect — quick to trust
Slow to condemn — quick to justify
Slow to offend — quick to defend
Slow to expose — quick to shield
Slow to reprimand — quick to forbear
Slow to belittle — quick to appreciate
Slow to demand — quick to give
Slow to provoke — quick to conciliate
Slow to hinder — quick to help
Slow to resent — quick to forgive." (a.u.)

Does this describe you, a member of the incendiary fellowship?

Planning Notes

Follow with a remark from John Patton's book, *Is Human Forgiveness Possible?* He suggests that human forgiveness is best understood, not as an act or even an attitude, but "as discovering that I am more like those who have hurt me than differing from them." How true!

For the truly courageous, ask members of the congregation to offer forgiveness to one another in the sanctuary and to receive forgiveness from one another. If the people are unwilling to do this during worship, suggest that they find a way to do so this coming week.

Proclamation of the Word

Suggested: Help people discover how they can experience, on a daily basis, the words of Jesus: "Peace, I leave with you; my peace I give to you, not as the world gives, do I give to you."

Norman Bakken has written, "Peace is measured, not by ceremonial pomp, ecclesiastical power, or a heavenly ideal, but by the movement of life in and for one's neighbor, for Christ is always in our neighbor."

Stewardship Challenge

Suggested: "The stewardship of peace." Ask the people to think about ways they create war during the week, including in their own homes, and how, through the Spirit of Christ, they can acknowledge and live out peace.

Charge to the Congregation

Consider this: Make certain that the people know that Christ comes to give peace. Say it several times with different voice inflections. Ask them to repeat the truth several times.

Planning for Your Congregation

Suggestions	Your Situation

I. Other Scriptures   *Lay readers:*

- Psalm 67
- Acts 15:1-2, 22-29
- Acts 14:8-18
- Revelation 21:10-14, 22-27

II. Hymn Possibilities   *Hymn selections:*

Use hymns that you've already used. About one-fourth to one-half of today's congregation did not attend worship last Sunday. Use new hymns until they are known (so that people may come to the end of their life realizing that hymns other than "In the Garden" were written).

"Come to Us, Mighty King"
 Anonymous tract, 1757, altered 1972
"Lead On, O King Eternal"
 Ernest Warburton Shurtleff, 1888, altered, 1972
 (Background: this hymn was written as a graduation hymn for the commencement of Shurtleff's class in 1887 from the Andover Theological Seminary. He served a series of congregational pulpits throughout America, and did student and relief work in Paris before and during World War I.)

III. Other Music Possibilities   *Music selections:*

Music for Preparation
 "The Holy Ten Commandments"   Bach
Response to the Scripture Reading
 "Upon Your Great Church Universal"
 by J. M. de Carbon-Ferriere, 1823.
 Translated by Margaret House, 1949; altered 1972
 (Ask the congregation to read the words)
Offertory "Be Thou in Ernest"   Karg-Elert
Doxology "Praise God" to the tune of "All Creatures of Our God and King" Francis of Assisi, 1225
(Change the doxology now and then)
Music for Dismissal Medley of Easter Hymns

IV. Bulletin Cover   *Bulletin design ideas:*

V. Bulletin Symbols

VI. Miscellaneous Details *(Assignments):* _____

- Ushers
- Banners
- Flowers
- Assistant(s) at Holy Communion

- Greeters
- Candlelighters
- Soloists
- Other

THE SEASON OF THE RESURRECTION

ASCENSION DAY
ASCENSION SUNDAY

(The Thursday before Easter • Replaces Easter 7)

Liturgical Color: White

Gospel: Luke 24:46-53

Theme: The ascension of Christ and the challenge to his disciples.

Pastoral Invitation to the Celebration

Planning Notes

Consider this: Incorporate Paul Vieth's statement, "Awareness of the Presence of God is the heart of worship; response to the Power of God is the heart of the act of worship," with the idea that worship is not something that happens between the church and God, but rather, worship is something that happens between the world and God.

Follow with this response, which emphasizes the Christian's response in the world:

Pastor: Who are you to have come here today?
Ministers: **We are the people of God, the forgiven ones, those called by God to live under God's Lordship in the world, and to serve God as Christ's natural resource.**
Pastor: And how did you decide to come?
Ministers: **Because we choose to celebrate God's love together, and to equip ourselves as Christ's support system in the world.**
Pastor: Let us sing our hymns of praise and make our commitments to God in Christ in the midst of the world.
Ministers: **We shall. Amen.**

Confessions and Forgiveness

One pastor introduced the prayer with words similar to these:

We put considerable emphasis on our personal sins, often to the neglect of our confessing our social sins.

Follow with this prayer:

O God, whose handiwork we see in the grand design of the universe as well as in your mastery of the smallest detail, forgive our carelessness. Forgive our carelessness with words: for blundering into your presence in prayer with a shower of syllables banking on a sick sentimentality, thoughtless and insensitive. Teach us, God, the discipline of saying what we mean, so that we can mean what we pray. Forgive us our carelessness with the world: for using the earth as if it were our private playground to do with as we please, with resources to be plundered and beauty to be ravished. Teach us, God,

Planning Notes

to respect the balance of nature that feeds and clothes and shelters us; and nourish our spirits as well, but only when we have the patience to think your thoughts after you. Forgive our carelessness with persons: allowing ourselves to be obsessed with the success of numbers, measuring everything in the mass, and standing in awe of statistics. Teach us God, the importance of one sparrow, one sunset, one rose, one person, one Lord, one faith, one baptism, one God of us all, even you, Lord, who are above all and through all and in us all. Amen (a.u.)

Have the people respond to the confession with the Kyrie, "Lord, Have Mercy Upon Us."

To introduce the Assurance of Pardon, speak words similar to these: We have said the words of the confession; do we believe the truth of the confession? I invite you to pray this prayer of forgiveness:

Most gracious and holy God, who has given your son, Jesus Christ, to save your people from their rebellion and estrangement from you and from each other, forgive us for our personal and social sin. Cleanse us from all our rebellion and I-centeredness, and renew a right spirit within us, through the grace and power of Jesus Christ, our Lord and Savior. Amen

Message to the Children of All Ages

Consider this: In your schoolwork or around your home, do you sometimes not understand your assignment? What do you do, and how do you feel? *(Make certain that you spend enough time to get below the surface of those questions.)* Compare that with the disciples' experience of not understanding Jesus or his mission. *(Give several examples of how they did not understand.)* And then, what happens when you do understand? Compare that with what the disciples did when they finally believed the Good News. They rejoiced and praised God.

Proclamation of the Word

Suggested: Consider the theme "From the institution to the world." In the light of Christ's work, we are called to be his people in his world. This involves a variety of things:

1. the uniting of talk with action,
2. the necessity of looking different and acting differently,
3. the strong possibility of failure by all "success" standards,
4. the acceptance of servanthood,
5. the necessity to listen and confront.

Stewardship Challenge

Consider this: Ask, "How do you plan to spend the next 167 hours for God in the world?"

Charge to the Congregation

Suggested: Perhaps you will want to re-read *God's Frozen People* after all these years. The author suggests that to be a Christian is to recognize that we are pilgrims, and that if we take Christ seriously we will face the accusations of being "disloyal" and "worldly," "oddly scrupulous," a sucker, and someone to be exploited. "This is our true vocation."

Planning for Your Congregation

| Suggestions | Your Situation |

I. Other Scriptures
- Psalm 47
- Psalm 110
- Acts 1:1-11
- Ephesians 1:15-23

Lay readers:

II. Hymn Possibilities

"A Hymn of Glory Let Us Sing"
   The Venerable Bede (672-735). Stanzas 1, 2, translated by Elizabeth Rundle Charles, 1858; altered 1972; Stanza 3, translated by Benjamin Webb, 1854; altered 1972.

"Christ the Lord is Risen Again"
   Michael Weisse, 1531. Translated by Catherine Winkworth, 1858

"Jesus Shall Reign"
   Based on Psalm 72   Isaac Watts, 1719

Hymn selections:

III. Other Music Possibilities

Music for Preparation and Dismissal
   "Only to God on High be Glory"
   Zachau and Teleman
Choral Introit
   "As In the Solemn Stillness"   Fiesinger
Response to the Scripture Reading
   "Creator, Supreme"   John L. Lewis
Response to the Prayer after the Proclamation
   "O for a Thousand Tongues to Sing"
   Charles Wesley, 1739; altered 1972
Offertory
   "Meditation"   Arcadelt

Music selections:

IV. Bulletin Cover

Bulletin design ideas:

V. Bulletin Symbols

VI. Miscellaneous Details *(Assignments):*

- Ushers
- Banners
- Flowers
- Assistant(s) at Holy Communion

- Greeters
- Candlelighters
- Soloists
- Other

THE SEASON OF THE RESURRECTION

EASTER 7

(When not observed as Ascension Sunday)

Liturgical Color: White

Gospel: John 17:20-26

Theme: But we are one. Jesus' prayer for unity. Looking for ways to claim our unity in the midst of great diversity.

Planning Notes

Pastoral Invitation

If you've never done this, begin with your frustration and confusion about the lack of unity, despite Jesus' prayer. And tie this in with the possibility of God's frustration also. Yes, this begins worship with a negative; yet, it also verbalizes what many in the church, and as the church, feel and believe. At the conclusion of that frustration, say something similar to this: "Now, God, we're frustrated; You're frustrated. We've thwarted your will and purpose for us. Teach us how to live out the essence of Jesus' prayer for his church. Give us some practical ways today through your Holy Spirit to begin during this worship hour.

Congregational Response to the Invitation

Suggested:

Pastor: Be joyous about God, everyone! Be glad to serve God! Sing because God is here!

Ministers: **We know that the Lord is God! We did not make ourselves! God made us; we belong to God!**

Pastor: Enter into worship, despite all of your frustrations and confusions, with thanksgiving, praise, and an openness to new truth. Bless the Name of God!

Ministers: **Our Lord is good. God's love never stops, even when we have questions and doubts about ourselves, as individuals, as members of the faith. We depend on God forever. Alleluia! Amen!**

Celebrating the Act of Renewal

One pastor printed and distributed the following quiz to the people as a part of the confession of sin (recognition of who we are):

"An Ecumenical Quiz"
(Some questions offered with tongue in cheek)

1. There are more than 250 denominations in the U.S.A. In your opinion this is
    a) contrary to God's will
    b) according to God's will
    c) not a matter of much concern to God

2. In your opinion, these denominations are divided largely because of
   a) their origins in different European countries.
   b) differences in doctrine
   c) differences in race and economic class
   d) tradition

3. The most important division within the church today has to do with
   a) the mode of baptism and the Lord's Supper
   b) whether or not the church should change
   c) whether or not the church should be involved in social issues (race, war, poverty, drugs, etc.)
   d) whether or not the main business of the church is to preach individual salvation
   e) doctrines such as the authority of the Bible and Virgin Birth

4. A conservative is, in your view, one who
   a) is stupid
   b) doesn't want to change or let others change
   c) really believes the Bible
   d) believes Jesus was truly the Son of God

5. A liberal, in the church, is one who
   a) wants change for the sake of change
   b) is stupid
   c) doesn't believe in the infallibility of the Bible
   d) wants to apply Jesus' teachings to life today

6. The best thing which could happen to our divided church now would be
   a) to divide into liberal and conservative congregations/denominations
   b) for each side to quit all controversial activities and have peace
   c) to go on as we are now
   d) none of the above: this is my suggestion _____

Give the people ample time to think about these statements.

For the assurance of pardon (Act of receiving new life) encourage the people to offer the prayers. Ask the people to respond with an affirmative "amen" after each prayer, if indeed, they can make such an affirmation. Ask them to remain silent if they cannot make such an affirmation.

Proclamation of the Word

Suggested: Because we have heard Jesus' prayer so often, we will need to bring some new light to it. Put the prayer in today's perspective. For example, despite the fact there are more than 250 denominations in the United States, fifteen of them enroll about 90% of the church membership. Describe ways that your people have already crossed the ecumenical barriers. Remind the people that barriers fall as we get to know each other on a person to person basis. In a *Christian Century* article some years ago, the author put the issue in perspective with these words: "Concern for ecumenism is one form of a larger concern, namely, human alienation."

Stewardship Challenge

Try this: Continue to follow the theme with "the stewardship of unity in the middle of our diversity." How will we find ways this week to acknowledge the unity-in-diversity theme of Jesus' prayer.

Charge to the Congregation

Consider this (or similar words):

If we pray that God's church may be one, beginning with this congregation, (which unity in theory we have, though in practice we have it not), we are exposing ourselves to a great danger, the danger that God may take us at our word. I challenge each of us to take God at God's word, so that God can take us at our word — and lead us into the reconciled and reconciling life, into the liberated and liberating life. Alleluia! Amen!

Planning Notes

Planning for Your Congregation

Suggestions	Your Situation

I. Other Scriptures

- Psalm 97
- Psalm 47
- Acts 16:6-10, 16-34
- Acts 7:55-60
- Revelation 22:12-17, 20

Lay readers:

II. Hymn Possibilities

"I Sing the Mighty Power of God"
   Isaac Watts, 1709, Stanza 3, altered

Perhaps your denomination or the National Council of Churches has provided a contemporary hymn for Ecumenical Sunday.

Ongoing caution: Watch the sexist language. Even though the congregation may still use the hymn, at least make people aware of the words. Many times, we can change the words even while singing the hymn, for example, changing "men" to "we."

Hymn selections:

III. Other Music Possibilities

Music for Preparation
   "Adagio" (Sonata I)   J. S. Bach
Choral Introit
   "Holy, Holy, Holy" *(many versions exist)*
Response to the Old Testament Choir
   "Praise Christ! Alleluia!"   Butler
Offertory
   "What God Ordains"   Peeters
Doxology
   (Begin to use a variety of versions; use a new version, however, until people know it well.)
Choral Response following the Benediction
   "Nuni Dimittis"   Vaughn Williams
Music for Dismissal
   Medley of seasonal Easter Hymns

Music selections:

IV. Bulletin Cover

Bulletin design ideas:

V. Bulletin Symbols

VI. Miscellaneous Details *(Assignments):*

- Ushers
- Banners
- Flowers
- Assistant(s) at Holy Communion

- Greeters
- Candlelighters
- Soloists
- Other

THE SEASON OF THE HOLY SPIRIT

THE DAY OF PENTECOST

Liturgical Color: Red

Gospel: John 14:8-17, 25-27; John 15:26-27; 16:4b-11; John 20:19-23

Theme: "On Ice . . . or, On Fire" — the coming of the Holy Spirit into the lives of the disciples, and ours!

The Season of the Holy Spirit

Planning Notes

Pentecost, meaning "Fiftieth Day," has its roots in the ancient Jewish Feast of Weeks, a celebration of the first harvest, seven weeks after the spring sowing of the grain. Later, the Jews associated Pentecost with the giving of the Law to Moses on Mount Sinai. For Christians, Pentecost has a two-fold significance independent of Jewish tradition. It commemorates the event in Acts 2 when two things occurred:

1. the Holy Spirit came in the fulfilment of Christ's promise to his disciples;
2. the Christian Church launched upon its world mission.

Pentecost, often called "Whitsunday," may refer, either to the wearing of white robes by candidates for baptism, or to the old Anglo-Saxon word, "wit," meaning "wisdom" — an allusion to the outpouring of the Spirit of wisdom. (Ephesians 1:17)

The color for the Pentecost season, which lasts seven days, is red. Red signifies divine fire, in addition to the fervor of the Church's faith. The dove serves as the most common symbol of the Holy Spirit, and is found in the story of Jesus' baptism.

Consider this as your planning proceeds:

The culture has left this church Holy Day alone for the most part. Unfortunately, many people in the mainline denominations know little about Pentecost. So, plan wisely and carefully, and tie this event into the Easter event.

This may be a good time to change the worship headings. Consider, for example:

CELEBRATION THROUGH ADORATION

CELEBRATION THROUGH CONFESSION AND FORGIVENESS

CELEBRATION THROUGH THE WORD

CELEBRATION THROUGH THANKSGIVING AND INTERCESSIONS

CELEBRATION THROUGH COMMITMENT

Pastoral Invitation to the Pentecost Celebration

Begin with this:

John Stott has said that "Before Christ sent the Church into the world, he sent the Spirit into the church. The same order must be observed today." The biblical themes today center on the coming of the Holy Spirit (Counselor and Dynamite) into the lives of the disciples, the original ones and many more. Has the Holy Spirit come into your life? If so, what difference does that make in your witness and work? And, by the way, don't expect the coming of the Holy Spirit to happen in the same way with everyone.

Planning Notes

Follow with this responsive reading. (Use much energy. Begin a second or third time if the people drag it out or simply mutter the words.)

Pastor: The Holy Spirit is here!
The Holy Spirit is the power and presence of Christ!
The Holy Spirit is the healing force of the world!
Ministers: **We come to celebrate the Spirit's bringing wholeness to our lives.**
Pastor: I invite us to open ourselves, our needs, the needs of others, and our relationships to God and to each other.
Ministers: **We come with expectations, of some of which we're aware; some of which we're not. We come to experience what the Holy Spirit of God can do with our lives made unreservedly open and receptive.**

Confession and Forgiveness

Consider this: Always find ways to introduce the confession. For example, M. G. Kyle once said, "When the tongues of flame appear, most people run for the fire department." Is that what we do? Does this confession speak for you; if it does, I invite you to pray it verbally.

"Almighty and Holy God, we speak of your presence with us; but most of the time, we try to go it on our own. We pray for your help, but we do not accept your will. We profess that your love abides within us, but we are impatient with our family members and neighbors. We say that we love our enemies, but we barely love our relatives. We tell others about our faith, but we fail to act it out. We portray a living Savior, but we fail to make him real. We call you "Father/Mother," but we act like orphans. We confess our sins, but we ignore our errors. Save us, O God, from being swallowed up by our inhibitions."

(author unknown, revised)

(Allow two minutes for meditation)

Always find ways to introduce the assurance of pardon, which focuses on accepting forgiveness. (Multitudes of church members, who have participated in many assurances of pardon have never experienced forgiveness.) Try this: "We have prayed the prayer; we have confessed our sins. Now, I invite you to receive God's forgiveness; for indeed, every moment up to the present moment, is forgiven. The past is forgiven. Believe the Good News, the best news ever given, because God cared enough to send the very best."

Pastor: If anyone is in Christ, he/she is a new person (not perfect, but new). The old has passed away (unless we keep dragging it into our awareness); the new has come. The mercy of the Lord is from eternity to eternity. I declare to you in the name of Jesus Christ, you are forgiven.
Ministers: **So be it!**
Pastor: O Lord, open our lips,
Ministers: **and our mouths shall show forth your praise. Amen**

Proclamation of the Word

Suggested: Clear up some of the extremes of celebrating Pentecost. Spell out a simple way for people to be evangelists while realizing that they are called to witness, not to change people (changing people is God's job). Perhaps you will want to use this statement which comes from a filmstrip produced by the Presbyterian Church. In it one of the people says, "Your greatest witness is your deepest relationship of love," which means, "to touch another person's heart, you will need to use your own."

Stewardship Challenge

One pastor did this:

Ask each person in worship to think of a person or family for whom they will pray and express their love and friendship, that is, someone outside of the church. Ask them to write that person's or family's name on a piece of paper and place it in the offering plate. They need not write their name on it. This act can serve as their commitment along with their money.

Charge to the Congregation

Consider using the responsive reading "Get the Word Out."
  (This reading appears below.)

Follow this with a birthday party for the birth of the church: to include cake, decorations, and balloons.

(For the especially brave:) You may want to print this message in the bulletin:

"No other organization on the face of the earth is charged with the high calling to which the church is summoned; to confront men (people) with Christ." (H. G. Kyle) Therefore, there should be some penalty that church members must pay if they do not win at least one person to Christ in five years.

GET THE WORD OUT
Commitment to Evangelism

Leader: "Get the word out" was the way James Bevel, the American civil rights leader, cryptically identified the evangelistic responsibility of the church and every member of the people of God. Get the word out: Christ is for man. He himself was man, human in every way. He knows what man is and can be. He is the man for others. He calls us into being — fully human beings — in community. He calls us to embody the good word about himself and the good word about us and to get it out to all the world.

Response: **We will get the word out! We will embody the word!**

Leader: Get the word out — that American Indians and Blacks are humans with no less of the image of God stamped in their being than others. This is good news to persons who have too long been ignored, treated like children, used, exploited. All people are children of the Father. God has no favorites. Let us get the word out!

Response: **We will get the word out that we are in the same family of God and we will act out the word and we will speak it and sing it with Christian joy!**

Leader: Get the word out — that Christ and his people are concerned about the poor. The plaguing paradox of poverty in the midst of plenty, underprivileged in the background of the highly privileged; dark, hidden poverty alongside conspicuous wealth drive Christ's followers to action — for people, not just money is at stake here, wasted people, underdeveloped human resources, God-given possibilities unrealized. Christ cares! He is among the poor. Even as we discern his real presence in the communion, so also has he called attention to his presence in the impoverished and dispossessed, those with any kind of need. Get the word out — Christ is for the disadvantaged.

Response: **We will get the word out — the good word to the poor, of the one in their midst who calls his own to be with him there at the place of need.**

Leader: Get the word out — Christ has fired his people with concern about illiteracy and inadequate training in a country with a public school system and a world with mass communication; about the verbally unskilled and inarticulate dominated by the more articulate; about the socially handicapped shunted off from those with social grace; about persons who have lost hope of a better life or incentive to reach out toward it to receive it. Get the word out — Christ's people have begun to catch his concern.

Planning Notes

Planning Notes

Response: **We will get the word out. We will be the living word seen of all men.**

Leader: Get the word out. Human life is sacred. We have a growing uncomfortable feeling about war, that it is not the right way to settle disputes, that war settles nothing. God's Son was called the Prince of Peace. It was he who called us to love even our enemies and to have a deep and prayerful concern for any who despitefully use us. If communists or segregationists or any other people provoke us or frighten us, can we embody a new law and a new day and be the "first fruits" of the reconciling grace of Christ? We can! Get the word out!

Response: **We will get the word out — that Christ is for peace and his people are for peace and that Christ and his people will work for the outlawing of war and threatening military gestures.**

Leader: Get the word out — that the tribal warfare called denominational competition is a dead issue and that God's people are becoming more and more committed to serving their communities and together proclaiming the Gospel of the Lord they all have professed to be serving. Get the word out that the church is repenting of having too long turned its eyes inward upon itself, with too much concern for its own affairs. It is turning out toward the world which God loves and for which Christ died, the world for which he gave his church as his continuing embodiment or incarnation. And in its service-mission-witness to the world, the church is being renewed. God is doing it! Let us get the word out.

Response: **We will get the word out about Christ's Church being renewed as it seeks to embody his Gospel and proclaim the good word that he is the world's Savior and Lord.**

Leader: Get the word out, that all walls must come tumblin' down. Berlin walls, Jerusalem walls and Mandelbaum gates; curtains between the holy of holies and the place where all the rest of us worship; walls between the clergy and the laity; walls between races and colors and castes. Walls between men and women. Walls between employers and employees, educated and uneducated, the native and the "foreigner;" the church and the world. All these walls are broken down in Christ. The walls are done. Get the word out.

Response: **We will get the word out that in Christ all walls are broken down, that people "outside" can be "inside" and those "inside" can see "outside." For he has made all one and has broken down the middle wall of partition between us.**

Leader: Get the word out — by every means possible: the "Early Bird" satellite, the TV networks, the radio, every little transistor, the news reporter to every newspaper reader. By every electronic device and every human means our ingenuity can imagine and invent, from person to person the witness must spread the Good News.

Response: **We will get the word out — imaginatively using every means available to us in this day. And if God can use us we are willing to be the instruments of his Gospel proclamation, his witnesses, who by deed and word proclaim the saving grace and Lordship of Christ.**

Leader: Get the word out! The cross of Christ is our redemption, and reconciliation is available to all people, if they will but receive it. For the artist's analysis and the poet's vision there can be salvation. For the statesman and politician, for the professor and teacher, for those in places of public and civic leadership, there can be saving accountability. Christ is with the poor, the disinherited, the hungry, the confused peasant of Vietnam. Good news of meaning, hope, freedom, justice is for all people and for each individual. This is the Good News. Get the good word out.

Response: **We will get the word out, the word of the Cross and the Christ of the Cross, the word of salvation in him for all people everywhere, however impotent and powerless they may consider themselves or in whatever power structures they may wield influence. Christ is Savior! Christ is Lord! We will get the word out for all must know. Help us, Lord Jesus, to be true to our commitment.**

(author unknown)

Planning for Your Congregation

Suggestions	Your Situation
I. Other Scriptures	*Lay readers:*
• Psalm 104:1, 24-34 • Genesis 11:1-9 • Acts 2:1-21 • 1 Corinthians 12:3-7, 12-13	
II. Hymn Possibilities	*Hymn selections:*

"God of our Fathers"
   (ask the people to sing "mothers" also)
   Daniel C. Roberts, 1876
   (this hymn has been updated with non-sexist language)
"Heralds of Christ, Who Bear the King's Commands"
   Laura S. Copenhaver, 1894; altered 1972
"Breathe on Me, Breath of God" Edwin Hatch, 1886
"Jesus Shall Reign"
   Based on Psalm 72 Isaac Watts, 1719	

III. Other Music Possibilities *(if possible, use a variety of musical instruments)*	*Music selections:*

Music for Preparation
   Medley of Pentecost hymns
     (use the energetic hymns)
Choral Introit
   "Breathe the Holy Spirit"   Regier
Response to the Proclamation Choir
   "Spirit of God"   Scholin
   (If the hymn appears in your hymnbook, ask the people to follow the words)
Offertory
   "Beside Still Waters"   Hamblen
Response following the Benediction
   Amen Chorus from "Lilies of the Field"
   (ask the people to sing this as they leave the sanctuary; use hand instruments if available)	

IV. Bulletin Cover *(perhaps you will want to order a special one for this day)*	*Bulletin design ideas:*
V. Bulletin Symbols *(Use many symbols; for example, the fire, the wind, the dove.)*	

VI. Miscellaneous Details *(Assignments):* _____

- Ushers
- Banners
- Flowers
- Assistant(s) at Holy Communion

- Greeters
- Candlelighters
- Soloists
- Other

THE SUNDAYS AFTER

PENTECOST
PART I

The Sundays after Pentecost, The Season of the Kingdom of God on Earth

The Sundays after Pentecost (Roman Catholics refer to these as "Sundays in Ordinary Time"), the longest portion of the church year, begins on the Sunday following Pentecost and continues until the eve of Advent. Depending on the date of Easter, this season can contain twenty-two to twenty-seven Sundays. This season serves (1) as the instructional half of the church year; and (2) as an attempt to keep God's commandments. Spiritual nourishment received from the observance of the first half of the church year now brings forth Christ-like living.

The Sundays after Pentecost can be divided into four parts:

I. Christians are taught how they are called to their new life in Christ.

II. Christians are instructed about how to live their new life in Christ.

III. Christians are reminded that God's love in Christ is to be shared with others.

IV. Christians are instructed concerning the return of Christ and the judgment that will follow.

Historically, the four parts of the half year known as the "Sundays after Pentecost" were arbitrarily broken out as follows:

I. From the Holy Trinity (whose date varies each year) until the Festival Day of Saints Peter and Paul (June 29);

II. From Saints Peter and Paul to the Festival Day of Saint Lawrence, Deacon and Martyr (August 10);

III. From Saint Lawrence to the Festival Day of Saint Michael and All Angels (September 29);

IV. From Saint Michael to Christ the King (whose date varies each year).

As a bit of simple arithmetic will show, this makes for uneven lengths in the first and last quadrants, a situation which cannot be avoided when attempting to organize a season which expands and contracts based on cycles of the moon (the assignment of Easter Day, a calculation made from lunar cycles, affects the length of the seasons of both Epiphany and the Sundays after Pentecost).

In an attempt to break this long "season" of Sundays into four shorter and more manageable units for worship and preaching planners, and with an eye to honoring the historic four-fold division, we have presented the material in the second half of this workbook according to the following four divisions (keep in mind that Part I could be longer, since when Epiphany Season is short, Propers 3, 2, and/or 1 could also be moved from Epiphany into the second half of the church year, which is in such a year correspondingly longer):

Part I
The Holy Trinity — Proper 7 (Common)
The Holy Trinity — Pentecost 5 (Lutheran)
The Holy Trinity — Ordinary Time 12 (Roman Catholic)

Part II
Propers 8 — 14 (Common)
Pentecost 6 — 12 (Lutheran)
Ordinary Time 13 — 14 (Roman Catholic)

Part III
Propers 15 — 21 (Common)
Pentecost 13 — 19 (Lutheran)
Ordinary Time 20 — 26 (Roman Catholic)

Part IV
Proper 22 — Christ the King (Common)
Pentecost 20 — Christ the King (Lutheran)
Ordinary Time 27 — Christ the King (Roman Catholic)

Liturgical colors for the season are as follows:

White for the Holy Trinity and Christ the King
Green for the rest of the season, except red on Reformation Sunday and All Saints' Sunday.

Symbols for the season include the following:

- *The Cross*
- *The Triangle*, signifying that salvation is the work of Christ, prompted by the love of the Father (Parent), and received by us through the work of the Holy Spirit.
- *The Circle*, signifying the eternal, unending nature of the Trinity.
- *The Dove*, representing the Spirit which fills the body of Christ, the church.
- *The Ship*, representing the church as the Body of Christ on the stormy waters of life.

THE SEASON OF THE HOLY SPIRIT

THE HOLY TRINITY

Liturgical Color: White

Gospel: John 16:12-15

Theme: Three in One — God the Father, Son, and Holy Spirit

Planning Notes

Pastoral Invitation

Suggested: Welcome to worship, in the name of God, the Father, the Son, and the Holy Spirit. We shall explore this theme, despite its misunderstandings and confusions. I invite you to put aside as much as possible of what you have heard in the past concerning the Trinity. Meanwhile, let us celebrate the presence and power of God who appears to us in a multitude of ways. Begin to think of the ways in which God appears to us as persons, to us as the church.

Follow up with this invitation

Pastor: In the name of the Father, and of the Son, and of the Holy Spirit,
Ministers: **we celebrate your Presence and Power.**
Pastor: The Lord be with you,
Ministers: **and with your spirit.**
Pastor: Praise the Lord!
Ministers: **The Lord's name be praised!**

Confession and Forgiveness

Try this: Spend some time with the Apostles' Creed, a statement which many church members have recited for many years, often without understanding what they said. On this occasion, center only on the Trinitarian aspect of the creed. Some do not say parts of the creed because they don't understand it. Some feel guilty about parts they "don't believe," because no one has ever defined it. Some are confused about what they're supposed to believe. Granted, they could have found out if they had wanted. It is the pastor's responsibility to talk about what it means. Give them time to ask questions and to clarify. (Traditionally, the Athanasian Creed is recited on this Sunday. The courageous may want to use that one instead of the Apostles' Creed.)

(Then, spend some time in silence.)

Follow with this prayer:

O God the Father who so loved the world, have mercy.
O God the Son, obedient to love, have mercy.
O God the Holy Spirit, Love in action, have mercy.
    Have mercy on us, O Holy Trinity, and enfold us
    in Your most sacred Love. Have mercy.
That our hearts may respond to your love, teach us, O God.
That our eyes may see your love, show us, O God.
That our lives may refract your love, lead us, O God.

That our love may be pure and holy, cleanse us, O God.
O God of Love, pour down upon us all the gift of
yourself that we may love what you love;
. . . that your love may abide in us and guide
us in all of our doings with people and things and you.
Let our lives be lived in joyful surrender, and our
sacrifice be holy so that we may share yourself with
you, O Blessed Trinity, who are a Unity of Love. Amen

Used at the 1961 Annual Banquet for
CBA's in Tulsa (author unknown)

Proclamation of the Word

Suggested: Dorothy Sayers has said what a good many people think about the Trinity: "The Father is incomprehensible, the Son is incomprehensible, and the whole thing is incomprehensible." Describe the difference between "persona" and "person." Use an analogy. If someone asked, "What is H_2O?" we might answer quickly, "It's water." Upon further reflection, we would change our answer, "It's either water, ice, or steam, depending on the temperature." Or compare the Trinity of God with the trinity of a man, who is father, son, and brother. God has chosen to reveal the God-Self in different ways, at different times to different people.

Charge to the Congregation

Consider this: Conclude with similar remarks: The real issue for us is not that of debating the reality of the Trinity. Dr. John Baillie, the Scottish theologian put the matter succinctly with these words: "Would the people who see you daily, and with whom you have most to do, be able to guess, even if you had not told them, that you believe in the divinity of Christ? . . . [Even though we are not eye-witnesses] we can show that his love is still a power in the world. And unless we bear this living witness, no other witness that we bear can be of much effect."

So go in peace and courage and bear that witness,
this week, every week, in the name of the
Father, Son, and Holy Spirit.

Planning Notes

Planning for Your Congregation

Suggestions **Your Situation**

I. Other Scriptures *Lay readers:*

- Psalm 8
- Proverbs 8:22-31
- Romans 5:1-5

II. Hymn Possibilities *Hymn selections:*

"Holy, Holy, Holy! Lord God Almighty!"
    Reginald Heber, 1826
"Come to Us, Mighty King"
    Anonymous tract, 1757, altered 1972
"Of the Father's Love Begotten"
    Aurelius Predentius (348-410)
    Translated by John Mason Neale, 1851, and Henry W. Baker, 1859, altered 1972

(see your worship book for a variety of selections)

III. Other Music Possibilities *Music selections:*

Music for Preparation
    Medley of Trinity Hymns
Response following the Prayer of Praise
    "Gloria Patri"
Response to the Pardon
    a choral version of the Apostles' Creed
Response to the Pastoral Prayer
    "Hear Our Prayer, O Lord"
    George Whelpton, 1897
Response to the Proclamation
    "All Glory Be to God on High"
    Based on Gloria in excelsis
    Attributed to Nikolaus Decius, 1525
    Translated by Catherine Winkworth, 1863, altered
Offertory
    Allegretto from "The Prodigal Son"   Sullivan
Music for Dismissal
    Chorale, "My Dearest Jesu"   Bach

IV. Bulletin Cover *Bulletin design ideas:*

V. Bulletin Symbols

VI. Miscellaneous Details *(Assignments):* _____

- Ushers
- Banners
- Flowers
- Assistant(s) at Holy Communion

- Greeters
- Candlelighters
- Soloists
- Other

Understanding the Lectionary during the Sundays after The Holy Trinity

This *Workbook* is intended for use within three broad lectionary families, (1) Lutheran, (2) Common, and (3) Roman Catholic. During the first half of each lectionary year (the Sundays from Advent 1 — the Holy Trinity), Gospel texts, which are the anchors for material in this book, are nearly identical both in terms of lectionary and where they appear on the church calendar. During the second half of the church year, however (the portion commonly called "The Time of the Church," "Sundays after Pentecost," "the non-festival half," or "Sundays in Ordinary Time," this scheme changes. Because Lutherans assign the Gospel texts according to the church year calendar while the Roman Catholic and Common lectionaries assign them instead to dates dictated by the secular calendar, the purchaser of this *Workbook* needs assistance. The following table will enable you to locate any Sunday in the remaining pages of this book for use with your own lectionary.

Gospel Text	Church day usage *(Lutheran only)*	Lectionary designation *(Common only)*	Lectionary designation *(Roman Catholic only)*	Calendar Parameters *(Common, RC only)*
John 16:12-15	The Holy Trinity	The Holy Trinity	The Holy Trinity	Sunday after Pentecost
Luke 9:11-17			Corpus Christi	Sunday after Trinity
Luke 7:1-10	Pentecost 2	Proper 4	Ordinary Time 9	May 29 — June 4
Luke 7:11-17	Pentecost 3	Proper 5	Ordinary Time 10	June 5-11
Luke 7:36—8:3	Pentecost 4	Proper 6	Ordinary Time 11	June 12-18
Luke 9:18-24	Pentecost 5	Proper 7	Ordinary Time 12	June 19-25
Luke 9:51-62	Pentecost 6	Proper 8	Ordinary Time 13	June 26 — July 2
Luke 10:1-12, 16-20	Pentecost 7	Proper 9	Ordinary Time 14	July 3-9
Luke 10:25-37	Pentecost 8	Proper 10	Ordinary Time 15	July 10-16
Luke 10:38-42	Pentecost 9	Proper 11	Ordinary Time 16	July 17-23
Luke 11:1-13	Pentecost 10	Proper 12	Ordinary Time 17	July 24-30
Luke 12:13-21	Pentecost 11	Proper 13	Ordinary Time 18	July 31 — August 6
Luke 12:32-48	Pentecost 12	Proper 14	Ordinary Time 19	August 7-13
Luke 12:49-56	Pentecost 13	Proper 15	Ordinary Time 20	August 14-20
Luke 13:22-30	Pentecost 14	Proper 16	Ordinary Time 21	August 21-27
Luke 14:1, 7-14	Pentecost 15	Proper 17	Ordinary Time 22	August 28 — Sept. 3
Luke 14:25-33	Pentecost 16	Proper 18	Ordinary Time 23	September 4-10
Luke 15:1-10	Pentecost 17	Proper 19	Ordinary Time 24	September 11-17
Luke 16:1-13	Pentecost 18	Proper 20	Ordinary Time 25	September 18-24
Luke 16:19-31	Pentecost 19	Proper 21	Ordinary Time 26	Sept. 25 — October 1
Luke 17:1-10	Pentecost 20	Proper 22	Ordinary Time 27	October 2-8
Luke 17:11-19	Pentecost 21	Proper 23	Ordinary Time 28	October 9-15
Luke 18:1-8	Pentecost 22	Proper 24	Ordinary Time 29	October 16-22
Luke 18:9-14	Pentecost 23	Proper 25	Ordinary Time 30	October 23-29
Luke 19:1-10	Pentecost 24	Proper 26	Ordinary Time 31	October 30-Nov. 5
Luke 20:27-38	Pentecost 25	Proper 27	Ordinary Time 32	November 6-12
Luke 21:5-19	Pentecost 26	Proper 28	Ordinary Time 33	November 13-19
Luke 19:11-27	Pentecost 27			
John 12:9-19		Christ the King		
Luke 23:35-43	Christ the King		Christ the King	

For those who use the Lutheran or the Roman Catholic lectionaries, the table above indicates not only how to determine on which Sunday a Gospel text is used but also what liturgical terminology is used to designate that day on the church calendar in the second half of the year.

For users of the Common lectionary, however, an additional step needs to be taken to determine the church day designation. The table provided here identifies Gospel texts for Common lectionary users in terms of "propers." The Sundays in this half of the church year are identified, however, as Sundays after Pentecost. These designations are assigned by counting forward from the Sunday of the Holy Trinity. (That is, the first Sunday following the Holy Trinity is always designated as Pentecost 2, for both Lutheran and Common lectionary users, even though the Gospel text assigned to Pentecost 2 will usually vary from one lectionary to the other in any given year.)

For example, in church year 1989, the following applied:

Sunday 25 May — *The Holy Trinity*
    Gospel — John 16:12-15 (Lutheran, Common, Roman Catholic)

Sunday 1 June — *Pentecost 2* (Lutheran, Common)
    Gospel — Luke 7:1-10 (Lutheran)
    Gospel — Luke 6:39-49 (Common)

Sunday 1 June — *Corpus Christi* (Roman Catholic)
    Gospel — Luke 9:11-17

Sunday 8 June — *Pentecost 3* (Lutheran, Common)
    Gospel — Luke 7:11-17 (Lutheran)
    Gospel — Luke 7:1-10 (Common)

Sunday 8 June — *Ordinary Time 9* (Roman Catholic)
    Gospel — Luke 7:1-10

THE SEASON OF THE HOLY SPIRIT

CORPUS CHRISTI
(Roman Catholic)

Liturgical Color: Green

Gospel: Luke 9:11-17

Theme: Sharing Life with Christ

Pastoral Invitation to the Celebration

Suggested: Focus on the receiving of the body and blood of Christ with our need to share bread and water with the world which God has created. Perhaps you will want to begin with a responsive version of Psalm 110.

Act of Recognizing our Humanness and Act of Receiving New Life

Try this: Point out that the sacrament, while personal, is never private; it is always corporate and social; it has to do both with us as a local congregation and with the world which God has called us to serve. Allow several moments of silence for the people to consider this idea.

Following the silence, perhaps you will want to read the passage from 1 Corinthians 11:23-26, comment about its content, and invite the people to consider their oneness, their unity, their wholeness in and through the body of Christ.

Invite the congregation to sing "This Is My Body," by John F. Wilson, based on Matthew 26:26.

Proclamation of the Word

Consider these ideas:

1. Much of the world suffers from a lack of food and lack of safe, pure water.
2. Much of the church suffers from a lack of commitment to those who die from hunger or thirst.
3. Jesus feeds his people both physically and spiritually and calls the church to do the same.

Obviously, we can't do everything; what is one thing that each member of the congregation will do this week to bring healing and wholeness to the people who touch their lives and whose lives they touch?

Ask them to place that commitment in the offering plate.

Stewardship Challenge

Try this: Follow the proclamation with the suggestion that each person write on a piece of paper how he/she will feed those around them this week. Describe the difference between "feeding on" someone and "feeding" someone, the difference between rescuing and nurturing someone.

Charge to the Congregation

Consider this: Worship is never a private affair between God and me. Worship, which does not result in resolve and obedience, is not worship, no matter how pious or sincere. Dietrich Bonhoefer once said that "the step of obedience must be taken before faith is possible." What form will our obedience take when we leave the sanctuary today?

Planning Notes

Planning for Your Congregation

Suggestions	Your Situation

I. Other Scriptures   *Lay readers:*

- Psalm 110:1-4
- Genesis 14:18-20
- 1 Corinthians 11:23-26

II. Hymn Possibilities   *Hymn selections:*

"Holy, Holy, Holy!"   Reginald Heber, 1826
"Come, Thou Almighty King"
    Anonymous, 1757, altered
"Our Father, By Whose Name"
    F. Bland Tucker, 1941; 1972

III. Other Music Possibilities   *Music selections:*

Music for Preparation and Dismissal
    Selected from Your Tradition
Response to the Act of Receiving New Life
    Congregation
    "This Is My Body"   John F. Wilson
HE'S ALIVE, 1972, Hope Publishing Company,
380 South Main Place, Carol Stream, Illinois 60187
Response to the Proclamation
    Choir and Congregation
    Tie the sacrament to our eating
    Use the round, "Thank You, Lord, for Daily Bread" by Bill Floyd with "Let Us Break Bread Together," a Spiritual, both in Hope Publishing Company's "Folk Encounter."

IV. Bulletin Cover   *Bulletin design ideas:*

V. Bulletin Symbols

VI. Miscellaneous Details *(Assignments):* _____

• Ushers	• Banners	• Flowers	• Assistant(s) at Holy Communion
• Greeters	• Candlelighters	• Soloists	• Other

THE SEASON OF THE HOLY SPIRIT
(Sometimes called Season of the Father, Son, Holy Spirit)

PROPER 4
PENTECOST 2
ORDINARY TIME 9

Liturgical Color: Green

Gospel: Luke 7:1-10

Theme: Intentional living from a surprising source

Pastoral Invitation

Planning Notes

Suggested: Welcome to the ongoing celebration of Pentecost. God has pursued us and wooed us where we go, where we are. God seeks to speak to us through every event, every experience. God even seeks us in worship. I invite us to listen for the Word of God now, so that we have a better chance of listening later.

You may want to continue with the following liturgy:

Liturgist: Let us speak of our faith and our lives, in the name of the Father and the Son and the Holy Spirit.
Community: **Amen**
Liturgist: The Lord is our enemy.
Community: **He demands our death.**
Liturgist: The Lord is our friend.
Community: **He commands our love.**
Liturgist: Accept the friendship of the Lord happily.
Community: **Lord, give us your Word so that we may open our hearts.**
Liturgist: The Word says, "In all things God works for good with those who love him."
Community: **That is his Word.**
Liturgist: The Word says, "Nothing in all creation will ever be able to separate us from the love of God in Christ Jesus our Lord."
Community: **That is his Word.**
Liturgist: His Word is daring us to dance before all of life.
Community: **He dares us to dance in the brilliance and dullness of life.**
Liturgist: He dares us to dance in the light and shadows of our living.
Community: **He dares us to dance in the good and the bad.**
Liturgist: He dares us to dance before justice and injustice.
Community: **That is his word and we accept it gladly.**
Liturgist: Will you not only accept it but seek to live it?
Community: **We will.**
Liturgist: Amen.
Community: **Amen.**

Used by permission of the Ecumenical Institute, present work now done under the name, "Institute of Cultural Affairs," 1049 Magnolia Avenue, Los Angeles, CA 90813.

Planning Notes

Confession and Forgiveness

If you haven't done this before, spend some time with doubt and faith. Many of the people carry guilt about their doubts right into the grave, especially when clergy emphasize the ministry of people similar to the centurian. Give permission to all to affirm that doubts are an essential part of faith. Perhaps you will want to read Leslie Weatherhead's book, *The Christian Agnostic.*

Follow with this or a similar prayer: God, I recognize the many needs I have: the need to be loved, to have others take an interest in me, to have them listen and care about what is happening to me and within me. I know also my need to love, to share myself with someone, to do things that give satisfaction and a contribution to life. Sometimes, I find these needs being met, and life becomes rich and full. At other times, they go unfulfilled, and I feel frustrated and hurt. I pray that I may grow in the ability to receive and give, despite all of my doubts and unanswered questions. Help me to seek you, and in discovering your will, to discover myself and others; and in doing all of that, to make a commitment to you and others, despite whatever doubts and confusions I may have.

You may want to proceed with this response,

Pastor: In Christ we have learned that we are loved.
Ministers: **Christ has declared us worthwhile persons, despite our doubts. It is good to be who we are.**
Pastor: Let us love ourselves and move from that relationship to a new love for those around us.
Ministers: **Let's give thanks and live!**
Pastor: Let's do just that!
Ministers: **So be it! Amen!**

Message to the Children of All Ages

Consider this: Build the message around a statement spoken by a teenager, which reflects the faith of the centurian, namely, "Obedience means to drop everything and to do what God wants." Describe the difference between *trying* to do something and *doing* it. Someone has said, "People who try are very trying."

Proclamation of the Word

Consider this insight from Elton Trueblood's book, *The Company of the Committed:*

"(The centurion) understood that the suffering he observed was really that of a military prisoner from a new kind of army, an army not for destruction but for redemption." (page 34) You may want to read the entire section. The centurion learned, as many of us have not, the statement, "I'm not anxious to die easily when Christ died so hard." (author unknown) So, you may want to deal with the questions, "What are some good tools for intentional living? What should be my first intentional decision about being intentional?"

Stewardship Challenge

Consider this: "The Stewardship of doubt and faith." One time a member of a congregation wrote, "I've been wondering how to handle my faith. Today, I think I've found a way to begin. I must decide, instead of waiting for some mysterious answer to hit me in the face."

Perhaps you will want to follow the offering with a prayer similar to this one: "Lord, thank you for receiving and accepting me with all of my doubts and stumbling attempts obeying you. Teach me to share all that I am, including my doubts, with my fellow Christians, rather than playing games with my fellow Christians and with you."

Charge to the Congregation

Suggested: Build the charge around a statement made by Palladin of TV's *Have Gun, Will Travel,* when he said, "I choose my own life and my own way of losing it, and that's my responsibility."

Planning for Your Congregation

Suggestions	Your Situation

I. Other Scriptures   *Lay readers:*

- Psalm 100
- Psalm 117
- 1 Kings 8:22-23, 27-30, 41-43
- Galatians 1:1-10

II. Hymn Possibilities   *Hymn selections:*

"Blessing and Honor and Glory and Power"
    Horatius Bonar, 1866; altered 1972
"Put Forth, O God, Your Spirit's Might"
    Howard Chandler Robbins, 1937; altered 1972
"We Believe in One True God"
    Tobias Clausnitzer, 1668. Translated by Catherine Winkworth, 1863; altered

III. Other Music Possibilities   *Music selections:*

Music for Preparation
    "Ricercare"   Palestrina
Response to the Old Testament   Choir
    "Send Out Thy Light"   Gounod
Offertory
    "Cantique"   Igor Stravinsky
Doxology
    "Praise God, from Whom All Blessings Flow"
    Thomas Ken, 1693, 1709 (*The Worshipbook,* page 266, Westminster Press)
    Use this doxology until people know it well
Choral Response following the Benediction
    "Allelu"   Ray Repp
    copyright 1966, 1967. F.E.L. Church Pub., Ltd.
    (Choir sing first, then congregation)
Music for Dismissal
    Medley of Trinity or Pentecost Hymns

IV. Bulletin Cover   *Bulletin design ideas:*

V. Bulletin Symbols

VI. Miscellaneous Details *(Assignments):* _____

• Ushers	• Banners	• Flowers	• Assistant(s) at Holy Communion
• Greeters	• Candlelighters	• Soloists	• Other

THE SEASON OF THE HOLY SPIRIT

PROPER 5
PENTECOST 3
ORDINARY TIME 10

Liturgical Color: Green

Gospel: Luke 7:11-17

Theme: Jesus offers life-giving power — How does the Lord raise us from the dead, the deadness of our old way of living?

Planning Notes

Pastoral Invitation

If you've never done this, ask the congregation to call out words of praise. Pastor repeat the words; then, invite the congregation to "repeat the repeat." Give different emphases to each word, depending on what the word requires.

Continue with a choral response of praise.

Then, consider using the following response.

Pastor: Just who are you? Who are we?
Ministers: **A mixture — of joy and sorrow, of high and low moods, of hypocrisy and honesty, of hope and despair, of sadness and gladness, of hate and love.**
Pastor: You're right. We are all of those and more.
Ministers: **What do you mean "more"?**
Pastor: I mean that whatever we are, in whatever situation we find ourselves, God is there first. God beat us to the draw. And because of that, we can know for a fact that God cares, that God has compassion, that God has concern for each of us, for all of us.
Ministers: **Great news! God loves us! God loves the church! God loves the world!**
Pastor: Rejoice and be glad about that.
Ministers: **We shall! We are! We rejoice. Amen and amen!**

Confession and Forgiveness

One congregation did this:

Pastor give the people some "non-traditional" ideas to consider. Many of our people continue to think of sin as something someone else does, usually the sins of the flesh, because they make such juicy stories. Ask them to consider the biblical fact that Sin is "the attempt to justify our behavior, decisions, action, existence." All of us spend much time justifying ourselves; and when we justify ourselves, we can/will/do anything to get even with the other, including members of our own household. Hitler sought his justification in the Jews; Americans earlier sought their justification in the Japanese, now, the Communists; Christians do our justification by tantrums, pouts, gossip, assumptions, insinuations.

Allow the congregation five minutes of silence to confess their sin. For the forgiveness, ask the choir to sing "Psalm 1" from "New American Psalms" by Megan, after saying to the people in several ways that God already has justified us in the person and power of the risen, living Christ.

Planning Notes

Message to the Children of All Ages

Try this: Use the Scripture of the day to discuss how Jesus gives us new life. You might begin with that of the seed, the birth of a pet, our own birth. Then, tie that into our growth through education, our learning by the limits put on us by others and then upon ourselves, through the things we learn from our friends (even friends who disagree with us). God uses all of these ways to teach us how to love.

Proclamation of the Word

Consider this insight:

Jesus, the Lord, provides us life-giving power because of his compassion for us, for the world. Our response is fear ("awe-some" fear, as our teenagers have suggested) which leads us into a new relationship with God, others, self.

Stewardship Challenge

Suggested: Perhaps you will want to develop your remarks around the following statements: "Life is a one-way street, and you're not coming back," (New York lawyer). Therefore, "choose your rut carefully; you'll be in it for the next twenty miles." (sign on a country road, a message which has many applications.)

Charge to the Congregation

Try this: Christ promises his peace and power for the road. Receive his gift and share it.

Then, ask the congregation to offer this promise to one another with these words, "The peace and the power of the Christ belong to you."

Planning for Your Congregation

            Suggestions   Your Situation

I. Other Scriptures   *Lay readers:*

- Psalm 113
- Psalm 30
- Galatians 1:11-24

II. Hymn Possibilities   *Hymn selections:*

"O Worship the King All-glorious Above"
    Based on Psalm 104
    Robert Grant, 1833; altered
"All Hail the Power of Jesus' Name"
    Stanzas 1, 2, Edward Perronet, 1779, 1780; altered
    Stanzas 4, 5, John Rippon, 1787

III. Other Music Possibilities   *Music selections:*

Music for Preparation
    Sarabande on "Rockingham"   Thiman
Assurance of Pardon
    "Psalm 1" from "New American Psalms" Megan
    Ask the congregation to sing the antiphon
Response to the New Testament Reading   Choir
    "What Wonderous Love is This"   (author unknown)
Offertory
    "Jesus, Priceless Treasure"   Gardner Read
Music for Dismissal
    Medley of Pentecost Hymns

IV. Bulletin Cover   *Bulletin design ideas:*

V. Bulletin Symbols

VI. Miscellaneous Details *(Assignments):* _____

• Ushers	• Banners	• Flowers	• Assistant(s) at Holy Communion
• Greeters	• Candlelighters	• Soloists	• Other

THE SEASON OF THE HOLY SPIRIT

PROPER 6
PENTECOST 4
ORDINARY TIME 11

Liturgical Color: Green

Gospel: Luke 7:36—8:3

Theme: Jesus, the Christ, can forgive only those who recognize their need for forgiveness — a Contrast between the Pharisee and the prostitute.

Pastoral Invitation

Planning Notes

Suggested: One pastor began this way: In the name of God the Creator, Liberator, Sustainer, welcome to the corporate celebration of the Good News. Corporate worship is an act of the total community of faith — not done just when we feel like it, but weekly, as was Jesus' custom; not because we agree or disagree with the pastor, because the pastor does not lead us to worship; not because we do or do not feel stimulated, but in spite of how we feel. We do not worship, basically, to get or to give something, but rather to celebrate.

The style of our celebration is thanksgiving.

We come to thank God for our lives in Christ.

You may want to follow with this response:

Pastor: I remind you that this day is beautiful and sacred, because God is alive!

Ministers: **But we do not see much beauty and sacredness outside of these cozy walls.**

Pastor: I remind you that God is beauty; God is love. That which is ugly does not come from God!

Ministers: **Does God love us with our ugliness? Even admidst our lives that betray and deceive God?**

Pastor: Look again at the Cross. It says that God loves us,
as we are . . . and forgives us, for what we are. Do you understand?

Ministers: **We understand. We understand that we are important creations of a concerned God! So now we express our thanks for such awesome confidence in us. Lead on!**

Confession and Forgiveness

One congregation did this:

The pastor began with this statement: "The only thing that we contribute to our salvation (reconciliation/liberation/wholeness) is our sin." Ask the people to think about that statement in silence. After two full minutes of silence, ask them to consider the theme and content of their confession. Did they consider the sins of the flesh or the spirit? Tie this in with the Scripture, the self-righteous sin of the Pharisees, and the humbling response of the prostitute. Give two more full minutes of silence for prayer.

Planning Notes

Now, begin the assurance of pardon with these words: "Only God knows the extent of our dishonesty, for God alone has paid the price for such knowledge." (a.u.)

Perhaps you will want to follow with this, or a similar, corporate prayer of pardon: "Convince us, O God, by your presence and power that our guilt has been wiped out, that our sin, spiritual and fleshly, has been cleansed, and that our forgiveness has been bought with a price. Teach us, the people of faith, that the past is forgiven, every bit of it, in the name of the Father, Son, and Holy Spirit."

Message to the Children of All Ages

Try this: Build the message around the Gospel for the day by asking the children if they think they've ever done something so terrible that God won't forgive them. Perhaps share one of your childhood experiences in which you thought that. You may want to conclude with the last part of the parable of the prodigal sons, and how the father greeted his long-lost child.

Proclamation of the Word

Suggested: William Hamilton, in his book, *The Christian Man,* makes a couple statements which you may want to incorporate in your message: "To call ourselves sinners is not to say that we're not good; it is to say something far more serious . . . we cannot save ourselves; we cannot make our lives whole by ourselves." (page 43) God can forgive only those who recognize their need for forgiveness.

From *The Christian Man,* by William Hamilton, Layman's Theological Library. Copyright 1956 by W. L. Jenkins. Used by permission of the Westminster Press.

Stewardship Challenge

Try this: Ask the people to write on a piece of paper an area in their lives which needs forgiveness. Without putting their name on the paper, ask them to put it in the offering plate.

In the prayer of dedication, seek for God's Spirit and the peoples' courage to deal with that issue.

Charge to the Congregation

Suggested: Conclude with these words: "You are forgiven; live as forgiven, and forgiving people. Because God has forgiven us nail prints, surely we can be compassionate and kind enough in the Spirit of God to forgive pinpricks."

Planning for Your Congregation

Suggestions	Your Situation

I. Other Scriptures   *Lay readers:*

- Psalm 42
- Psalm 32
- 1 Kings 19:1-8
- 2 Samuel 11:26—12:10, 13-15
- Galatians 2:11-21

II. Hymn Possibilities   *Hymn selections:*

"Praise to the Lord, the Almighty"
    Joachim Neander, 1680
        Translated by Catherine Winkworth, 1863; altered
"Cast Your Burden on the Lord"
    Based on Psalm 55:22
    Rowland Hill's Psalms and Hymns, 1783;
    altered, 1972
"There's a Wideness in God's Mercy"
    Frederick W. Faber, 1854

III. Other Music Possibilities   *Music selections:*

Music for Preparation
    "Carillon"   Sowerby
Response to the New Testament Reading   Choir
    "Eternal Ruler"   Eugene Butler
Music for Dismissal
    Medley of Pentecost Hymns

IV. Bulletin Cover   *Bulletin design ideas:*

V. Bulletin Symbols

VI. Miscellaneous Details *(Assignments):* _____

• Ushers	• Banners	• Flowers	• Assistant(s) at Holy Communion
• Greeters	• Candlelighters	• Soloists	• Other

THE SEASON OF THE HOLY SPIRIT

PROPER 7
PENTECOST 5
ORDINARY TIME 12

Liturgical Color: Green

Gospel: Luke 9:18-24

Theme: Jesus said, "If anyone would come after me, let that person deny self, take up his/her cross daily, and follow me."

Dietrich Bonhoefer said, "When Jesus calls people, he bids them come and die."

To be bearers of the Cross means that we die to ourselves so that we can be advocates of new life, the kind that Christ gives to his people.

Planning Notes

Pastoral Invitation

One pastor did this:

Welcome to the celebration of the Good News, which, in the beginning seems bad news. We are here for myriad reasons, some healthy, some not so healthy. We are here, primarily, because God has called us and we said "yes."

And now that we're here, we will hear a hard lesson from the Scriptures; as we seek to respond to the question which God asks each of us daily, "Who do you say that I am?"; and a hard calling, "If anyone would come after me, let that person deny self, take up his/her cross, and follow me."

Perhaps you will want to follow this with the following response, which urges people to follow the hard way (one which many of us Christians prefer not to do).

Pastor:	Listen! Do you hear God?
Ministers:	**We do hear God.**
Pastor:	How do you hear God?
Ministers:	**In the plaintive cries and crises of the world around us.**
Pastor:	Let us become even more sensitive to those cries and crises as we worship.
Ministers:	**Indeed we shall. Amen** (a.u., revised)

Confession and Forgiveness

One pastor did this:

Introduce the confession with a statement by John Howard Griffin (*Black Like Me*) who, in 1976 wrote, "The very worst development of recent years is simply that people no longer feel a sense of horror (or even uneasiness) in the face of injustice that simply wrecks human lives."

Then, you may want to use this prayer, or a similar one which speaks directly to your congregation: "God, our God, whose love never fails, whose desire is our reconciliation: We confess to patch-work lives — hope and despair; high resolve and weak failure; good intention, bad living; great joy, vast discouragement.

O Lord, our lives lack the steady strength possible through your promised Spirit. We are slow in accepting the fulness of our new life in Christ. Cover our frailty with your forgiveness, and see us in Christ Jesus as persons made alive to eternity."

(always allow ample time for silence)

Follow with this assurance: "If anyone sins, we have an advocate with the Father, Jesus Christ the Righteous. And he is the propitiation *(use another word; people have heard it for years and still don't know what it means)* for our sins. And not for ours only, but also for the sins of the whole world. The grace of the Lord Jesus Christ be with us all."

(Read this slowly, deliberately, rather than rushing through it. Ask the congregation to repeat some of the phrases and words. Give them an opportunity to clarify.)

You may want to conclude with this response:

Pastor: O Lord, open our lips.
Ministers: **And our mouths shall show forth your praise.**
All: **In Christ's presence and power. Amen**

Message to the Children of All Ages

Suggested: Build around the Scripture. Begin with the question, "Do you children know how you learn what's important to you?" *(Allow time for answers and responses.)* Continue, "We learn what's supposed to be important for us by seeing what's important to our parents. Later, we see what's important to our friends."

Give a couple examples: Our parents may say to us, "Don't smoke," and then go "Puff, puff on their cigarette." Or "Don't drink alcohol," and then, have a social drink.

Jesus also told us what's important, namely, following him and his teachings. Sometimes that's hard. It means learning to say "no" and meaning it, even when all of our friends say "yes" to the wrong things.

Conclude with a prayer centering on this theme.

Proclamation of the Word

Consider this: Christ bids us come and die. We may not become literal martyrs (witnesses) by getting killed. We are called to die daily to our old attitudes and behaviors. We can find many examples of people who indeed die to themselves daily. I remember some years ago a man who went to Mississippi for six months to work on voter registration; he resigned his position as service manager for a local business firm when he returned, and sought for a deeper meaning for his vocation. And surely, we can challenge our people to stop participating in clubs or organizations that discriminate in their membership and exclude persons because of race, religion, or any other external measurement.

Planning Notes

Stewardship Challenge

Try this: Ask, how would you take seriously these words of Jesus in your daily life?

Charge to the Congregation

Consider this: Build around a statement from the popular song "Easy to Be Hard" from *Hair*. "If you really have a heart, don't you think it's time you used it" in the Name of Christ, for the sake of Christ's world?

Planning for Your Congregation

Suggestions

I. Other Scriptures

- Psalm 43
- Psalm 63:1-9
- 1 Kings 19:9-14
- Zechariah 12:7-11
- Galatians 3:23-29

II. Hymn Possibilities

"Blessing and Honor and Glory and Power"
    Horatius Bonar 1866; altered, 1972
"God Is Working His Purpose Out"
    Arthur Campbell Ainger, 1894
    (You may want to use this as an hymn of the month; as much as possible, give up the sexist language)

III. Other Music Possibilities

Music for Preparation
    "My Heart Ever Faithful"   Bach
Response to the Scripture
    "The Lord's Prayer"   Gates
Response to the Proclamation
    Choir and Congregation
"O Christ, Whose Love Has Sought Us Out"
    John Edgar Park, 1953; altered, 1972
    (Use a variation; perhaps the choir to sing the first stanza; everyone hum the second; read the third together; all sing the fourth.)
Music for Dismissal
    "Postlude"   Haydn

IV. Bulletin Cover

V. Bulletin Symbols

VI. Miscellaneous Details *(Assignments):*

- Ushers
- Banners
- Flowers
- Assistant(s) at Holy Communion
- Greeters
- Candlelighters
- Soloists
- Other

Your Situation

Lay readers:

Hymn selections:

Music selections:

Bulletin design ideas:

THE SUNDAYS AFTER

PENTECOST
PART II

THE SEASON OF THE HOLY SPIRIT

PROPER 8
PENTECOST 6
ORDINARY TIME 13

Liturgical Color: Green

Gospel: Luke 9:51-62

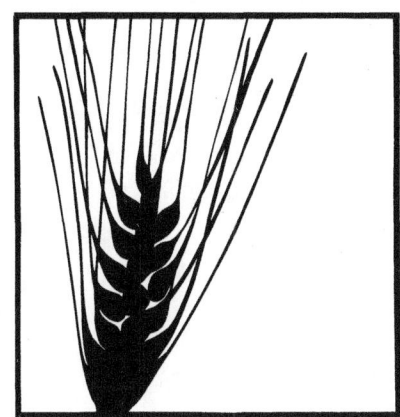

Theme: Jesus invites and calls us to put his ministry and mission first.

Joseph Stalin said, "He who wants the future must not inquire into the past."

Jesus said something similar long before Stalin. "No one who puts his/her hand to the plow and looks back is fit for the Kingdom of God."

Pastoral Invitation   *Planning Notes*

One pastor did this:

In the name of God the Creator, Liberator, Sustainer, welcome to this worship. Today, we will deal with one of Jesus' hard sayings about looking back. The message sounds harsh and impossible for us to understand, because of our safe and comfortable situation. We need to hear the whole gospel, and today we will hear the part of it that we might prefer not to hear.

Follow with this, or a similar, response:

Pastor: We are here to become brainwashed.
Ministers: **Wash our brains, Lord, with your power, your promise, your purpose — so we can be clean enough to brainwash this community with that same power, promise, purpose.**
Pastor: So be it!
Ministers: **Amen!**

Confession and Forgiveness

Suggested: Introduce the confession with the question, "What are your excuses when you are asked to follow Christ?" This author once wrote a sermon *(unpublished and not preached)* entitled, "Is Your 'But' Sticking Out?" Perhaps you will want to use some of the excuses offered by some of the biblical characters.

Then, give the people some time to reflect on their own excuse-making, devices to avoid confrontation and obedience.

After an extended silence, offer God's forgiveness to even those who make excuses. God invites us to turn our excuses over to God's power of forgiveness. God kept after people such as Moses, for example, by offering his presence and power to respond. For especially brave worship leaders: ask the people to write their excuses on pieces of paper and have a "burning up" ceremony in the sanctuary.

Planning Notes

Message to the Children of All Ages

Suggested: Make today's Gospel text come alive for the children. Most of them know about making excuses. Share one of your own and invite them to share theirs. Help them to move beyond excuse-making to making new decisions.

Proclamation of the Word

Consider this: Someone has said that "Jesus Christ is a totalitarian. He is all in all. Unless we are ready to let him be precisely that for us, all in all, we had better drop him altogether. He will not settle for less. Because Jesus came to conquer the foe that enslaved us, he is, therefore, Lord of all." So we trust and obey — reluctantly, at times; yet we trust and obey. (a.u.)

Stewardship Thought

Consider this as a follow-up to the sermon:

Ask, "What are you keeping from your commitment and obedience to God? What would happen if you put your excuse in the offering plate?" Replace your gift of money with your written excuse for one week to see what happens in your life.

You may want to follow this with one of these prayers:

"These gifts, O God, represent what we think of you. Take them."
or,
"Do these gifts, O God, represent what we really think of you?"

Charge to the Congregation

Suggested: You may want to use one of these statements:

1. "The greatest gift to the totalitarians is religious and political indifference and apathy. At the last judgment, the balcony-sitter (excuse-maker) may plead, 'I never harmed a fly.' But the Judge will say, 'The fly you never harmed carried the plague to millions.'"
Franklin Littell, *Wild Tongues*
or,
2. "If you really have a heart, don't you think it's time you used it?"
— in the name of the Christ, for the sake of his world.
From the popular song (1969),
"Easy to Be Hard," from *Hair*

Planning for Your Congregation

Suggestions   **Your Situation**

I. Other Scriptures   *Lay readers:*

- Psalm 44:1-8
- Psalm 16
- 1 Kings 19:14-21
- Galatians 5:1, 13-25

II. Hymn Possibilities   *Hymn selections:*

"God Is Working His Purpose Out"
    Arthur Campbell Ainger, 1894
    (Consider this as a hymn of the month. Again, caution people about the sexist language)
"Take Thou Our Minds, Dear Lord"
    William Hiram Foulkes, 1918
    (This is both a prayer hymn as well as a hymn of commitment)

III. Other Music Possibilities   *Music selections:*

Music for Preparation
    "Arioso"   Handel
Response to the Proclamation
    "Be Thou My Vision"   Ancient Irish
    Translated by Mary Byrne, 1927
    Versified by Eleanor Hull, 1927

IV. Bulletin Cover   *Bulletin design ideas:*

V. Bulletin Symbols

VI. Miscellaneous Details *(Assignments):* _____

- Ushers
- Banners
- Flowers
- Assistant(s) at Holy Communion

- Greeters
- Candlelighters
- Soloists
- Other

THE SEASON OF THE HOLY SPIRIT

PROPER 9
PENTECOST 7
ORDINARY TIME 14

Liturgical Color: Green

Gospel: Luke 10:1-12, 17-20

Theme: Claiming God's Power — Today? Yes, today!

Planning Notes

Pastoral Invitation

Consider this: Keep the focus upon the One whose presence and power we celebrate. Incorporate this idea: When worship is truly corporate, it is a celebration of the wholeness of life. We people of faith view life, not from B.C., but from A.D.; and therefore, we will rejoice — not because Jesus suffers, but because Christ won the victory over life and death. So, let's celebrate as if he were the Victor — because he is.
(The verb "will rejoice" is deliberately used here, rather than "can rejoice." Will is a decision; can may be a dream.)

Following the choral introit, use this declaration of joy:

Pastor:	Gladness is ours!
Choir:	**Hallelujah!**
Ministers:	*Gladness is ours!*
Pastor:	Sing to the Lord with thanksgiving.
Ministers:	*Glorious things God has done for us.*
Pastor:	Hills, plains,
Choir:	**Rock, sand,**
Ministers:	*Grass, trees, fields,*
Pastor:	Clouds, sky,
Choir:	**Moon, stars,**
Ministers:	*Rain, wind, sun.*
Pastor:	Gladness is ours.
Ministers:	*Hallelujah, amen!*
Choir:	**Hallelujah, amen!**
All:	**Hallelujah, amen!**

(author unknown, revised)

Confession and Forgiveness

Suggested: Begin with the statement, "To confess our sin is to cut it out." We can't/won't do it without the help of the Holy Spirit. You may want to concentrate on the sin of our cowardice, as did the disciples in today's Scripture, and then focus on the joy of their obedience.

Consider this prayer of confession:

Planning Notes

"Almighty God, who loves us as we are, so that no one of us need remain as he/she is, we praise you for the gift of life. It's good to be alive! We know that we are infinitely loved in spite of what we have been or said. We experience love and acceptance for ourselves; and we know that we are to love as we have been loved. You have granted us your own spirit of love to dwell in us. But Lord, you know how blocked we become. We are hampered in our loving by our judgments, our preconceptions, our selfishness, our cowardice, our pride and our anxiety. We wait for people to meet our standards. We create images for people to fulfil. We wait for others to make the first move in accepting us before we give ourselves. Forgive us Lord, and free us. Help us to see that the purpose of our existence is to love — you and one another. We open ourselves anew to your Holy Spirit of love and pray that you will love others through us. Warm our hearts, soften our rigid wills, and bend our pride. So may loving be our reason for being."

(author unknown)

You may want to continue with the Lord's Prayer, West Indies Version, arranged by Paul Abels. Have the choir sing the first line and the congregation respond with the phrase,
"Hallowed be Thy Name."

Message to the Children of All Ages

Try this: Before sharing the message, spend some time thinking about how to apply the Scripture for the day to the children. Perhaps you will want to identify some of their fears when they are asked to do a task, that they might fail their parents or teacher. Avoid a legalism that makes good little boys and girls out of them if they "do it right." You may not want to use Martin Luther's statement, "I would rather have a dead than disobedient son;" but you may want to think about its implications. Also, identify the joy that they experience when they do respond, despite their fear of beginning.

Proclamation of the Word

Suggested: This is a hard passage, as are many of the hard sayings of Jesus. Describe some ways that we witness, our fears about getting started, and the joys of the contact. Clergy can apply this to pastoral calling, the one thing that gets cut first because "I'm too busy." God promises that God's word will take root somehow, some way, somewhere, if we are faithful to share the Good News.

Stewardship Thought

If you haven't done this, select a specific mission of your denomination, and focus on it for the day and week. Ask people to read about it, to write letters to the people involved, to send stories about how the Good News is spoken, heard, and responded to. Be certain to give the people the opportunity to share in the weeks ahead once they begin to receive information. Ask the missionaries to talk about their fears and the results when they took the step of obedience.

Charge to the Congregation

Consider developing the charge around this quote:

"The grace of God is the power of God in persons; it represents an accession of resources which we do not have of ourselves."

(author unknown)

You may want to conclude with this benediction:
Pastor: You are free to celebrate life in Christ.
People: We rejoice that Christ makes this possible.

Planning for Your Congregation

Suggestions	Your Situation
I. Other Scriptures	*Lay readers:*

- Psalm 5:1-8
- Psalm 66:1-11, 14-18, 20
- 1 Kings 21:1-3, 17-21
- Isaiah 66:10-14
- Galatians 6:1-18

II. Hymn Possibilities — *Hymn selections:*

"God Is Working His Purpose Out"
   Arthur Campbell Ainger, 1894
    (Hymn of the Month)
"Sing Praise to God Who Reigns Above"
   Johann J. Schutz (1640-1690)
   Translated by Frances E. Cox (1812-1897)
"Christ, of All My Hopes the Ground"
   Ralph Wardlaw, 1817

III. Other Music Possibilities — *Music selections:*

Music for Preparation
   "Toccata in D Minor" — Froberger
Choral Introit — Choir
   "Hallelujah! Hallelujah! In God's temple,
   God be praised. In the high and heavenly
   places be the sounding anthem raised. Amen." (a.u.)
Response to the Scripture
   "Salvation is Created" — Tschesnokoff
Doxology
   Use tune to "All Creatures of Our God and King"
   (Change the tune every now and then)
Music for Dismissal
   "Credo" — Haydn

IV. Bulletin Cover — *Bulletin design ideas:*

V. Bulletin Symbols

VI. Miscellaneous Details *(Assignments):* _____

- Ushers
- Banners
- Flowers
- Assistant(s) at Holy Communion

- Greeters
- Candlelighters
- Soloists
- Other

THE SEASON OF THE HOLY SPIRIT

PROPER 10
PENTECOST 8
ORDINARY TIME 15

Liturgical Color: Green

Gospel: Luke 10:25-37

Theme: The parable of the Good Samaritan — The parable remains only another works doctrine until each of us sees ourself as the person lying along the freeway needing the help of the other.

Pastoral Invitation

Planning Notes

Consider this: We are here to celebrate the One who makes life, and the new life in Christ, possible. Enter into this worship with your mind, emotions, body, life.

Follow with this pastoral invitation:

> Listen, do you hear God?
> > in the words of Scripture,
> > in the silent meditation
> > > and spoken message,
> > in the breathing of your fellow
> > > worshipers
> > in the pulse of your heartbeat
> > in the morning headlines,
> > in the most recent athletic event,
> > in the playfulness of your children,
> > > whatever their age,
> > in the confrontation of an unhealthy
> > > behavior,
> > in the plaintive cries of the world
> > > around you?
> I invite us to become even more sensitive
> > to the presence and activity of God as
> > we worship — in the Name of the Creator,
> > Liberator, Sustainer.

Prayer of Adoration

One pastor used this prayer:

Almighty God, we stand amazed at the wonder of you. We are astonished at ourselves, that we make such poor and grudging response to your love. Mercy, faithfulness, righteousness, lovingkindness — these are all ours for the asking: you wait upon our consent.

Planning Notes

Lord, teach us to pray, to open our lives to your generous gifts. Enlarge our hearts. Quicken our longing for a share of your completeness. Do this for no selfish end, but rather that we may have the generosity to share with others, for the life of the world. (a.u.)

Confession and Forgiveness

One pastor used this approach:

Introduction to the Confession: "My sins, while terrible, aren't nearly as bad as yours," (a.u.) because I commit the forgivable ones and you commit the unforgivable ones.

Think of those sins which repel us most, and which repelled Christ most.

You may want to follow those words with this printed prayer:
O God, who in Jesus Christ breaks into our lives in new ways, offering love and fellowship, we remember actions that failed you. We harbor memories which disturb. We say things behind peoples' backs that we wouldn't dare say to their faces. We set high standards for others and ourselves. We find it difficult to accept human frailty. We are filled with judgment. We overtax strengths and schedules. We plan more than we ought, do more than we should, spend more than we have. We love things and use people, instead of loving people and using things. Forgive us, Lord; make us aware of your healing love amidst the company of our friends and enemies.

Introduce the assurance of pardon with these words:
It is easier to remember things that make us feel guilty than to forgive ourselves, yes, even to let God forgive us. Remember, the past is not only over and done, it is forgiven; and all the guilt in the world will not change it one iota. We have a choice — to keep recycling our guilt, or to trust in God's grace. Which will we choose?

You may then want to use this response:

Pastor: Let us remember the Good News of our liberation.
Ministers: **In Christ, our self-worth has been declared.**
Pastor: We have been forgiven, accepted, received.
Ministers: **The present has been given new meaning. The future is full of possibilities.**
Pastor: Let us live fully and responsibly. Let us be free.
Ministers: **Indeed we shall! So be it! Amen!**

Message to the Children of All Ages

Consider this: Of all the parables, we probably use this one more than any other to get our children to do what they're told, to do what we as parents, pastors, teachers want them to do. Drive home the idea that the point of the parable is our need for others. Ask them to share memories of persons who have been with them in their needs.

Proclamation of the Word

Suggested: Most of the time, we hear and interpret this parable in one of two ways:
(1) We are exhorted not to act like the priest/levite, not to act like the

busy, indifferent, calloused religious folk who pass by on the other side; and not to act like the gangster who clobbered the fellow, stole his belongings, and left him in the ditch. (2) We are urged to identify with the Samaritan, the good guy, Mr. Clean, who took time to help; that is, to treat our neighbor as if we were that neighbor. There is a third way to view the parable: To recognize that we are the wounded, battered person, and that we are going to receive help from a least-expected someone, maybe someone we hate, ignore, ridicule when we're healthy. The crucial point of the parable is our neediness, and that help may come when we least expect it, from someone whom we least expect.

Stewardship Thought

Consider this statement: "Give until you enjoy it."

Charge to the Congregation

Christianity begins with an act of receiving and continues with millions of acts of receiving. So as receivers, then givers, from this day forward, as the people of Christ who have received the gift of new life, daily, live in Christ's power, with Christ's promise, for Christ's purpose — for the sake of Christ's world. Amen

Note: You may want to consider using Clarence Jordan's telling of the story of the Parable. Clarence Jordan wrote the *Cotton Patch* translation of some of the New Testament. His books and tapes are available through most book stores. His approach drops the story right into our laps.

Planning for Your Congregation

| Suggestions | Your Situation |

I. Other Scriptures

- Psalm 139:1-12
- Psalm 25:1-9
- Psalm 69:14, 17, 30-31, 33-34, 36-37
- 2 Kings 2:1, 6-14
- Deuteronomy 30:9-14
- Colossians 1:1-20

Lay readers:

II. Hymn Possibilities

"God Is Working God's Purpose Out"
   Arthur Campbell Ainger
   (Hymn of the Month)
"Walk Tall, Christian"
   Miriam Drury, 1969

Hymn selections:

III. Other Music Possibilities

Music for Preparation
   "Chaconne" — Buxtehude
Offertory
   "O Lamb of God" — Dupre
Music for Dismissal
   "Tollete Hostias" — Saint-Saens

Music selections:

IV. Bulletin Cover *(If you use a fixed worship folder design, consider changing the cover occasionally)*

Bulletin design ideas:

V. Bulletin Symbols *(use either symbols for the season or different symbols each week, depicting the day's theme. The publisher grants the original purchaser of this workbook permission to duplicate in Sunday worship folders the Sunday symbols which accompany the chapters of this book. You may want to consider using those from time to time.)*

VI. Miscellaneous Details *(Assignments):* _____

- Ushers
- Banners
- Flowers
- Assistant(s) at Holy Communion

- Greeters
- Candlelighters
- Soloists
- Other

THE SEASON OF THE HOLY SPIRIT

PROPER 11
PENTECOST 9
ORDINARY TIME 16

Liturgical Color: Green

Gospel: Luke 10:38-42

Theme: The contrast between Mary and Martha — "You've got to stop and smell the roses." Keeping busy or keeping attuned.

Pastoral Invitation

Planning Notes

Consider this: (for the courageous) Deliberately slow down the pace of today's worship. Give people plenty of time for silence and meditation. You may want to stand or sit for several minutes after the prelude before giving the call to worship. Delay until the people become uncomfortable with the silence. A three-minute delay for some will seem like three hours.

Then, you can introduce worship with words similar to these:

Welcome to the celebration of the Good News.
Do any of you feel uncomfortable? If so, think about that for a few more minutes. Give at least two more minutes of silence. Be ready for some hostility; this may result, because we Americans think that we accomplish nothing unless we keep ourselves perpetually busy, running here and there every moment of the day.

Perhaps this would be a good day not to use a bulletin, so that the people would not have that crutch to lean on.

Confession and Forgiveness

Try this as a follow-up to the adoration/praise section of worship:

Use large chunks of silence. Somewhere in the confession, you may want to play Simon and Garfunkle's "The Sound of Silence." Then, ask these or similar questions:

- How do we use silence, or does silence use us?
- Do we ever think that God uses silence to speak to us?
- What does the "still small voice of God" mean to us in our daily routine?
- Why do you suppose that we have a compulsion to stay so busy?

Again, allow several moments for silence between the questions, and following the questions.

After the confession, invite the people to thank God, silently, for the possibility of new life through silence. Ask each to write down his/her prayer, and for those who want, to share that prayer with the congregation.

Planning Notes

Message to the Children of All Ages

Suggested: Continue the message of silence. Ask if, and how, the children use silence. Sometimes parents insist that the children be silent, but that's different.

We can use many examples of our busy-ness; identify some ways that we can use quiet times.

Proclamation of the Word

Suggested: Robert Short in *The Parables of Peanuts,* pages 2-3, offers some useful insight into the Mary-Martha syndrome. Our activity, at least much of it, is often a cover for superficiality, rootlessness. We are still hooked into what can be called the "Protestant Purgatory" as we attempt to achieve our salvation. In addition, multitudes of church members define their Christianity by doing, occasionally, institutional activities (such as worship attendance when they have nothing else to do; taking a church office; giving a little money to a budget).

There is no secret to slowing dowm to smell the roses. That takes a deliberate decision to focus on the essentials of life.

Stewardship Thought

Try this: Ask: What specific way this week, this year, will you take to consider the stewardship of slowing down, in order to hear God speaking to you?

Charge to the Congregation

Try this: You began in silence; conclude in silence. Ask the congregation not to speak to each other until they arrive home after worship. A silent coffee hour might free people to think about many things they would never have considered previously.

Planning for Your Congregation

Suggestions | Your Situation

I. Other Scriptures

- Psalm 139:13-18
- Psalm 15
- 2 Kings 4:8-17
- Genesis 18:1-14
- Colossians 1:21-29

Lay readers:

II. Hymn Possibilities

"God Is Working His Purpose Out" Ainger
(Hymn of the Month)

For the second and third hymns, try the following:

For the second, select a hymn of confession and pardon, and ask the people to read it silently.
For the concluding hymn, ask the people to select any hymn they want and to read it silently.

Hymn selections:

III. Other Music Possibilities

Music for Preparation
"Be Still, My Soul" From Psalm 46
Katharina von Schlegel, 1752
Translated by Jane Laurie Borthwick, 1855

Maintain silence during the receiving of the offering

If you want to use a concluding hymn,
use "Be Still My Soul."

Music selections:

IV. Bulletin Cover *(unless you decide not to use a bulletin)*

Bulletin design ideas:

V. Bulletin Symbols *(If you do not use a bulletin, place symbols around the sanctuary which contrast the approach between Mary and Martha, between busy-ness and quietness.)*

VI. Miscellaneous Details *(Assignments):*

- Ushers
- Banners
- Flowers
- Assistant(s) at Holy Communion

- Greeters
- Candlelighters
- Soloists
- Other

THE SEASON OF THE HOLY SPIRIT

PROPER 12
PENTECOST 10
ORDINARY TIME 17

Liturgical Color: Green

Gospel: Luke 11:1-13

Theme: Persistence, the essence of prayer.

Planning Notes

Pastoral Invitation

One pastor began this way:

The Psalmist said, "I was glad when they said to me, let us go to the house of the Lord." Some of us may have come gladly this morning; some of us may have come gloomily, grudgingly.

The fact is that now we are here, standing inside the walls of the building. We are here to worship. God accepts us as we are, no matter how we came. Thank God for that.

You may want to continue with this response, introduced with these words: We have come for a variety of reasons, with a variety of feelings. We are here to face the reality of life — life in Christ.

Pastor:	The call of Christ is not an easy one.
Ministers:	**It is an invitation to self giving.**
Pastor:	It requires hard work in the face of disappointment.
Ministers:	**It means going on when everyone else has given up.**
Pastor:	We will need to support each other if we are to follow Christ.
Ministers:	**Let us offer this support as we celebrate the Christian life together.**

Invite the congregation to greet each other, not only those nearby, but to walk about the sanctuary; allow sufficient time.

Confession and Forgiveness

One pastor did this:

Involve the people in a meditation. Select one idea from the Scripture, and invite the people to experience it. Lead them through these steps:

1. Place yourself in God's presence. God is always present; we are not aware of God's presence.
2. Offer an invocation prayer; for example, "God, may your Spirit help me to understand and apply your Word today."
3. Read the biblical passage until you know it well. Keep the passage short. Read it from several versions. Read it aloud until you know the whole story and can remember the details without referring to the passage.

4. Visualize the passage. Set up a motion picture of it in your mind. Sit back and let the events of the Scripture pass before you in review.

5. Enter the picture yourself. Take the place of one of the people. Ask yourself how you act like that person. Here, the Word gets downright personal.

6. Pray on the basis of the meditation. Get specific! Do not pray, "Lord, help me to be patient with everyone!" Pray, "Lord help me to be patient with my [husband/wife]." Do not pray, "Lord, help me tolerate those who are intolerable;" but, "Lord, help me to love John Smith my business rival, or Mary Jones who has been spreading rumors about me, or Bill Brown who pretends to be my friend." Specifics, not generalities, put teeth into our resolutions.

7. Pick a thought from the devotional to pin to your heart and mind the rest of the day. By doing this, we keep the Scripture continually in front of us.

8. Finally, sit quietly for a minute in silence. This becomes a period of digestion, during which time God helps us to assimilate the morning meal.

Allow fifteen minutes for this meditation. In addition, offer a workshop for the membership to learn this meditational method in depth.

Message to the Children of All Ages

Suggested: Focus on one aspect of the Scripture, perhaps the theme of persistence. Use an example of your own life in which persistence paid; make sure the children understand what you're saying. This is an age of immediate gratification; "I must have everything now; I'm not willing to wait." If everything doesn't happen immediately, we go on to something else. Show a rock worn smoothly by water. How long did it take?

Proclamation of the Word

Consider this: Invite people to look at their prayer life. Someone has said that "some people pray like a jackrabbit eating cabbage." Few of us think of prayer as "the oxygen of our spiritual lungs." Invite the serious worship participants to involve themselves in a daily prayer time; offer a workshop on prayer and teach people how to pray.

Stewardship Thought

Suggested follow-up of the proclamation:

Invite the people to write their name on a slip of paper indicating their desire to take prayer seriously and to put that paper into the offering plate. Remind them that this is a commitment to prayer for a specific time. Meet with them after worship or later in the week to decide the direction of their prayer-commitment.

Charge to the Congregation

Suggested follow-up to the offering:

God calls us as a people of faith, hope, and love; God also calls us as a people of prayer. I invite you to respond by repeating after me, these words:
  We are a people of faith. *[The people respond]*
  We are a people of hope. *[Response]*
  We are a people of love. *[Response]*
  We are a people of prayer. *[Response]*

Planning Notes

Planning for Your Congregation

Suggestions   Your Situation

I. **Other Scriptures**   *Lay readers:*

- Psalm 21:1-17
- Psalm 138
- 2 Kings 5:1-15ab
- Genesis 18:20-32
- Colossians 2:6-15

II. **Hymn Possibilities**   *Hymn selections:*

"Holy, Holy, Holy! Lord God Almighty!"
   Reginald Heber, 1826
"In the Cross of Christ I Glory"
   John Bowring, 1825
"Crown Him With Many Crowns"
   Stanzas 1, 2, 4, Matthew Bridges, 1851; altered, 1972
   Stanza 3, Godfrey Thring, 1874

III. **Other Music Possibilities**   *Music selections:*

Music for Preparation
   "Cazona"   Purvis
   Response to the New Testament   Choir
   "God Be in My Head"   Ellsworth
Offertory
   "Come Sweet Death"   Bach
Choral Response after the Benediction
   "When Jesus Wept"   Stanzas, 1, 4
   Stanza 1, William Billings, 1770
   Stanzas 2-4, Frank A. Brooks, Jr., 1972
Music for Dismissal
   Medley of Prayer Hymns

IV. **Bulletin Cover** *(If you didn't use a bulletin last week, what kind of a response did you get? Discuss this with your Worship Committee or worship planning team.)*   *Bulletin design ideas:*

V. **Bulletin Symbols**

VI. **Miscellaneous Details** *(Assignments):* _____

- Ushers
- Banners
- Flowers
- Assistant(s) at Holy Communion

- Greeters
- Candlelighters
- Soloists
- Other

THE SEASON OF THE HOLY SPIRIT

PROPER 13
PENTECOST 11
ORDINARY TIME 18

Liturgical Color: Green

Gospel: Luke 12:13-21

Theme: The parable of the rich fool —
"It's folly time, so let's have fun, fun, fun!"

Pastoral Invitation

Planning Notes

One pastor began this way:

We're here to celebrate life in its fulness and wholeness, because God has called us here. Therefore, on behalf of God's world, and on behalf of all of those who decided to stay home, or go skiing, or travel, or watch TV, we celebrate the Good News as a body, family, community of persons,
>   called into being by God,
>   sustained along the way by God,
>   completed, fulfilled by God,
in order to allow the Spirit of God to energize us,
>   to allow the lives of each other to strengthen us,
>   to let the rest of the world know who we are,
>>   whose we are,
>>   what we do,
>>   where we go —
> in the Name of God the Creator, Liberator, Sustainer.

You may want to introduce the prayer of praise with these words:

Pastor:	The Lord be with you.
Ministers:	**And with your spirit.**
Pastor:	Praise the Lord!
Ministers:	**The Lord's Name be praised.**
Pastor:	Almighty God, you have expressed your love for us by the gift of Jesus Christ. Help us to express our love to you in this hour of worship. We thank you for the power of his cross in our lives. Help us to take up our crosses and follow him who gave his life that we might be free from subtle and manipulative I-centeredness and alienation.

Confession and Forgiveness

Try this: Begin to have the congregation think about the gospel lesson for the day by asking, "How do we act like the rich fool? What do we covet? In what ways do our secondary commitments get in the way of our obedience to God? Allow some silent time to consider these questions silently.

Planning Notes

Then, ask the people to pray this prayer, first verbally:

Eternal King of the Universe, we confess that we have accepted you as Lord of all life, but have refused your reign in specific areas of life. We have prayed "Your Kingdom come" but have not turned over the control of our particular lives. We have been afraid to pray for your will in the so-called little things of life. We have wanted you to bring world peace, but have not found your profound inner peace. We know that your strategy is to change society by changed people, but we are reluctant, Lord. Create in us a new life, filled with the desire that the kingdoms of this world and all our own lives, may become the Kingdom of our Lord. Amen

The pastor, for the assurance of pardon, can then speak these words:

"The persons who want to have their alienations, their I-centeredness forgiven and to live new lives of love will let their decisions be known to God, and let their friends know of their decisions in Christ.

Message to the Children of All Ages

Suggested: Clarence Jordan has recorded this parable on record and cassette tape. Either play it during worship or listen to it before worship and interpret it to the children.

Proclamation of the Word

Consider this: You may want to discuss the source, the meaning, and the response to this drive of ours toward having "fun, fun, fun." Luther uses this term for sin: "bent (turned in) upon oneself." P. T. Forsythe gives an excellent response, when he says, "Unless there is within us that which is above us, we shall soon yield to that which is around us."

Stewardship Thought

Consider this as a follow-up of the proclamation:

Someone has said, "A dead church with money is worse than a live church without it."

Charge to the Congregation

One pastor did this:

Freed from the past, from the burden of living primarily for ourselves, we leave to welcome the future. Jesus gives himself to those who give themselves to him in commitment and obedience. I invite those interested in making a commitment to Christ and the church to meet after worship. I invite all of us to recommit ourselves in obedience to the mission of Jesus Christ by (a) a renewed relationship to the institutional program, and (b) a new concern for one family unrelated to the church.

Those who make this commitment will respond by reverently shouting "Alleluia! Amen!" and by singing with the choir, in a lively and energetic way, the benediction.

Planning for Your Congregation

<table>
<tr><th align="center">Suggestions</th><th align="center">Your Situation</th></tr>
</table>

I. Other Scriptures   *Lay readers:*

- Psalm 28
- Psalm 49:1-11
- Psalm 95:1-2, 6-9
- 2 Kings 13:14-20a
- Ecclesiastes 1:2; 2:21-23
- Colossians 3:1-11

II. Hymn Possibilities   *Hymn selections:*

"Praise to the Lord, the Almighty"
    Joachim Neander, 1680
        Translated by Catherine Winkworth, 1863; altered
"Holy Spirit, Truth Divine"
    Samuel Longfellow, 1864, altered, 1972

III. Other Music Possibilities   *Music selections:*

Music for Preparation
      "Woodland Flute Call"   Dillon
Choral Introit
      "Come, Let Us Worship God"   Kettering
Response to the Gospel   Choir
      "Creator Supreme"   Lewis
Response to the Proclamation
      "Breathe on Me, Breath of God"
    Edwin Hatch, 1886
Offertory
      "Green Fields and Meadows"   McKay
Music for Dismissal
Theme from "The Creation"   Haydn

IV. Bulletin Cover   *Bulletin design ideas:*

V. Bulletin Symbols

VI. Miscellaneous Details *(Assignments):* _____

• Ushers	• Banners	• Flowers	• Assistant(s) at Holy Communion
• Greeters	• Candlelighters	• Soloists	• Other

THE SEASON OF THE HOLY SPIRIT

PROPER 14
PENTECOST 12
ORDINARY TIME 19

Liturgical Color: Green

Gospel: Luke 12:32-48

Theme: Ready or not, here I come!

Planning Notes

Pastoral Invitation to the Celebration

One pastor began this way:

In the name of God, the Creator, Liberator, Sustainer, we're here — probably for a variety of reasons.

Choose the one that fits you:
I'm here because

- ☐ I'm in the choir,
- ☐ I'm teaching church school,
- ☐ My mother made me come,
- ☐ A neighbor invited me,
- ☐ I had nothing else to do,
- ☐ I wanted to celebrate with God's people.

We're here — for many reasons (all of which may have had to do with God's invitation to us, no matter what form it took). We're here! Now what?

Consider following with this response:

Pastor:	Jesus, called the Christ, has offered us a way of being fully human.
Ministers:	**He has presented a new style of life based on love and peace and justice for all.**
Pastor:	He invited the church to declare this way of life.
Ministers:	**Let us be the church at worship, so we can be the church in mission.**
Pastor:	Let us celebrate life in Christ.
Ministers:	**Let's do! Amen! Be it so!**

Confession and Forgiveness

One pastor did this:

He introduced the confession with words similar to these: Our greatest temptation is to become someone rather than ourself. Many of us make this obvious when we're children: "I wish I were so and so . . . I wish I had a million dollars . . . I wish . . ." As adults, we're only more subtle. We talk about "Being a good Christian," whatever that's supposed to mean. Someone usually defines what that's supposed to mean to us; so we spend a whole lifetime trying to be something that God has not called us to be. In no way can we (really) imitate Christ; we are not Christ. It is much more risky for us to seek God's will in everything we are and do. This will involve failure, false starts. (See Walter Wink's book, *Unmasking the Powers*)

You may want to use this written confession of sin, which could be called, "The Act of Recognizing our Humanness":

O God, who has the qualities of Mother and Father, You give us the capacity to perceive right from wrong, truth from falsehood, good from evil. We acknowledge that all too often we neglect the development, with your Holy Spirit's help, of those capacities. We are perplexed and undecided about morality, truth, and joy. Forgive our sin of neglect and unconcern in matters so vital to You. Help us, hour by hour, minute by minute, earnestly to seek help from your Holy Spirit, that we may become more and more like you in righteousness, truthfulness, and goodness, through Jesus Christ our Lord. (a.u., revised)

For the assurance of pardon, which may be called "The Act of Receiving New Life," you may want to begin with an idea from John Patton's book, *Is Human Forgiveness Possible?* He suggests that human forgiveness is best understood not as an act or an attitude, but "discovering that I am more like those who have hurt me than different from them." We can forgive when we realize that we have no "right" to forgive. The only difference among us is our choice of sin, and sin is anything or anyone that alienates us from God, from each other, and from our best self.

Perhaps you will want to use this response:

Pastor: The word of Christ is good news.
Ministers: **Our humanness has been received. We can be ourselves.**
Pastor: The past is forgiven. The future is before us.
Ministers: **Let us live with courage and with a deep concern for others.**
Pastor: Let us give thanks and embrace our lives.

Message to the Children of All Ages

Try this: Bring a bouquet of flowers. Point out all the differences in them — color, shapes, sizes. Then suggest how each of us is a part of God's bouquet. If possible, have a member of a minority present the message.

Proclamation of the Word

Consider this: The Scouts have a motto: "Be Prepared." We all know that motto intellectually, as we prepare for a job, marriage, family, death. Yet, we know, emotionally, that we haven't prepared well for any of those. Give people some specifics about preparation. For example, invite the people to prepare for their death, by writing a will, their funeral or memorial service, their obituary, and by talking with their families well in advance.

Stewardship Thought

Try this as a sermon follow-up:

Think about your stewardship of preparation. Write down on paper in what area of your life you need to do some specific preparation. Place it in the offering plate as an indication that you have made a commitment to do it.

Charge to the Congregation

Consider this: We're here to support and encourage each other to be the people of Christ. So, choose this day whom you will serve — God or self? And the peace of the Lord Jesus Christ be with you wherever you go, whatever you do — in the name of God the Creator, Liberator, Sustainer.

Planning Notes

Planning for Your Congregation

Suggestions   Your Situation

I. Other Scriptures   *Lay readers:*

- Psalm 14
- Psalm 33
- Jeremiah 18:1-11
- Genesis 15:1-6
- Wisdom 18:6-9
- Hebrews 11:1-3, 8-19

II. Hymn Possibilities   *Hymn selections:*

"Fairest Lord Jesus"
   German, 17th Century. Translator Unknown
"God Has Spoken By His Prophets"
   George Wallace Briggs, 1952; altered 1972
(Point out the sexist language; change it as much as possible while singing)

III. Other Music Possibilities   *Music selections:*

Music for Preparation
   Medley of Pentecost Hymns
Response to the Act of Receiving New Life
                                    Solo/duet
   "Love Divine"   Stainer
Response to the Old Testament
   Any "alleluia" chorus
Response to the Benediction
   Tune: "Michael, Row the Boat Ashore"
(find new or write new words for your congregation)

IV. Bulletin Cover   *Bulletin design ideas:*

Consider using these quotes on your bulletin cover, or somewhere inside: "We think of religious activity as directed toward God, instead of people . . . maybe we have turned religion (Christianity) inside out," from *Please Touch,*
           and
"How much do we demand the benefits of Christianity and ignore its sterner demands?"

V. Bulletin Symbols

VI. Miscellaneous Details *(Assignments):* ___

- Ushers
- Banners
- Flowers
- Assistant(s) at Holy Communion

- Greeters
- Candlelighters
- Soloists
- Other

THE SUNDAYS AFTER

PENTECOST
PART III

THE SEASON OF THE HOLY SPIRIT

PROPER 15
PENTECOST 13
ORDINARY TIME 20

Liturgical Color: Green

Gospel: Luke 12:49-56

Theme: Tested by fire — How is your staying power?

Pastoral Invitation to the Celebration

Planning Notes

Consider this: Welcome to Worship. God arrived long before we did. God invited us to come and promised his/her presence. We need each other as we listen and respond today to one of Jesus' hard teachings. So, how have we prepared ourselves for today's worship? What kinds of expectations do we have as we come? What are we willing to contribute as actors, not as spectators, in the drama of worship?

You may want to use this response:

Pastor: Who do you think you are?
Ministers: **We are the church of Jesus Christ.**
Pastor: What are you doing here?
Ministers: **We have gathered here to remember what it is to be a person and a Christian.**
Pastor: Will you be honest during this hour?
Ministers: **We will seek to be honest.**
Pastor: Will your minds and hearts be open to God's Word?
Ministers: **We will seek to be open to God's Word.**
Pastor: Good. Then we can proceed. Let us celebrate the Good News in the name of the living Christ.

Confession and Forgiveness

One pastor did this:

To introduce the confession, use this statement: "One of the subtlest tricks of the evil one (whatever form he/she/it takes) is to convince us that all we have to do is love Jesus in our heart. The basic issue, however, is to discover the kind of demand resulting from loving Jesus in our heart." (Wayne Keller)

Then, ask the people to think silently about the depth of their commitment to the Christ. How far would they go in their obedience? Ask them to think about this experience: One day a parishioner said to her pastor, "Pastor, I don't feel that I love Jesus enough." And the pastor responded, "My dear lady, loving Jesus is not a matter of feeling; it is a matter of character." *(Allow three minutes for silence)*

Planning Notes

Introduce the assurance of pardon with D. T. Niles' response to the question, "Who could be properly called a Christian in an Asian setting?" He said, "Anyone who is willing to bear Christ's name."

Perhaps you will want to use a hymn such as "Jesus, I My Cross Have Taken." If so, ask the people to read and study the words before singing. Encourage them *not* to sing any words which they have little or no intention of practicing.

Message to the Children of All Ages

Try this: Ask the children what their family is like when people don't get along with each other. Encourage them to talk about those areas which cause disagreement and fighting. Suggest that the same thing can happen when we don't understand Jesus in the same way. Find some examples out of your own experiences. This writer remembers, in his first parish, a family supported the local and world mission of the church, *until* the daughter decided she wanted to become a missionary. The parents didn't like that at all.

Proclamation of the Word

Consider this: Help the congregation to recognize this as one of Jesus' hard teachings. Remind them that most of us have not been put to the supreme test about our faith as have millions of people over the centuries. We invest ourselves in a "watered-down version" of the Good News. For many of us, our response is a convenience, something we do if we have nothing else to do. Drive home the essence of this Scripture perhaps by using examples of how one family member's commitment brings serious changes in his/her life style.

Stewardship Thought

Suggested: Give an example from your own life, or the life of someone in your denomination whose commitment created pain and separation from the family. This writer remembers that when he made his decision to enter the seminary, several of his relatives thought he had "flipped out."

Charge to the Congregation

Try this: David O. Fuller has posed the question, "If you were arrested for being a Christian, would there be enough evidence to convict you?" Good question. Build the charge around that idea.

Planning for Your Congregation

Suggestions   Your Situation

I. Other Scriptures   *Lay readers:*

- Psalm 10:12-18
- Psalm 82
- Psalm 40:2-4, 18
- Jeremiah 20:7-13
- Jeremiah 23:23-29
- Jeremiah 38:4-6, 8-10
- Hebrews 12:1-17

II. Hymn Possibilities   *Hymn selections:*

"All Hail the Power of Jesus' Name"
　Edward Perronet, 1779, 1780; altered.
　Stanza 4, John Rippon, 1787
　For the concluding hymn, also use
　"All Hail the Power of Jesus' Name,"
　but use another tune

III. Other Music Possibilities   *Music selections:*

Music for Preparation
　"Prelude and Fugue in B Minor"   Bach
Response to the Proclamation
　"Let There Be Light"   Darst
Offertory
　"The Saints' Delight"   Dale Wood
Response to the Benediction
　"Now Let Us Sing"   Anonymous

IV. Bulletin Cover   *Bulletin design ideas:*

V. Bulletin Symbols

VI. Miscellaneous Details *(Assignments):*

- Ushers
- Banners
- Flowers
- Assistant(s) at Holy Communion

- Greeters
- Candlelighters
- Soloists
- Other

THE SEASON OF THE HOLY SPIRIT

PROPER 16
PENTECOST 14
ORDINARY TIME 21

Liturgical Color: Green

Gospel: Luke 13:22-30

Theme: Who's In and Who's Out? — We'll all be surprised. We prefer to debate the issue rather than to witness to the Good News.

Planning Notes

Pastoral Invitation to the Celebration

One pastor began like this:

In the name of the One who Created, Liberates, and Sustains us, welcome. We are here to praise the Lord and Author of history; we are here to discover how God calls us to be a part of that history, as we celebrate the Good News.

You may want to follow with this responsive call to worship, inviting the people to "reverently shout":

All: *Praise the Lord! Praise the Lord! Praise the Lord!*
Right *Praise God in the sanctuary!*
Left: **Praise God in the heaven of power!**
Right: *Praise God for mighty deeds.*
Left: **Praise God for sovereign strength!**
Right: *Praise God with a bugle blast,*
Left: **Praise God with lute and lyre,**
Right: *Praise God with drum and dance,*
Left: **Praise God with strings and flutes,**
Right: *Praise God with resounding cymbals!*
Left: **Praise God with the noise of cymbals!**
All: *Let everything that breathes, praise the Lord!*
Praise the Lord! Praise the Lord! Praise the Lord!

If you have hand instruments, use them by giving them to the congregation and/or the choir members.

Confession and Forgiveness

One congregation used the following response to the Beatitudes: (This could be printed or two readers could respond; use the response slowly and deliberately, giving the people plenty of time for silent meditation.)

| The Way It Seems | The Way God Intended | Planning Notes |

Instead of using "happy," use another word such as fulfilled, complete, or satisfied.)

1. How satisfied are the pushers, the people who know what they want): for they get on in the world . . .

1. How complete are those who realize their spiritual poverty: they already have entered the Kingdom of Reality.

2. How satisfied are the hard-boiled: for they never let life hurt them.

2. How complete are those who bear their share of the world's pain: in the long run, they will know more fulfilment than those who avoid it.

3. How satisfied are those who complain: they get their way in the end.

3. How complete are those who accept life and their own limitations: they will find more in life than anyone else.

4. How satisfied are the blase: for they never worry over their sins.

4. How complete are those who long to be truly "good": they will fully realize their ambition.

5. How satisfied are the slave-drivers: for they get results.

5. How complete are those who are ready to make allowances and forgive: they will know the love of the Lord.

6. How satisfied are the knowledgeable people of the world: for they know their way around.

6. How complete are those who are real in their thoughts and feelings: for in the end, they will see the Ultimate Reality, God.

7. How satisfied are the troublemakers: for people have to take notice of them.

7. How complete are those who help others to live together: they will be known to be doing God's work. (author unknown)

Message to the Children of All Ages

Try this: You may want to focus on "the last first, and the first last." Begin by pushing your way through the children to get to the front. Bring examples from your own life where you like to be first, to sit at the head table, to get served first, to be treated better than others. Maybe the children like to be "on stage . . . to be seen . . . to get lots of attention." Tie in with Jesus' being servant rather than master, and how he calls us to love rather than lord it over others.

Proclamation of the Word

Consider this: I used to have God all figured-out. In the beginning of my Christian journey, I *knew* who the Christians were; I could tell you who was "in" and who was "out." The world of radio and TV preaching, and too many pulpits in America, presents such an image. It sells, it makes money, it gets the spotlight — and it's *wrong*! At the moment of death, we will all be surprised.

It's dangerous and anti-biblical to decide for God; and, it's necessary and biblical to share our faith every opportunity we get, without making value judgments about others.

Planning Notes

Stewardship Thought

Consider this: There is only one test for the person of faith: "If your enemy is hungry, thirsty, in trouble, take care of him/her." We do this when we least expect it; we don't do this when we least expect it. Someone has said that "Christianity is the heart of a world without a heart." We are that heart, God's heart in a heartless world.

Charge to the Congregation

Consider this follow-up to worship:

We are God's heart, mind, thought, word, action in this world. Luther suggests that God calls us to be "little Christs" to the world around us. What a joy! What a challenge! And God promises to energize and support us along the way.

Planning for Your Congregation

Suggestions   **Your Situation**

I. Other Scriptures

Lay readers:

- Psalm 84
- Psalm 117
- Jeremiah 28:1-9
- Isaiah 66:18-23
- Hebrews 12:5-7, 11-13, 18-24

II. Hymn Possibilities

Hymn selections:

"Immortal, Invisible, God Only Wise"
    Walter Chalmers Smith, 1867, 1884; altered
"Rejoice, the Lord is King"   Charles Wesley
    (music by Ian Mitchell, found in *New Wine*,
    page 2. Published by the Board of Education of the
    Southern California-Arizona Conference of
    the United Methodist Church, copyright 1969)

III. Other Music Possibilities

Music selections:

Music for Preparation
    "Toccata"   Frescobaldi
Response to the Scripture Reading
    "Great God, Attend, While Zion Sings"   Butler
Offertory
    "The Last Hope"   Purvis
Music for Dismissal
    "For All the Saints"
    William Walsham How, 1864; altered

IV. Bulletin Cover

Bulletin design ideas:

V. Bulletin Symbols

VI. Miscellaneous Details *(Assignments):* _____

• Ushers	• Banners	• Flowers	• Assistant(s) at Holy Communion
• Greeters	• Candlelighters	• Soloists	• Other

THE SEASON OF THE HOLY SPIRIT

PROPER 17
PENTECOST 15
ORDINARY TIME 22

Liturgical Color: Green

Gospel: Luke 14:1, 7-14

Theme: Who gets the best seats? — Letting God put our lives in perspective.

Planning Notes

A New Order of Worship
Perhaps you will want to consider a change for the last part of this season.

Consider this:

Remembering Who God Is
(Adoration)
Facing up to Ourselves
(Confession and Forgiveness)
Looking out to Others
(Prayer)
Remembering Why We Are Here
(Scripture and Sermon)
Acting Out Our Faith
(Announcements as opportunities, Offering and Benediction)

Pastoral Invitation to the Celebration

Suggested: Begin with words similar to these:

In the name of the Father, Son, and Holy Spirit,
  by whom we are created,
  in whom we live and move and have our existence,
  to whom we go when this life ends,
we are here today to recognize and appreciate
  the Source and Power of our lives.
In these moments, we focus upon our Creator, Liberator, Sustainer.

Perhaps you will want to continue with this response:

Pastor: Let us affirm one another as called by God to be the church . . . to live under God in the Kingdom . . . to serve God.
Ministers: **All of us need to know that we are noticed and affirmed by God and each other; that we have a sense of purpose and something worthwhile to do; that we belong somewhere and to someone.**
Pastor: Therefore, it is exceptionally good to find out who we are and to whom we belong.
Ministers: **Also, it is exceptionally good to discover God's purpose for our lives.**
Pastor: The job of this congregation is to help us discover all of God's essentials and to help all of us to affirm each other in our discoveries.
All: **Come, you blessed of my Father, inherit the Kingdom which has been prepared for you from the foundation of the world. (a.u.)**

Confession and Forgiveness
(Facing Up to Ourselves)

Consider this: Begin with these words: "Most of us don't like to look at ourselves, especially in the light of God's truth. Yet, we can do so, because God is with us in our introspection. I invite us to pray this written prayer, and to let the Spirit of God seek us out and change us (print the following in the worship folder):

With openness of heart and mind, I acknowledge before you, O God, the thoughts I often allow to enter my mind and to influence my actions. I confess, Lord, that I allow my mind to wander down unproductive ways; that I deceive myself about where my obvious duties lie; that, by concealing my real motives, I pretend and fake my way through life; that my honesty, sometimes, is only a matter of policy; that my affection for my friends, sometimes, is only a refined form of self-interest; that often, my sparing of my enemy is due to nothing more than cowardice; that often, I do good deeds only to be seen of others, and shun evil deeds only because I fear that someone may find me out; that I sometimes refer to myself as your disciple, and live as though it were not true; that I sometimes make a verbal profession of faith, and do not follow through in consistent witness. O Holy One, let the fire of your love enter my heart, and burn up my meanness and hypocrisy; and make my heart as the heart of a little child. (a.u.)

(During an extended silence, invite the people to pray the prayer silently, inserting their first name after each "I")

Follow with this assurance of pardon:

Many of us spend more time and energy on our sins then we do on God's pardon. God promises to forgive the past, every bit of it; are we willing to accept God's promise?

Conclude with this response:

Pastor: Let us remember the Good News of our Liberation.
Ministers: **In Christ, our self-worth has been declared.**
Pastor: We have been forgiven, accepted, received.
Ministers: **Christ has forgiven the past. Christ has given the present new meaning. Christ has made the future full of possibilities.**
Pastor: Let us live fully and responsibly. In Christ, we are freed.
Ministers: **Indeed we are! So be it! Amen!**

Message to the Children of All Ages

Try this: Set up a table in the chancel with some goodies on it. Ask the children of all ages to come forward and sit wherever they want at the table. Once they are seated, ask the one near you to move to the end; and the one at the end to sit near you. Apply this to the Gospel for the day.

Proclamation of the Word

Consider this: Share with the people the danger that we clergy run, accepting the kind of treatment we receive from the congregation, at least in the early part of our ministry. We are treated as royalty, getting invited

Planning Notes

Planning Notes

places that we couldn't afford to go. We like such treatment. The danger for us is that we become a guru for the people, maybe even insisting they call us "reverend." Perhaps by sharing our danger, members will see their own danger in their expectations. We can easily come to expect special privileges, which then become demands. The most obvious pathology illustrating this is the TV evangelist who insists that God will kill him if the people don't respond. It's easy for us to focus on such obvious pathology, and miss our own.

Stewardship Thought

One pastor used this:

Someone has said that "only the disciplined change the world . . ." A teenage girl once said that "Obedience means to drop everything and do what God wants."

Charge to the Congregation

Consider this: Build the charge around this question:

Do we want to inherit the Kingdom of God by osmosis, or by obedience?

Planning for Your Congregation

Suggestions	Your Situation

I. Other Scriptures *Lay readers:*

- Psalm 15
- Psalm 112
- Psalm 68:4-7, 10-11
- Ezekiel 18:1-9, 25-29
- Proverbs 25:6-7
- Sirach 3:17-18, 20, 28-29
- Hebrews 13:1-8
- Hebrews 12:18-19, 22-24

II. Hymn Possibilities *Hymn selections:*

"All Praise Be Yours; for You, O King Divine"
    F. Bland Tucker, 1938, 1972
    (use for several weeks until the congregation knows it well)
"O Christ, Whose Love Has Sought Us Out"
    John Edgar Park, 1953; altered, 1972

III. Other Music Possibilities *Music selections:*

For the prayer of praise,
sing a version of the Lord's Prayer
Response to the Scripture
    "Cause Us, O Lord"   Ron Nelson
Offertory
    "Andante"   Marchand
Music for Dismissal
    "Immortal, Invisible, God Only Wise"
    Walter Chambers Smith, 1867, 1884, altered

IV. Bulletin Cover *Bulletin design ideas:*

V. Bulletin Symbols

VI. Miscellaneous Details *(Assignments):* _____

- Ushers
- Banners
- Flowers
- Assistant(s) at Holy Communion

- Greeters
- Candlelighters
- Soloists
- Other

THE SEASON OF THE HOLY SPIRIT

PROPER 18
PENTECOST 16
ORDINARY TIME 23

Liturgical Color: Green

Gospel: Luke 14:25-33

Theme: Discipleship costs; if it doesn't cost us something, it isn't true commitment.

Planning Notes

Setting the Theme

At the beginning and end of each worship service, one pastor uses a quote, which he either writes or chooses, to summarize the theme for the day. (sometimes he takes 15-30 minutes to find the right statement; he does this so that the people will have a handle by which to remember worship)

Consider these quotes for this worship service:

At the beginning:

"Christianity either begins with the receiving of a gift, the gift of God's grace, or it doesn't begin at all." Wayne H. Keller

At the end:

"To take up the cross of Christ is no great action done once and for all; it consists in the continual practice of small duties [responses] [some of] which are distasteful to us [while others bring extreme joy]. John Henry Newman. (brackets mine, WK)

Pastoral Invitation to the Celebration

Suggested: The reason we don't sell tickets to worship is because we don't want spectators.

You may want to follow with this response:

Pastor:	Jesus — called the Christ — has offered us a way of being fully human.
Ministers:	**He has presented a new style of life based on love and peace and justice for all persons.**
Pastor:	He has invited the church to declare this new way of life.
Ministers:	**Let us be the church at worship, so that we can be the church in mission.**
Pastor:	Let us celebrate life in Christ.
Ministers:	**Let's do! Amen! So be it!**

Following the hymn of praise, consider this prayer:

Planning Notes

> Praise be to you, O Lord! Invade us with the power of your love and create in us a love for you and one another. Come and possess us so that our wills may be obedient to your will for us. Show us the futility of trusting in pride, position, or power; and then give us the gift of the Holy Spirit, so that we may leave here filled with yourself and free to serve others in your love, that unmerited, undeserved, unearned gift of yours to us.

Confession and Forgiveness

Consider this: After introducing the confession, invite the saints to pray this prayer (which you may want to print):

O Gracious Lord, I have been forgetful this past week of what love and forgiveness mean in my life. I have been reluctant to respond to my neighbor's needs. I have talked behind [*speak person's name*] back when [he/she] could not defend [him/her] self. I have held on selfishly to spiritual and material idols when I should have known better. Forgive me again, Lord. Help me to see a joyful tomorrow, where you and I and the world can work together for this thing we call mercy. (a.u.)

You may want to continue with this response:

Pastor: The word of Christ is Good News.
Saints: **Our humanness has been received. We can be ourselves.**
Pastor: The past is forgiven. The future is before us.
Saints: **Let us live with courage and with a deep concern for people.**
Pastor: Let us give thanks and embrace our lives.
Saints: **Let's do. Amen. Let it be!**

> Choral response: a contemporary "Gloria Patri."

Message to the Children of All Ages

Suggested: Ask the children, "Do you enjoy obeying your parents? Do you know that some children don't obey their parents? They may not even like their parents. We can tell because they don't pick up their clothes; they don't wash the dishes; they don't brush their teeth; they don't pick up after themselves. So who does it? Usually mother!" Compare this with obedience to God. God has shown us how to live and we say we'd rather do things our way. God doesn't hit us over the head and say, "Shape up or ship out!" God, through people, seeks to love us so that we respond with love in return.

Proclamation of the Word

Consider this: This, obviously, is one of Jesus' hard teachings. He invites us/insists that we put him first. Of course, we don't; and we depend on God's grace and forgiveness, plus a new resolve on our part. Perhaps you will want to incorporate these ideas in your message: The believer does the ordinary things of life. The key is — he/she *does* them. "I like my way of doing things better than your way of not doing them." Millions of church members, some on the church rolls for years, use the church for "hatching/matching/dispatching," for comfort, peace, security and a haven from which to ignore the sterner demands of the Cross.

Planning Notes

Stewardship Challenge

One pastor did this:

Ask, "What parts of ourselves will we commit to God and to Christ's mission today and for the year? Pretend that your offering and pledge represent that part of yourself. Now, what obstacles are you permitting to block the other parts from responding?"

Charge to the Congregation

Suggested: By God's unconditional acceptance of us, we are made whole through our trust to the point of obedience. To this unconditional gift from God who "cared enough to send the very best," we give one response: "Thanks" — with our energy, time, resources, not in order to get into the Kingdom, but rather, to acknowledge our presence in the Kingdom. "We love, we obey, because God first of all loved us."

Planning for Your Congregation

Suggestions

I. Other Scriptures
- Psalm 94:12-22
- Psalm 10:12-15, 17-19
- Psalm 90:3-6, 12-17
- Ezekiel 33:1-11
- Proverbs 9:8-12
- Wisdom 9:13-18
- Philemon 1-21

II. Hymn Possibilities

"All Praise Be Yours; for You, O King Divine"
   F. Bland Tucker, 1938, 1972
   (Hymn of the Month)

"The God of Abraham Praise"
   Daniel ben Judah Dayyan, ca.1400
   Translated by Newton Mann, 1885 and
   William Channing Gannett, 1910; altered
   (substitute "God" for "His")

"Take Thou Our Minds, Dear Lord"
   William H. Foulkes; stanzas 1-3, 1918;
   stanza 4, 1920

III. Other Music Possibilities

Music for Preparation
   "Pastorale"   Franck
Choral Introit
   "Holy, Holy, Holy"   Choir
Response to the Act of Receiving New Life
   "Gloria Patri"
   (use a contemporary version)
Offertory
   "Be Thou Near"   Bach
Congregational Response following Benediction
   "Day By Day" from "Godspell"
   St. Richard of Chichester (altered)
   Copyright 1971 by Valando Music, Inc.
   and New Cadenza Music Corp.

IV. Bulletin Cover

V. Bulletin Symbols

VI. Miscellaneous Details *(Assignments):* _____

- Ushers
- Greeters
- Banners
- Candlelighters
- Flowers
- Soloists
- Assistant(s) at Holy Communion
- Other

Your Situation

Lay readers:

Hymn selections:

Music selections:

Bulletin design ideas:

THE SEASON OF THE HOLY SPIRIT

PROPER 19
PENTECOST 17
ORDINARY TIME 24

Liturgical Color: Green

Gospel: Luke 15:1-10

Theme: The parables of the lost sheep and coin — Seeking the lost. (Consider this dimension to the parable — seeking the lost in our own home.)

Planning Notes

Consider these bulletin quotes

1. *At the beginning:* "Children need someone to look up to, which ought to be incentive enough for any parent." Griff Niblack
2. *At the end:* "Live so that your children, when someone tells them that they remind them of you, will stick out their chest instead of their tongue." *The Furrow*, John Deere Company

Pastoral Invitation to the Celebration

One pastor began this way:

"Alleluia! God created us within families. God continues creation through us — as biological families, as church families. God welcomes, pursues us as family. Therefore, Good morning, as together, the family of Christ, we celebrate the Good News.

Confession and Forgiveness

Suggested: Introduce the call to confession with words similar to these. Here is the human condition: God placed us in families for nurture, affirmation, growth. Often we use each other as scapegoats. "It's not my fault!" Compare the Adam-Eve story. God gave/gives us everything we need, but we want more. Adam/Eve is the story of our lives. Now, I invite us to listen to a contemporary version of Genesis 3. (Play Petula Clark's rendition of "Games People Play," produced by Claude Wolff, Warner Bros. Seven Arts Records, Inc. Burbank, California.)

You may want to follow the music with this introduction to the act of forgiveness: Someone has said that "you are never loyal to your family until you are first loyal to Christ." The family need not serve as the battleground educating each other in violence (that is, verbal, physical, silent violence). God calls the family in Christ to model agape (unconditional good will) for the world. God invites us to share the fruits of the Spirit with one another and beyond — love, joy, peace, patience, kindness, goodness, gentleness, self-control — This will happen when we integrate the grace of God into our words, thoughts, actions. We've heard the words before. Will we now allow the Spirit of God to infuse them into our being, our personality?

Continue with this response:

> *Pastor:* Let us remember the good news of our liberation.
> *Ministers:* **In Christ our self-worth has been declared.**
> *Pastor:* We have been forgiven, accepted, received.
> *Ministers:* **Christ has forgiven the past. Christ has given the present new meaning. Christ has made the future full of possibilities.**
> *Pastor:* Let us live fully and responsibly. In Christ we are free.
> *Ministers:* **Indeed we are! So be it! Amen!**

Message to the Children of All Ages

Try this: Pretend that you've lost something. You think that you lost it somewhere in the chancel. Ask the children to help you find it. Make it difficult but not impossible to find. When someone does find it, let out a joyful squeal. Ask the children if they've had a similar experience. How did they feel when they found it, or if they didn't find it. Ask if they know that Jesus loves each of us far more than we love our lost item. And he uses people to seek us out, sometimes using parents, friends, relatives, teachers, pastors, to find us. Maybe you will want to tell them briefly how you were found.

Proclamation of the Word

Suggested: I have deliberately taken the family theme to talk about lostness, because I have never heard a message which ties this Scripture of lostness to the family. The first time the pastor came to visit the Keller family, I was the only member to refuse to sit in the same room with him. He read my fear, lightly veiled with anger. That was the beginning of my being found by God, though I didn't know that until years later.

Perhaps you will find this useful: Samuel Taylor Coleridge, the English poet of the Romantic period, one day talked with a man who believed in giving children no religious instruction. This individual theorized that nothing should prejudice a child's mind; so that when the child came to years of discretion, he/she could choose for him/herself. Coleridge said nothing; but after a while, he asked his visitor if he would like to see his garden. The man said yes; so Coleridge took him into the garden where only weeds were growing. The man looked at Coleridge in surprise and said, "Why, this isn't a garden; there are nothing but weeds." Coleridge answered, "Well, I didn't wish to infringe upon the liberty of the garden in any way. I was just giving the garden a chance to express itself and to choose its own production."

Stewardship Challenge

Consider this idea from the *Mustard Seed Conspiracy* by Tom Sine:

Two billion people, about half the world's population, make less than $200 per year. For example, people in Haiti make less than $150 per year, and pay four times the price we pay for tomato sauce. Are we willing to live simply, so that others may simply live?

Planning Notes

Planning Notes

You may want to follow with this prayer:

God, you hold us accountable for all that you have given us — our lives, education, homes, business, friends, and wealth. As we have been prospered, so may we give to you, through your needy world, for the sake of your son, our liberator, Jesus the Christ.

Charge to the Congregation

One pastor employed this idea suggested by Robert Hudnut's book, *Surprised by God*: All of us pastors have dealt with every conceivable problem and crisis known to human beings, usually physical and emotional illnesses. How often do people invite us to respond to their *spiritual* illness? Hudnut one day from the pulpit offered to visit any home in which family worship was difficult to get started and to sustain. He said that he had not received a single request in nine months.

We deal with every problem except the one which could truly bring us together. Now, my friends, today I'm making the same offer to you. Any takers?

Planning for Your Congregation

Suggestions	Your Situation

I. Other Scriptures *Lay readers:*

- Psalm 77:11-20
- Psalm 51:1-19
- Hosea 4:1-3,
- Hosea 5:15—6:6
- Exodus 32:7-14
- 1 Timothy 1:12-17

II. Hymn Possibilities *Hymn selections:*

"All Praise Be Yours; for You, O King Divine"
   (Hymn of the Month)
"God of our Fathers/Mothers; Whose Almighty Hand"
   Daniel C. Roberts, 1876
   (this hymn has been rewritten in inclusive language)

III. Other Music Possibilities *Music selections:*

Music for Preparation and Dismissal
   Medley of Pentecost Hymns
Response to the Assurance of Pardon   Soloist
   "Amazing Grace"
Response to the Proclamation
   "Cannon of Praise"   Arranged by Hopson

IV. Bulletin Cover *Bulletin design ideas:*

V. Bulletin Symbols

VI. Miscellaneous Details *(Assignments):* _____

- Ushers
- Banners
- Flowers
- Assistant(s) at Holy Communion

- Greeters
- Candlelighters
- Soloists
- Other

THE SEASON OF THE HOLY SPIRIT

PROPER 20
PENTECOST 18
ORDINARY TIME 25

Liturgical Color: Green

Gospel: Luke 16:1-13

Theme: Prudence — Emulate the cleverness of the rascal of a steward for a better purpose; because you can serve only one master.

Planning Notes

Pastoral Invitation to the Celebration

One pastor began this way:

Welcome to worship. Why have we come to worship today? To get something? Only partly, I hope, because if we don't get what we want, we may fail to realize that we are participants, not spectators, in the act of worship.

You may want to use this story:

One day a deaf-mute was asked why he attended worship. His answer, "To let the world know who's side I'm on."

We come, not primarily to get something; we come to declare who's side we're on, to let the world know that we're on Christ's side. So, let's worship as if we are the actors, because we are, in the Name of God the Creator, Liberator, Sustainer.

Perhaps you will want to continue with this response: *(Invite the people to "reverently shout.")*

Pastor:	I'm glad to see you.
Ministers:	**Thanks. It's [fill in your answer] to be here.**
Pastor:	Let's fulfil the purpose to which God has called us.
Ministers:	**Let's do. Let's celebrate the presence of God, the Creator, who makes life possible, and God, the Reconciler, who makes life purposeful.**
Pastor:	I'm for that!
All:	**So am I. Amen**

Confession and Forgiveness

Try this: Because popular songs depict the human condition, use them on occasion, either the recording or a soloist, or sometimes have the choir and congregation sing them. For today, use "Both Sides Now." Give a brief introduction to the music, along with what you want the people to focus upon. Following some silence, build the assurance of pardon around our belief in the "priesthood of all believers." Compare the Old Testament concept with the New Testament. If you feel especially courageous, you may want to invite the people to turn to their neighbor and offer each other forgiveness as the priests of God. *(Be ready for some hostility.)*

Message to the Children of All Ages

Suggested: Bring into the chancel a variety of things that occupy the childrens' time: perhaps a TV set, sports equipment, books, toys, and the like. Ask them to think about how much time they spend with each during a week. Point out how easy it is to make them more important than anything or anyone else, including Jesus. Show them how easy it is for you to put your own joy before Christ.

Proclamation of the Word

Consider this: Read *Pilgrim's Progress* in preparation for this message. Perhaps you will want to use examples similar to these: (1) a fisherman/woman spends time preparing for, and fishing, while Christians make worship a leisure-time activity when they have nothing else to do; golfers take lessons and read books to develop their skill, while Christians seldom take time to pray, except in crises; salespeople never stop talking about their product, while Christians seldom mention their Lord and Savior; the worldly thoroughly care for their senses and bodies, while Christians give tidbits to the mission of Christ.

Stewardship Challenge

Consider this: Tom Sine, author of *The Mustard Seed Conspiracy,* tells of a pastor in a small Lutheran Congregation in Washington who called the Lutheran Relief Service in New York to inform them that their church would be sending a check for $100,000. They decided that, if they could borrow money to construct a building, they could borrow money to help feed starving people!

Charge to the Congregation

Suggested: James Thurber has said, "Let us not look back in anger, or forward in fear, but around in awareness." Perhaps you might also want to integrate the following quotation in the charge also: "The greatest burden we have to carry in life is self; the most difficult thing we have to manage is self." (Hannah Smith)

Planning Notes

Planning for Your Congregation

Suggestions	Your Situation

I. Other Scriptures *Lay readers:*

- Psalm 107:1-9
- Psalm 113
- Hosea 11:1-11
- Amos 8:4-7
- 1 Timothy 2:1-8

II. Hymn Possibilities *Hymn selections:*

"All Praise Be Yours; for You, O King Divine"
   (Hymn of the Month)
"God Is Working His Purpose Out"
   Arthur Campbell Ainger, 1894

III. Other Music Possibilities *Music selections:*

Music for Preparation
   "Prelude in G Minor" — Bach
Act of Recognizing our Humanness
   "Both Sides Now"
Response to the Old Testament Reading — Choir
   "The Lord Is My Shepherd" — Schubert
Offertory
   "Meditation" — A. Guilmant
Response to the Benediction
   "Praise God, Hooray" — Dick Avery/Don Marsh

IV. Bulletin Cover *Bulletin design ideas:*

V. Bulletin Symbols

VI. Miscellaneous Details *(Assignments):* _____

- Ushers
- Banners
- Flowers
- Assistant(s) at Holy Communion

- Greeters
- Candlelighters
- Soloists
- Other

THE SEASON OF THE HOLY SPIRIT

PROPER 21
PENTECOST 19
ORDINARY TIME 26

Liturgical Color: Green

Gospel: Luke 16:19-31

Theme: The story of the rich man and Lazarus — God will receive only those who recognize their need.

Pastoral Invitation to the Celebration

Planning Notes

Suggested: Build the invitation around the idea that both in worship and in mission, the central fact is not that we are seeking God, but that God is seeking us. So, today, we begin with some moments of silence in order to listen to the still small voice.

After three to four minutes of silence, invite the people to respond by reverently shouting this response:

Pastor: You have heard it said that God is dead; but I say to you, God is living and is here!
Ministers: **Praise be to the living God!**
Pastor: God is here! Can you hear God?
Ministers: **We hear God through the Word, spoken and sung; in Scriptures and the hymns; in laughter and in joy; in hurt and in sadness; in the noise and the silence.**
Pastor: God is here! Can you feel God?
Ministers: **We feel God through the Holy Spirit, in support and challenge from God's Word; in common unity of purpose and mission; in persons who love as God taught us to love and in persons who confront us even as the Cross confronts us.**
Pastor: Let us celebrate God's presence and power!
Ministers: **So be it! Amen!**

Confession and Forgiveness

One pastor did this:

Introduce the confession with "the law of God," perhaps the Ten Commandments or the Great Commandment, or with some other aspect of God's Law.

Then, you may want to print the following prayer:

Our God, we confess that we have done those things which we never should have done, and cannot understand now why we did and why we do. Why do we dirty love with calculation, powder and pamper our pride with pouts, fear to allow friendship to be more than cosmetic smiles? Why do we wear

Planning Notes

life and never live it? Why, O Father/Mother God? Forgive us, O Lord; it's not that we hate; it's just that we do not love. Do you understand us, Lord? For we do not understand ourselves. And therefore, we pray for forgiveness — for that which we have done, did not do, and plan to do, consciously and unconsciously. Make us, O Lord, healthy and new. In the name of the Christ. (a.u.)

After several moments of silence, begin the assurance with this statement of P. T. Forsythe: "All the deepest tides of a world's great sins were forced through the channel of a single heart." Then, invite the people to sing, "Let All Mortal Flesh Keep Silence."

Message to the Children of All Ages

Try this: Tell the children that after thinking all week, you couldn't come up with a children's message. Tell them that you're disappointed and maybe they are also. Tie this in with the Gospel. Suggest all the possibilities for growing in our knowledge and love of Jesus each day, and how easily we get so "busy" that we may not take time for the most important things.

Proclamation of the Word

Consider this: If you have Andrew Blackwood's book, *Expository Preaching for Today,* refer to page 136 for an outline of this story. He suggests that we need to "let the sermon be dramatic rather than dogmatic." As with all good writing, we are to show rather than tell. Show the contrast between the two men. Point out that the five brothers' destiny is determined by their relationship to the Word, and does not depend on their wealth. Be sure to emphasize that God can receive only those who recognize their need.

Stewardship Challenge

Suggested: The church too often *reflects* society instead of *changing* society. How will we go about this week seeking by God's Spirit to change those things in our immediate neighborhood that need changing?

Charge to the Congregation

Conclude with this statement by Samuel Rutherford:

"If you have not got a Cross, you have not got Christ; for the Cross is one of the first of his gifts." Maybe the church as we know it must die before the church as Christ wants it can really begin to live, as the revolutionary movement it was in the beginning.

Planning for Your Congregation

Suggestions	Your Situation

I. Other Scriptures   *Lay readers:*

- Psalm 107:1, 33-43
- Psalm 146
- Joel 2:23-30
- Amos 6:1-7
- 1 Timothy 6:6-19

II. Hymn Possibilities   *Hymn selections:*

"All Praise Be Yours; for You, O King Divine"
   (Hymn of the Month)
"Let All Mortal Flesh Keep Silence"
   From the Liturgy of Saint James
   Translated by Gerard Moultrie, 1864
"Be Still My Soul"
   From Psalm 46, Katharina von Schlegel, 1752
   Translated by Jane Laurie Borthwick, 1855
"Who Is On the Lord's Side?"
   Frances Ridley Havergal, 1877

III. Other Music Possibilities   *Music selections:*

Music for Preparation
   "Cortege and Litany"   Dupre
Choral Invitation to Worship
   "Let All Mortal Flesh Keep Silence"
   From the Liturgy of Saint James
   Translated by Gerard Moultrie, 1864
Response to the Proclamation
   "When I Survey the Wondrous Cross"
   Isaac Watts, 1707
   (After the congregation sings, point out that if we believe that message for ourselves, we are commanded to share it with others.)
Response following the Benediction
   Chorus of "Now on Land and Sea Descending," namely, "Jubilate, Jubilate, Jubilate, Amen."
   (repeat)

IV. Bulletin Cover   *Bulletin design ideas:*

V. Bulletin Symbols

VI. Miscellaneous Details *(Assignments):* _____

• Ushers	• Banners	• Flowers	• Assistant(s) at Holy Communion
• Greeters	• Candlelighters	• Soloists	• Other

THE SUNDAYS AFTER

PENTECOST
PART IV

THE SEASON OF THE HOLY SPIRIT

PROPER 22
PENTECOST 20
ORDINARY TIME 27

Liturgical Color: Green

Gospel: Luke 17:1-10

Theme: Cause and effect — This business of forgiveness.

Pastoral Invitation to the Celebration

Planning Notes

One pastor began this way:

Someone has said that corporate worship is the church's most important hour of the week. If that's true, how have we prepared ourselves to come today? What kinds of expectations do we have as we come? Are we harboring any grudges? Are we alienated from anyone? Do we need forgiveness? Are we willing to receive and share the good news? Are we willing to be actors, not spectators, in the drama of worship?

(Allow several moments of silence to prepare.)

You may want to use Saint Francis of Assisi's Prayer: "Lord, make me, *[put your name here],* an instrument of your peace. Where there is hatred, let me, *[first name],* sow love. Where there is doubt, faith; where there is despair, hope; where there is darkness, light; and where there is sadness, joy." Ask the people to repeat the prayer after you, inserting their first name where appropriate.

Confession and Forgiveness

Suggested: Introduce the confession with words similar to these:

> Many of our people have a terribly superficial view of sin. We prefer to use the words, "problems, shortcomings, weaknesses, mistakes, errors," but not the word "sin." Along with himself, Ernest Renan's son was a skeptic. One day, he went into a rectory, knocked on the door, and said to the priest, "Come out; I want to talk to you about a problem." The priest said, "Come in; I want to talk to you about your sins."

Introduce the assurance with these two ideas: (1) Forgiveness never comes easily; and if it does, it may not be forgiveness, but patronization. (2) Though forgiveness never comes easily, it does come freely, or it isn't forgiveness after all.

Then follow with this response:

Pastor: We have made confession of our problems, shortcomings, weaknesses, mistakes, errors, rationalizations, excuses. For those who take God's promises seriously, in the name of Jesus Christ, I declare the forgiveness of all your sin, your I-centeredness.

Ministers: **Christ, we thank you for your promise; we believe you. And now, we are better equipped to seek forgiveness and reconciliation each day, each hour.**

Planning Notes

Message to the Children of All Ages

Suggested: Bring some full-blown dandilions into the chancel. Ask the children to blow the seeds all over the place. Then ask them to pick them up and bring them back to place on the flower. Compare this with careless words. Yes, we can gather them, but they have done their damage. We have treated Jesus the same way; yet, even then, he forgives us if we seek his forgiveness. [You may want to alert your custodian in advance of this planned activity, so that you two can remain on friendly terms afterwards.]

Proclamation of the Word

Consider this: Compare the idea of forgiving three times, with Peter's seven times, with Jesus' "You forgive as often as you need to forgive; because you also need to be forgiven over and over." [Author's translation.]

Think about (1) the frustration, anxiety, exhaustion of alienation; about how we avoid each other, make no direct eye contact, glance around, worry about running into the person on the street, saying things behind other's back we would not dare say to his/her face; and (2) the peace, stability, newness, wholeness, health, relief of forgiveness. Use many examples from your and others' lives.

Stewardship Challenge

Try this: The Stewardship of Forgiveness. All the money in the world does nothing to achieve or acquire the kingdom. How well do we forgive? How well do we *receive* forgiveness?

Charge to the Congregation

Suggested: A country western song has this sentence in it: "When you learn that forgiveness doesn't mean giving in, that's when love can begin again." We are God's forgiven and forgiving people.

Planning for Your Congregation

Suggestions   Your Situation

I. Other Scriptures   *Lay readers:*

- Psalm 101
- Psalm 95:1-2, 6-11
- Amos 5:6-7, 10-15
- Habakkuk 1:1-3; 2:1-4
- 2 Timothy 1:1-14

II. Hymn Possibilities   *Hymn selections:*

"All Praise Be Yours; for You, O King Divine"
    (*Hymn of the Month*)
"They'll Know We Are Christians By Our Love"
    Peter Scholtes, 1966

III. Other Music Possibilities   *Music selections:*

Music for Preparation
    "A Prelude"   Delius
Response to the Prayer of Praise   Choir
    "Psalm 100"   David Williams
Introduction of the Sermon   Popular Song
    "Tie a Yellow Ribbon 'Round the Old Oak Tree"
(*perhaps use a soloist*)
Offertory
    "Be Thou But Near"   Bach
Music for Dismissal
    "O Master Let Me Walk With Thee"
    Washington Gladden, 1897

IV. Bulletin Cover   *Bulletin design ideas:*

V. Bulletin Symbols

VI. Miscellaneous Details (*Assignments*):

- Ushers
- Banners
- Flowers
- Assistant(s) at Holy Communion

- Greeters
- Candlelighters
- Soloists
- Other

THE SEASON OF THE HOLY SPIRIT

PROPER 23
PENTECOST 21
ORDINARY TIME 28

Liturgical Color: Green

Gospel: Luke 17:11-19

Theme: The ten lepers — "By the way . . . thanks"; or, the mystery of the missing persons.

Planning Notes

Pastoral Invitation to the Celebration

One pastor did this:

Build the invitation around the words, "First thanks, then giving," and "Poverty does not prohibit gratitude; prosperity does not produce it." (authors unknown.)

Our life of faith begins with gratitude, gratitude for the grace of God in our lives.

Build the response around the use of praise words and nature words, between pastor, choir, and congregation. The choir could sing its responses.

Use generous responses of "gladness is ours"; hallelujahs; amens, with words of praise, joy, hope, peace, with words of "sun, moon, mountains, hills, deserts, lakes, sea," and the like.

Confession and Forgiveness

Try this: Begin with this statement by John E. Southard: "The only people with whom you should try to get even are those who have helped you." If that is true, do we ever do it? I invite us to pray the following prayer with that idea in mind.

Lord Christ, you know us both as we are and as we can be. You know what's beneath the surface of our exterior masks of adequacy and pretension. You know how we manipulate words, situations, and people to accomplish what we want when we want it. Forgive the misuse of our intellects and our will to thwart your plan and purpose. Our self-centeredness is subtle! Reach deeply into our inner nature and reorient us around a dominant desire to know your will and do it. Show us again what life can be when we are motivated by your love and all our energies are marshalled to express this love in our relationships with others, our families, and the realm of society for which you have made us particularly responsible. (a.u.)

(silent prayer)

After a sufficient silence, introduce the assurance with these words from John M. Versteeg: "A Christian is one who majors in appreciation." Think about reasons for expressing appreciation to God, to the saints of God, to the body of Christ for new life, new awareness, new growth, new being.

Then use this response between pastor and ministers:

Pastor: Christ has set us free to live.
Ministers: **The past is forgiven. The future is before us.**
Pastor: Let us love life and the people who share it with us.
Ministers: **Let us embrace life and live.**

Message to the Children of All Ages

Suggested: Instead of reading the Gospel, either ask the children to act it out, or have a group of adults act it out as the children sit in the chancel. You may want to do some pre-preparation. Have the people wear signboards indicating what kind of modern leper they are, such as Indian, Black, Soviet, AIDS, etc. Perhaps you would like to be "Jesus" in the story. Make that moment when the one leper returns a holy moment, to include a hug and kiss on the cheek, and words similar to these: "Thank you for returning; feel free to leave; your trustful action has made you whole."

Proclamation of the Word

Consider these ideas:

Someone said that the greatest sin is that of ingratitude. In 1959, Lawrence S. Squires, pastor of the Highbury Congregational Church of Cheltenham, England, described in a *Church Management* article the kinds of lepers who went to Jesus that day. For example, he suggested that one was simply ungrateful, one too busy, one lazy, one did show himself to the priests (who convinced him not to return to this Jesus), one whose experience didn't touch his life, one afraid of himself, one afraid of outside things, one who expected Jesus to come by where he waited but Jesus went another way, and one too full of false pride.

Prayers of Thanksgiving by the People

Try this: Invite the people to offer sentence prayers of thanks; or include in the bulletin a half-sheet of paper with instructions to the people to write down a brief statement of someone or something for which they are thankful today. Ask them to hand these in following the sermon and use these as their response to the message.

Stewardship Challenge

Consider this: Ask, "What does it profit us if we add ten or twenty years to our lives if we aren't really living anyway?" (a.u.)

Charge to the Congregation

Try this: Say, "Worship which does not conclude with commitment is not worship. How will you live lives of thanks this coming week? Whom will you thank personally? Whom will you phone, or write, to let them know how much you appreciate them?"

Planning Notes

Planning Notes

Conclude with this response, in the style of Bill Cosby.

Pastor: You and I are human beings. Right?
Ministers: **Right!**
Pastor: You are for real. Right?
Ministers: **Right!**
Pastor: I am for real. Right?
Ministers: **Right!**
Pastor: Love is great. Right?
Ministers: **Right!**
Pastor: God is love. Right?
Ministers: **Right!**
Pastor: God's word came loud and clear in Jesus Christ. Right?
Ministers: **Right!**
Pastor: A lot of people are lonely. Right?
Ministers: **Right!**
Pastor: We have mouths. Right?
Ministers: **Right!**
Pastor: We have hands. Right?
Ministers: **Right!**
Pastor: Well, what on earth are we waiting for. Come on. Let's get out of here! For Christ's sake and the world's sake. Okay?
Ministers: **Okay!**

(Idea suggested by Herbert Brokering's *Uncovered Feelings*, Fortress Press)

Planning for Your Congregation

Suggestions
Your Situation

I. Other Scriptures

- Psalm 26
- Psalm 111
- Psalm 98:1-4
- Micah 1:2; 2:1-10
- Ruth 1:1-19a
- 2 Kings 5:14-17
- 2 Timothy 2:8-15

Lay readers:

II. Hymn Possibilities

"God of Our Life, Through All the Circling Years"
   Hugh T. Kerr, 1916; altered, 1928, 1972
"Now Thank We All Our God"
   Martin Rinkart, 1636. Translated by
   Catherine Winkworth, 1858; altered, 1972

Hymn selections:

III. Other Music Possibilities

Music for Preparation
   Medley of Thanksgiving Music
Choral Response to the Assurance of Pardon
   Popular Song   Chorus only, "Let It Be . . ."
Response to the Old Covenant
   Comtemporary Version
   "You Are the Lord, Giver of Mercy"
Response to the Prayers of Thanksgiving   Choir
   "Cannon of Praise"   Pachelbel
Response to the Benediction
   Tune: "Michael, Row the Boat"
   Prepare your own which includes thanksgiving

Music selections:

IV. Bulletin Cover

Bulletin design ideas:

V. Bulletin Symbols

VI. Miscellaneous Details *(Assignments):*

- Ushers
- Banners
- Flowers
- Assistant(s) at Holy Communion

- Greeters
- Candlelighters
- Soloists
- Other

THE SEASON OF THE HOLY SPIRIT

PROPER 24
PENTECOST 22
ORDINARY TIME 29

Liturgical Color: Green

Gospel: Luke 18:1-8

Theme: Pest With a Purpose — Persistence and Perseverance

Planning Notes

Pastoral Invitation to the Celebration

Suggested: Begin with an idea by Corita Kent (formerly Sister Corita) from *Footnotes and Headlines,* Herder and Herder, that playing an praying are, or can be, similar. It's much more important to live a life of prayer in all areas than to say a few prayers now and then.

We are taught that in prayer, and even in worship, it's okay to be sad, silent, somber, and not okay to smile, laugh, gaffaw. Who says so? I say to you, it's okay to be who we are, and to bring what we are to the act of worship.

You may want to follow with this response between pastor and ministers, asking the people to reverently shout:

Pastor: Who are you?
Ministers: **We are the people of God, called by love in Jesus Christ, not because we are adequate or worthy, but because of God's unconditional acceptance of us.**
Pastor: Why have you come?
Ministers: **To glorify God and to enjoy God!**
Pastor: What do you need?
Ministers: **Power to live an authentic life; freedom to be honest and open, released to love; joy to communicate; hope to begin again and daring to become involved in the wounds of the world.**
Pastor: These are gifts to be discovered in the Giver of Life. God is here as promised. Come on, let's celebrate life in the promised and present Messiah!

(a.u.)

Try this: If the congregation mumbles the response with little enthusiasm, repeat it until the people sound as though they mean it.

Confession and Forgiveness

Consider this: Invite the people to pray silently as you offer this bidding prayer of confession. Revise it to fit your local situation.

1. Let us confess our dependence on God's grace.
   (Allow at least 30 seconds of silence)

2. Let us confess our fear of others, our fear of honesty with oneself.
   (silence)

3. Let us confess our unbelief that others need Christ for salvation.
   (silence)

4. Let us confess our unconcern for the eternal welfare of others, our concern primarily for ourselves and immediate families.
   (silence)

5. Let us confess our lethargy, laziness, lacksadaisicalness, about speaking of Christ to others.
   (silence)

Then, conclude with this, or a similar prayer: God, we recognize our call to serve you, and our fears in fulfilling that call. Forgive us when we permit our fears to stifle the proclamation of your word. Help us to turn our eyes both outwardly and upwardly, as well as inwardly and downwardly, and now,
   (follow this immediately with this assurance of pardon)
Almighty God, who freely pardons all who repent and turn to Christ, fulfil in every heart the promise of reconciliation; forgive all of our rebellion, and cleanse us from a subtlety of evil, through the perfect sacrifice of Jesus Christ, our Lord, who has given us a reason for living and for sharing.

Message to the Children of All Ages

Suggested: Build your message around the model of fishing. Use a pole, tackle, bait. Point out that those who catch fish stay with it year after year, and hour after hour. You might ask if fisherpeople ever give up just because the trout fishing is slow, or if the trout is hard to land.

Proclamation of the Word

Consider this: Topic — "Pest With A Purpose." William Barclay has pointed out that, in this parable, Jesus was saying, "If, in the end, an unjust and greedy judge can be wearied into giving a widow-woman justice, how much more will God, who is a loving Father (Mother), not give his children what they need?" (It will not necessarily be what they always think they need.)

Contrast that widow with our usual approach:

1. We ask timidly, not boldly.
2. We ask once, and then quit.
3. We ask, expecting a turndown.

A salesman once reported that most sales are made after asking seven times.

Prayers by the People Following the Proclamation

Try this: Many laypeople who've been sitting in sanctuaries for many years confess "I can't pray" (which usually means, "I won't"). Invite the people to do what former Sister Corita once suggested: Repeat the letters of the alphabet, and let God arrange them into the appropriate words of the prayer. *(For the first time, you may want to do this silently; later, verbally.)*

Planning Notes

Planning Notes

Stewardship Challenge

Consider this: Ask the person to think about their stewardship of perseverance. List for them, or ask them to respond verbally to, those areas in their life in which they are persistent: maybe during an illness, with a dying mate, raising of children, or sports. It's easier to persevere in everything *except* our prayer life.

Charge to the Congregation

Suggested: I charge you today to sift out the essentials from the trivia of your life. Select three areas about which you will make a contract with God to pray, faithfully and persistently. Write them down; check them out; share them with us, in the Name of God the Creator, Liberator, Sustainer.

Planning for Your Congregation

Suggestions	Your Situation

I. Other Scriptures

- Psalm 119:137-144
- Psalm 121
- Habakkuk 1:1-3; 2:1-4
- Genesis 32:22-30
- Exodus 17:8-13
- 2 Timothy 3:14—4:2

Lay readers:

II. Hymn Possibilities

"I Sing the Mighty Power of God"
   Isaac Watts, 1709
   (Hymn of the Month)
"A Mighty Fortress Is Our God" from Psalm 46
   Martin Luther, 1529
   Translated by Frederick H. Hedge, 1853
"Prayer Is the Soul's Sincere Desire"
   James Montgomery, 1818
"Jesus Shall Reign Where'er the Sun"
   from Psalm 72   Isaac Watts, 1719

Hymn selections:

III. Other Music Possibilities

Music for Preparation
   "A Celtic Pastorale"   Lindsay
Choral Introit   An Alleluia Piece
Response to the Reading of the Scripture
   "Alleluia, Glorious is Thy Name"   Olson
Offertory
   "Prayer"   Armstrong
Response to the Benediction
   Either, congregational three-fold, or,
   choral seven-fold amen
Music for Dismissal
   "Alleluia! Alleluia!"   Armstrong

Music selections:

IV. Bulletin Cover

Bulletin design ideas:

V. Bulletin Symbols

VI. Miscellaneous Details *(Assignments):*

- Ushers
- Banners
- Flowers
- Assistant(s) at Holy Communion

- Greeters
- Candlelighters
- Soloists
- Other

THE SEASON OF THE HOLY SPIRIT

PROPER 25
PENTECOST 23
ORDINARY TIME 30

Liturgical Color: Green

Gospel: Luke 18:9-14

Theme: Parable of the Pharisee and Publican — Contrasting Prayer Postures

---

Planning Notes

Pastoral Invitation to the Celebration

Consider this: Begin with, "Wake up! We're here to celebrate life in the presence and power of God. We gather each week in this sanctuary, not because God is any more present here than in our homes, offices, classrooms, neighborhoods; we gather in this sanctuary in order to announce to each other and the world
- our *experience* of new life in Christ,
- our *endurance* in the midst of change,
- our *enjoyment* of the presence of God outside.

Worship is the celebration of God's presence and activity in the world — all of it — for Christ's sake.

You may want to continue with this response:

Pastor: Now that we're awake, good morning! Who do you think you are?

Ministers: **Now that we are awake, good morning to you! We are the church of Jesus Christ. We have come here to remember what it means to be Christian and to be the church in worship, so that we can be the church in mission.**

Pastor: Will you be honest during this time? Will your hearts and minds be open to God's Word?

Ministers: **We will be honest and open to God's Word.**

Pastor: Then, we shall continue to praise God.

Ministers: **Amen! Let it be so in you and in me.**

(a.u.)

Confession and Forgiveness

Try this: Introduce the Gospel for the day. In advance, ask one of the members to memorize the prayer of the Pharisee, and pray it as the prayer of confession. Introduce the prayer, not so much as the Pharisee's prayer, but as the way we often pray, though much more subtly. Following the prayer, ask the people to remain silent for at least two minutes.

After the silence, have someone (who was asked in advance) to pray the prayer of the Publican as the prayer of forgiveness.

You may want to conclude with the choir's singing "Lord Have Mercy" by John Michael Talbot. *(See Planning section.)*

Message to the Children of All Ages

Suggested: Ask the children what they thought about the way the two people prayed. Build the message around their responses.

Proclamation of the Word

Suggested: Consider reading the text from Clarence Jordan's *Cotton Patch Version*. Many of us have heard the parable so often that we no longer hear the parable for us. You may want to incorporate these ideas: (1) In the November 1948 issue of *Ladies Home Journal*, a huge slice of the American public was asked what it believed about prayer. Ninety percent of those asked said that they prayed; only five percent admitted praying for forgiveness. With our "Rambo mentality" today, which assumes that we are the "good empire" and they are the "evil empire," has anything changed? (2) In the *Church and Home Magazine* several years ago, the story is told of a successful businessman giving advice to his son, who was just launching a business career. "Remember that honesty is the best policy," said the Father, "but read up on corporation law. It's really surprising how many things you can do in business and still remain honest — if you know how to do them."

You may want to conclude the proclamation with the song "If Jesus Came to Your House," by Craig Starrett. Though the words are a bit naive, they do hit home. *(See the Planning section for details.)*

Stewardship Challenge

Consider this: Ask the people to consider their stewardship of prayer. When, how, for what do they pray? How much is adoration, confession, thanksgiving, intercession, dedication and commitment? Ask them to consider a specific person or event for their prayers next week.

Charge to the Congregation

Suggested: Summarize the two prayers: (1) "I thank You, God, that I'm not like so-and-so over there in the corner" and (2) "God, have mercy on a sinner such as I." Which kind of pray-er am I, are you, are we?

Planning Notes

Planning for Your Congregation

Suggestions	Your Situation
I. Other Scriptures	*Lay readers:*

- Psalm 3
- Psalm 34
- Zephaniah 3:1-9
- Deuteronomy 10:12-22
- Sirach 35:12-14, 16-18
- 2 Timothy 4:6-8, 16-18

II. Hymn Possibilities   *Hymn selections:*

"I Sing the Mighty Power of God"
   Isaac Watts, 1709
   (Hymn of the Month)
"Open My Eyes That I May See"
   Clara H. Scott, 1895
"God, Be Merciful to Me"
   From Psalm 51   *The Psalter,* 1912
"Blessing and Honor and Glory and Power"
   Horatius Bonar (1808-1889)

III. Other Music Possibilities   *Music selections:*

Music for Preparation
   "Pastorale"   Purvis
Response to the Assurance of Pardon
   "Lord, Have Mercy"   John Michael Talbot
   Birdwing Records, Chatsworth, California 91311
   Produced by John Michael Talbot and Phil Perkins
Response to the Proclamation
   "If Jesus Came to Your House"
   Words/Music by Craig Starrett
   Hill and Range Songs, Inc., 1650 Broadway,
   New York, New York
Offertory
   "Chorale"   Dupre
Music for Dismissal
   Medley of Pentecost Hymns

IV. Bulletin Cover   *Bulletin design ideas:*

V. Bulletin Symbols

VI. Miscellaneous Details *(Assignments):* _____

- Ushers
- Banners
- Flowers
- Assistant(s) at Holy Communion

- Greeters
- Candlelighters
- Soloists
- Other

THE SEASON OF THE HOLY SPIRIT

PROPER 26
PENTECOST 24
ORDINARY TIME 31

Liturgical Color: Green

Gospel: Luke 19:1-10

Theme: Come to the party — Jesus' invitation to Zacchaeus.

Pastoral Invitation to the Celebration

Planning Notes

Consider this: Every Sunday God invites us to a party, a celebration, worship. Sometimes, we say no; today we said yes. Now that we're here we celebrate in the Name of God the Creator, Liberator, Sustainer. So, let's welcome each other to the party!

Encourage people to move about the sanctuary to greet many of the guests of God. *After several minutes, invite the people to respond:*

Pastor: Come, let's keep celebrating the Good News!
Ministers: **We come to celebrate the Resurrection and each other!**
Pastor: Christ is alive and calls us to life.
Ministers: **We come to discover the post-resurrection miracle of new life in fellowship with the living Christ and his living body.**
Pastor: This life is life as Christ lived it — life as we live it with him and each other, and life as he lives it in us and each other.
Ministers: **That's how we choose to live, today and always!**

Confession and Forgiveness

Suggested: Print this prayer in the bulletin (you may want to have the people pray it verbally or silently — or both):

With openness of heart and mind, I acknowledge before you, O God, the thoughts I often allow to enter my mind and to influence my actions: I confess, Lord, that I allow my mind to wander down unproductive ways; that I deceive myself about where my obvious duties lie; that, by concealing my real motives, I pretend and fake my way through life; that my honesty is sometimes only a matter of expediency; that my affection for my friends is sometimes only a refined form of self-interest; that often my sparing of my enemy is due to nothing more than cowardice; that often I do good deeds only to be seen by others, and shun evil deeds only because I fear that someone may find me out; that I sometimes refer to myself as your disciple, and live as though it were not true; that I sometimes make a verbal profession of faith, and do not follow through in consistent witness. O Holy One, let the fire of your love enter my heart, and burn up my meanness and hypocrisy, and make my heart as the heart of a little child.   (author unknown, revised)

Planning Notes

Follow with silence.

For the act of forgiveness, sing "Breathe On Me, Breath of God." Point out that this is a prayer-hymn.

Message to the Children of All Ages

Consider this: Update the story by asking the children to be Zacchaeus. What do they do to see a parade, something exciting, when the crowds get in their way? Point out how important they are in the eyes of Jesus, and that Jesus sees them when no one else may. Remind them that Jesus invites them to come to his party, even when no one else may.

Proclamation of the Word

One pastor did this:

Begin with the fact that Jesus liked parties so much that some of his contemporaries called him a playboy, wino, party boy. List some of the barriers that keep people from coming to the party. One pastor (unknown to this writer) has suggested three barriers: (1) The claim to adequacy — "I don't need you, God." (2) The attempt to concealment — "I won't share my hurts, failures, needs with my fellow earthlings." (3) The decision to cop-out — "I'm not willing to accept the responsibility of death and life." Then, give the reasons for people's willingness to come to the party, as an acceptance of our humanity in response to God's Spirit.

Stewardship Challenge

Try this: Zacchaeus responded after his encounter with Jesus, "Look, half of what I own, sir, I'm giving to the poor, and if I have . . . er . . . cheated anone . . . er . . . anyone, that is, I'll pay back four times the amount." (*Cotton Patch Version,* Clarence Jordan) What a contrast with our approach, which usually is this: "Funny how a dollar can look so big when we put it in the offering plate, and so small when we take it to the grocery store." (author unknown, revised)

Charge to the Congregation

Suggested: The celebrant of the faith is characterized by three fundamental attributes: He/she is incredibly courageous, absurdly joyous, and always in trouble for Christ's sake. (source of idea unknown) How about you, and you, and you, and me? Offer greetings to each other on your way out of the sanctuary.

Planning for Your Congregation

Suggestions | Your Situation

I. Other Scriptures

- Psalm 65
- Psalm 145
- Haggai 2:1-9
- Exodus 34:5-9
- Wisdom 11:22—12:1
- 2 Thessalonians 1:11—2:2

Lay readers:

II. Hymn Possibilities

"I Sing the Mighty Power of God" Isaac Watts, 1709
  (Hymn of the Month)
"O Worship the King All Glorious Above"
  from Psalm 104   Robert Grant, 1833
"Breathe on Me, Breath of God" Edwin Hatch, 1886
  (the act of forgiveness)
"All Hail the Power of Jesus' Name"
  Edward Perronet, 1779, 1780; altered
  Stanza 4, John Rippon, 1787

Hymn selections:

III. Other Music Possibilities

Music for Preparation
  "Choral in E Major"   Franck
Response to the Proclamation
  "Joy in the Morning"   Natalie Sleeth
Offertory
  "Lord, Be Present Now"   Bach
Response to the Benediction
  "Allelu!"   Words and Music by Ray Repp
  Copyright 1966 by F.E.L. Church Pub., Ltd. from
  Folk Encounter songbook
  Hope Publishing Co., Carol Stream, Illinois 60187

Music selections:

IV. Bulletin Cover

Bulletin design ideas:

V. Bulletin Symbols

VI. Miscellaneous Details *(Assignments):*

- Ushers
- Banners
- Flowers
- Assistant(s) at Holy Communion

- Greeters
- Candlelighters
- Soloists
- Other

THE SEASON OF THE HOLY SPIRIT

PROPER 27
PENTECOST 25
ORDINARY TIME 32

Liturgical Color: Green

Gospel: Luke 20:27-38

Theme: The Wrong Questions — Another Attempt to Trap Jesus

Planning Notes

Pastoral Invitation to the Celebration

Consider this: Psalm 148: Develop a call to worship without a printed form. Let the worship leader speak the words with different emphases and voice inflections. Ask the people to repeat some of the words. Perhaps you will want the choir to have its own response. For further information, refer to the way Avery and Marsh have used this method.

Following the invitation, ask the people to share their joy with one another.

Confession and Forgiveness

Try this: After using Psalm 148 as an adoration-psalm, use Psalm 139 as a confession psalm. You can invite all the saints and sinners to respond in this way:

Pastor: "O Lord, you have examined me and you know me! You know everything I do; from far away you understand all my thoughts. You see me, whether I am working or resting; you know all my actions.

Male Voices: **Can this be true? Does God know when I deliberately deceive to impress my friends? Does God hear my unspoken, bitter words?**

Pastor: Even before I speak you already know what I will say. You protect me with your powers. Your knowledge of me is overwhelming; it is too deep for me to understand.

Female Voices: **I feel uncomfortable to be known that well by anyone. I fear being exposed to such knowledge.**

Pastor: Where could I go to escape from your Spirit? Where could I get away from your presence?

All: **We think that we must hide from God. We are afraid to be seen and known by God.**

Pastor: If I went up to heaven, you would be there; if I would lie down in the world of the dead, you would be there. If I flew away beyond the east, or lived in the farthest place in the west, you would be there to lead me; you would be there to help me.

Male Voices: **Can't I escape God? Why does God seek me? To judge me? To condemn me?**

Female Voices: **Can it be that God seeks me out to love me? To forgive me? To use me for healthy, productive purposes?**

Pastor: I could ask the darkness to hide me, or the light around me to turn into night, but even the darkness is not dark for you, and the night is as bright as the day. Darkness and light are the same to you.

All: **So it is with God's love. God seeks us out with forgiveness and longing. God turns our darkness into light. Such a gift of love is not earned or deserved; we can receive it as a gift if we choose.**

Pastor: Examine me, God, and know my mind; test me and discover my thoughts.

All: **Find out if there is any deceit in me, and guide me in the eternal way."**

(*Today's English Version,* American Bible Society, 1970.)

(Two minutes of silence)

For the response, select one of the contemporary versions of "You Are the Lord, Giver of Mercy." After you sing, ask the people if they experienced any relief after praying the confession-psalm. Offer that, if they didn't, you would be glad to talk with them this coming week. *(Many church members pray the prayer of confession week after week, but still carry guilt and fear forever.)*

Message to the Children of All Ages

Try this: Without focusing on the content of the Scripture as such, which the children probably would not understand, center on the last line, "God is a God of the living." You may want to begin, however, by asking if the children ever do anything that doesn't count for much, even argue about things just to keep things stirred up. Maybe they even put parents to the test to see if they will bend. Compare this with what some people tried to do to Jesus (not seeking to find out anything important, they tried to trap him, so that they would have an excuse to get rid of him).

Proclamation of the Word

Consider this: Review the *Interpreter's Bible* section on this passage. The author points out that "we are never allowed to lose sight of the paradox that we are dust and divinity."

The Sadducees were out to "get" Jesus, using methods not unlike those we use to "get" those who disagree with us. We like to debate and argue about those things that add nothing to our faith, so we need not live our lives in the precious present moment. You may want to read Spencer Johnson's book, *The Precious Present*, published by Doubleday and Company, Garden City, New York.

Stewardship Challenge

Suggested: A university coed once said, "Sure I believe in God; I'm just not nuts about him." Follow this with Eugene Rolf's remark: "Almost all of us, nowadays, conduct our lives for all practical purposes as if God did not exist."

Charge to the Congregation

Suggested: Conclude worship with Luke 20:38. God is a God of the living, for all live to God. How will we do just that this coming week?

Planning Notes

Planning for Your Congregation

Suggestions	Your Situation
I. Other Scriptures	*Lay readers:*

- Psalm 9:11-20
- Psalm 148
- Psalm 17:1, 5-6, 8, 15
- Zechariah 7:1-10
- 1 Chronicles 29:10-13
- 2 Maccabees 7:1-2, 9-14
- 2 Thessalonians 2:13—3:5

II. Hymn Possibilities   *Hymn selections:*

"I Sing the Mighty Power of God"   Isaac Watts, 1709
   (Hymn of the Month)
"Christ is Made the Sure Foundation"
   Latin, Seventh Century
   Translated by John Mason Neale, 1851
"God Be in My Head"   Sarum Primer, 1558

III. Other Music Possibilities   *Music selections:*

Music for Preparation
   "Psalm Prelude"   Howells
Response to the Confession   Contemporary Version,
   "You Are the Lord, Giver of Mercy"
Offertory
   "Adagio"   Reuble
Response to the Proclamation
   "Psalm 150"   Howard Hanson
Music for Dismissal
   Another version of Psalm 150

IV. Bulletin Cover   *Bulletin design ideas:*

V. Bulletin Symbols

VI. Miscellaneous Details *(Assignments):* _____

• Ushers	• Banners	• Flowers	• Assistant(s) at Holy Communion
• Greeters	• Candlelighters	• Soloists	• Other

THE SEASON OF THE HOLY SPIRIT

PROPER 28
PENTECOST 26
ORDINARY TIME 33

Liturgical Color: Green

Gospel: Luke 21:5-19

Theme: Expect Persecution and Claim God's Power. Consider this statement of Bonhoefer's — "In the end, there are only two possibilities of encountering Jesus — either we must die or we will kill him."
Christ the Center, page 36. Harper and Row, Published 1966

Pastoral Invitation to the Celebration

Planning Notes

Consider this: Here is an idea from the *Christian Century* several years ago, (somewhat revised): Coming alive happens when a congregation recognizes that it has not one or two or three ministers, but rather, the number of people on its rolls or participating in its life — people/ministers who celebrate the Gospel as a corporate act of worship, who care about one another, and who do their tasks in the Spirit and power of the Christ, "using pulpits made out of business transactions, relationships with neighbors and families, classroom responsibilities, and political issues and churches made out of highways, living rooms, offices, airplanes, kitchens, golf courses, assembly lines, doctors' offices, bedrooms, and grocery stores." (author unknown)

You may want to continue with this response:

Pastor:	The call of Christ is not an easy one.
Ministers:	**It is an invitation to self-giving.**
Pastor:	It requires hard work in the face of disappointment.
Ministers:	**It means going on when everyone else has given up.**
Pastor:	We will need to support each other if we are to obey Christ.
Ministers:	**Let us offer this support as we celebrate the life of faith, hope, love together.**

Confession and Forgiveness

Suggested: Drive home the concept of *Sin* as opposed to "sins." Many pew-sitters still carry around a superficial, saccharine view of sin, recorded in the little ditty, "I don't smoke or drink or chew; and I don't go with [girls/boys] who do."

Use something like this: If Sin is basically alienation from God, from others including fellow church members and family members, and from the best self (which it is), then we are a part of that experience daily. To God, Sin is deadly, because it keeps us from receiving and experiencing the horror and shame of the Cross.

Planning Notes

Our temptation, according to C. S. Lewis in the *Screwtape Letters*, is to believe that religion is great — up to a point. How do you measure the extent of your obedience? Where do you draw the line with your commitment?

(Allow plenty of time for silence)

For the assurance of pardon, you may want to use this:

Pastor: Jesus said, Be of good cheer; your Sin (that is, your rebellion, your alienation, your I-centeredness) is forgiven. Believe this Good News and begin to live!

Ministers: **We believe; help us in our unbelief which leads to inaction.**

(author's paraphrase)

Message to the Children of All Ages

Try this: If you use the Gospel for the message, confess how difficult a time you had preparing it, if you did. Sometimes, a little child will lead parents into the church; sometimes, the opposite happens. When we become Christ's person, we don't know how others will act.

Proclamation of the Word

Suggested: Admit that most people prefer to ignore this part of the Gospel. Consider these ideas:

1. We think that the problems of the world are too great/big, so why try? "What difference does my decision make?" That's similar to Lloyd George declaring that the most dangerous feat in the world is the attempt to get across a chasm in two jumps. (Idea from *Preaching to the Contemporary Minds,* Merrill Abbey, p. 147, Abingdon Press.)

2. We are not to sit around passively waiting for God to work out the purpose for our lives. Rather, God invites us, urges us to respond in obedience to each decision, each relationship or event of our lives in the here-and-now.

3. This passage contains a warning against false messiahs and *all* assumptions about the immanence of the end. It does insist that there is no deliverance out of trouble, but surely deliverance in the midst of it. (See Romans 8:18-39.)

(For additional insights, see the *Interpreter's Bible*.)

Stewardship Challenge

Suggested: Arnold Toynbee once said, "So long as my neighbor's needs remain unsatisfied, it is my social and moral duty to supply his needs at the expense of my surplus wants." Tie that in with the Gospel.

Charge to the Congregation

One pastor concluded with these words by Miguel de Unamuno: "May God deny you peace but give you glory!" (You may need to clarify what that means.)

Planning for Your Congregation

Suggestions	Your Situation

I. Other Scriptures

- Psalm 82
- Psalm 98
- Malachi 3:19—4:2
- 2 Thessalonians 3:6-13

Lay readers:

II. Hymn Possibilities

"I Sing the Mighty Power of God"
    Isaac Watts, 1709
(Hymn of the Month)
"When I Survey the Wondrous Cross"
    Isaac Watts, 1707, 1709

Hymn selections:

III. Other Music Possibilities

Ask those responsible for the music to build all of the music around the other Scriptures assigned to this day. Make certain that they have a list.

Music selections:

IV. Bulletin Cover

Bulletin design ideas:

V. Bulletin Symbols

VI. Miscellaneous Details *(Assignments):*

- Ushers
- Banners
- Flowers
- Assistant(s) at Holy Communion

- Greeters
- Candlelighters
- Soloists
- Other

THE SEASON OF THE HOLY SPIRIT

PENTECOST 27
(Lutheran only)

Liturgical Color: Green

Gospel: Luke 19:11-27

Theme: The Parable of the Talents — If We Don't Use It, We Lose It.

Planning Notes

Pastoral Invitation to the Celebration

One pastor did it this way:

God arrived here long before we did this morning. God authored, established the church, the Body of Christ, centuries ago. God invites, calls the church, the Body of Christ, to worship together each Sunday.

• Some choose not to respond to God's invitation and do something else — sleep in/attend the sport's event/visit relatives/travel/or a myriad of other things.

• Others of us have responded to God's call with our presence (though we may fit the other group often); so, let us not congratulate ourselves that we've come, but rather, praise God for our presence.

You may want to continue with this response:

Pastor: We are here because God, through people, has invited us to celebrate our lives together in Jesus Christ, as his body, the church, the fellowship of the Spirit.

Ministers: **Our celebration finds its pattern in self-giving sacrifice, in a deep love for people in a commitment to a new world, offering peace, justice, and fulfilment.**

Pastor: As we worship, may God's presence and power inspire, stimulate, and energize us to be his people in word and in action. If you agree, respond,

Ministers: **So be it!**

Confession and Forgiveness

Consider this: Invite the congregation to offer its confession in silence. Print these words in the order of worship:

Let us ask ourselves these questions and confess our sin. Is my life completely under Christ's control? If not, why not? What areas do I reserve for my own will and plans, unexamined in prayer? How do I resist Christ's plan for me? In what areas do I have divided loyalties? Who or what is often more important to me than Christ, indicated by the way I spend my time, energy, money?

After several minutes of silence, invite the congregation to pray this prayer verbally:

"Lord God, you have instructed that we shall have no other gods before You. We confess that our false gods, though subtle and seemingly acceptable, nevertheless demand our ultimate allegiance. We worship our possessions, our work, our loved ones and our hopes for the future, as though these things could satisfy our deeper needs. Forgive us, Lord, for the way we try to manipulate you to achieve our worship of these false gods. We pray for strength, wisdom, and energy to be able more completely to serve the lesser gods of our own making, instead of making these things a means of glorifying and praising you. Forgive us, Lord, and create a new spirit of love and devotion to you with us. So be it." (author unknown)

Following a few additional moments of silent meditation, have the choir sing Franz Schubert's "The Lord is My Shepherd."

Message to the Children of All Ages

Consider this: Bring the parable into the experience of the children. You may want to tie it into the use of their own talents and abilities, either in sports, or music, or art, or math. If they don't develop and use these, they will no longer have them. I learned, for example, at the age of forty-two, that I had seldom used my facial muscles because as a child I was not supposed to have any feelings. My therapist suggested that I begin to massage my face to get back the use of those muscles. Even today, however, I think that my inner feelings show on my face and often they do not. You can find a variety of ways to apply this with the children.

Proclamation of the Word

Consider this: Daniel Webster once was asked, "What is the greatest thought that has ever entered your mind?" After a brief pause, he said, "The thought of my accountability to God."

You may want to cover the parable this way:

    I. Managers of the World's Resources.
    II. Coming of the Day of Reckoning.
    III. Recipients of Rewards and Punishments.

Consider these applications (an idea suggested in the *Christian Century*, (author unknown, revised):

Think about how we refuse to vote but complain about who gets elected. Think about how we buy what we want and then beg for things we need. Think about how we use our friends and then complain that no one understands us.

Think about how little we give to worthy causes and gripe about the world going to hell in a hand-basket. Think about how we ignore God when all goes well and then wonder where God is when *we* need him/her.

Stewardship Challenge

One pastor did this:

Ask, (1) Does our offering, our giving, time/talents/treasure, reflect and refract what we think of God, what we consider the worth of God's mission? (2) Does our offering, our giving represent a greater concern for others, or for ourselves?

If worship is a celebration, which it is, then the act of the offering is perhaps

Planning Notes

Planning Notes

the most important part of the celebration. How much thinking prayer, concentration goes into the placing of our money into the offering (not collection) plate, as it slides past us?

Today, I invite us to bring our offering to the communion table, either as individuals or as families. We can represent or present it in several ways:

- by the actual cash;
- by the pledge of time, talent, treasure;
- by the ritual of friendship card, (yes, even with our credit card).

All of these represent ourselves.

As you come, as you place that which represents yourself upon the table, use the words printed in the dedicatory prayer: "Here am I, Lord, use me, send me, commit me. Amen."

If you prefer not to present yourself and your offering, please leave your offering in the plate at the door following worship.

(You may want to use this idea when you dedicate your people's pledges for the coming year.)

Charge to the Congregation

Consider this: A literary critic once said that he begins every day with the feeling that he is on trial for his life and probably will not be acquitted.

P.T. Forsythe has said, "Unless there is within us that which is above us, we shall soon yield to that which is around us."

Every day is crisis (opportunity) day; for every day is our call to commitment. We build a life, earthy and eternal, not by an emergency call at the end, but by a perpetual connection all along the way.

Planning for Your Congregation

Suggestions	Your Situation
I. Other Scriptures	*Lay readers:*
• Psalm 68:1-4 • Isaiah 52:1-6 • 1 Corinthians 15:54-58	
II. Hymn Possibilities	*Hymn selections:*

"Heaven and Earth, and Sea and Air"
    Joachim Neander, 1680
    Translated composite; *Church Book,* 1868
 "Take Thou Our Minds, Dear Lord"
    William H. Foulkes;
    stanzas 1-3, 1918; stanza 4, copyright 1920	

III. Other Music Possibilities	*Music selections:*

Music for Preparation
    "Chaconne"   Buxtehude
 Response to the Prayer of Confession
    "The Lord Is My Shepherd"   Franz Schubert
 Offertory
    "Prayer for Peace"   Jean Baptiste Lully
 Be cautious about music, especially anthems and solos, during the offertory; use silence sometimes. The music may distract from the presentation of the offering itself. This would be a good day not to have any music as the people come forward.
 Music for Dismissal
    "Prelude and Fugue in D Minor" J.S. Bach	

IV. Bulletin Cover	*Bulletin design ideas:*
V. Bulletin Symbols	

VI. Miscellaneous Details *(Assignments):* _____

- Ushers
- Banners
- Flowers
- Assistant(s) at Holy Communion
- Greeters
- Candlelighters
- Soloists
- Other

THE SEASON OF THE HOLY SPIRIT

CHRIST THE KING
(Last Sunday in the Church Year)

Liturgical Color: White

Gospel: John 12:9-19 (Common)
Luke 23:35-43 (Lutheran, Roman Catholic)

Theme: Living under and within the Kingship of Christ

Planning Notes

Pastoral Invitation to the Celebration

One pastor did this:

Begin by announcing the present reality of the Kingdom of God; that is, wherever God rules, that is heaven. Christ is Lord of all, even of those who refuse to acknowledge his Lordship, even of those who ignore his Lordship.

You may want to follow these remarks with one of the following two responses:

Pastor: The heavens are telling the glory of God; and the firmament proclaims God's handiwork.

Ministers: **Day to day pours forth speech, and night to night declares knowledge.**

Pastor: There is no speech, nor are there words; their voice is not heard;

Ministers: **Yet their voice goes out through all the earth, and their words to the end of the world.**

or:

Pastor: In the events of our lives, Christ the King invites, calls us to follow him.

Ministers: **His is a call of freedom. His is a call to responsibility. His is a call to new life — faith, hope, love.**

Pastor: Let us renew our lives together under his Lordship.

Ministers: **Let us celebrate life together under his Lordship — in the name of the Father, Son, Holy Spirit. Yes, Indeed! Let's do that!**

Confession and Forgiveness

Try this: Introduce the confession with a prayer hymn which helps the people to focus on Christ the King. Perhaps you will want to use "Savior, Thy Dying Love." (Bring some of the old words up-to-date.)

Follow with this prayer:

Forgive us, most gracious Lord and King, for doing and saying things to increase the pain of the world. Pardon the unkind word, the impatient gesture, the selfish deed, the failure to show empathy when we missed the opportunity; and enable us so to live that we may daily do something to lessen the tide of human sorrow, and to add to the sum of human joy, through him who died and rose again, and who reigns above and below.

For the pardon, after a brief introduction of asking the people to note the words in silence first, sing the hymn, "Your Kingdom Come! Great God we Pray," by Jane Parker Huber.

Message to the Children of All Ages

Consider this: The word "King" may be a strange one to the children. Define it, describe it, and illustrate it. Make sure the children know what it means. Then talk about how Christ is King over the world and over our lives. Be certain they understand that God's kingship doesn't depend on what we do. Help them find ways to be aware of God's kingship (for example, through our acts of kindness and caring).

Proclamation of the Word

Consider the following:

(1) The significance of the Apostles' Creed, when it says that ". . . he ascended into heaven."
(2) Martin Luther's statement . . . "that I may serve him . . . even as he is risen from the dead, and lives and reigns to all eternity."
(3) The Scriptural affirmation, "The fear (awesomeness) of the Lord is the beginning of wisdom."
(4) The biblical idea that under Christ's kingship, we are free, faithful and responsible (or, putting it another way, we are responsibly free and freely responsible).

Stewardship Challenge

Consider this: A friend who used to sing in cocktail lounges and taverns asked me one day, "Would you like to know the dirtiest word ever spoken in such establishments?" I hesitated, briefly, because she used all the four-letter words in the book and a few extras. I said, "yes." She responded, "Commitment." What is our stewardship of commitment?

Charge to the Congregation

Try this: Build on this statement: We can worship and obey only one of two gods, either Christ or self. We can allow Christ to be king, or we can attempt to usurp him by demanding that he and others conform to our expectations. We have the choice. Whom will we choose?

Planning Notes

Planning for Your Congregation

Suggestions	Your Situation

I. Other Scriptures
- Psalm 95
- Psalm 122:1-5
- 2 Samuel 5:1-5
- Jeremiah 23:2-6
- Colossians 1:11-30

Lay readers:

II. Hymn Possibilities

"Praise Ye (You), Praise Ye (You) the Lord"
    from Psalm 148, *The Psalter*, 1912
To Introduce the Confession:
    "Savior! Thy Dying Love" Sylvanus D. Phelps, 1862
For the Assurance of Pardon
    "Your Kingdom Come! Great God We Pray"
    Jane Parker Huber, 1982
    from *Joy In Singing*, Jane Parker Huber. The Office of Women and The Joint Office of Worship of the Presbyterian Church (U.S.A.)
"Christ Shall Have Dominion"
    from Psalm 72, The Psalter, 1912
"We Are a New Creation" Jane Parker Huber, 1981
    from *Joy In Singing*

Hymn selections:

III. Other Music Possibilities

Music for Preparation
    Ancient Hebrew Melody   Nowakowski
Choral Introit
    "The Lord is King"   Conder
Gloria Patri following the Prayer of Adoration
    and Praise — a contemporary or traditional version
Response to the Reading of God's Word
    "Lift Thine Eyes"   Mendelssohn
Offertory
    "Good Friend, for Jesus' Sake Forbear" Beethoven
Music for Dismissal
    "Dona Nobis"   Mozart

Music selections:

IV. Bulletin Cover

Bulletin design ideas:

V. Bulletin Symbols

VI. Miscellaneous Details *(Assignments):* _____

- Ushers
- Banners
- Flowers
- Assistant(s) at Holy Communion

- Greeters
- Candlelighters
- Soloists
- Other

THE SEASON OF THE HOLY SPIRIT

REFORMATION SUNDAY

Liturgical Color: Red

Gospel: John 8:31-36

Theme: The Protestant Reformation

Pastoral Invitation to the Celebration

Planning Notes

Try this: How many of you know what day today is, other than Sunday? (You may hope that someone will know.) Then ask, "What does this day mean to you in the history of the church?" You may receive some strange answers. Do not attempt to respond to them at this time.

Act of Recognizing our Humanness and Act of Receiving New Life

Consider this: In Ripley's *Believe It Or Not* there is described a torture whip made from iron chains with wooden handles. These were used by penitents, an extremely fanatical group which believed in attaining salvation through suffering. You may know of other ways by which people seek to attain their salvation. Mention some of the modern ones (for example, by becoming a pillar of the church, by giving money anonymously, by being a nice person with a perpetual smile, by not committing the more obvious sins).

Provide some silence for people to consider their own ways. Then, have a soloist sing a popular song, such as "Sittin' On a Fence," by Mick Jagger and Keith Richards (Rolling Stones), published by Gideon Music Inc. copyright 1966, for a contemporary confession.

For the assurance of pardon, as a prayer have the congregation sing, while seated, "Dear Lord and Father of Mankind."

Provide sufficient explanation.

Proclamation of the Word

Suggested: Topic — An affirmative protest. The Protestant Reformation was a protest against the corruption of the church and state. It was also an affirmation of the Scriptures and the grace of God.

Stewardship Challenge

Consider this: During the offering, ask the people to consider the stewardship of their heritage from the Reformation. Ask them to pray for a new reformation to begin in the Holy Catholic (you may even need to explain this word) Church, beginning, not with the person next to us, but with us.

Planning Notes **Charge to the Congregation**

One pastor did this:

> The Reformation has not ended. The Spirit of the Reformation has not died in the Holy Catholic Church, or the Roman Catholic Church, or the Protestant Church, or this congregation. The Reformation continues with each of us, and will continue until every knee shall bow before Christ, and every tongue confess that he is Lord of the universe.

Planning for Your Congregation

Suggestions	Your Situation
I. Other Scriptures	*Lay readers:*

- Psalm 46
- Jeremiah 31:31-34
- Romans 3:19-28

Hymn selections:

II. Hymn Possibilities

Use Reformation Hymns which best interpret the Reformation for you; this could include your own tradition and a variety of other traditions.

III. Other Music Possibilities   *Music selections:*

Music for Preparation
    "On a Norwegian Folk Hymn"   McKay
Choral Introit
    "The Lord Is King!"   Conder
Offertory
    "How Blest Are Ye"   Willan
Music for Dismissal
    "March in G"   Schreiner

IV. Bulletin Cover   *Bulletin design ideas:*

V. Bulletin Symbols

VI. Miscellaneous Details *(Assignments):* _____

- Ushers
- Banners
- Flowers
- Assistant(s) at Holy Communion

- Greeters
- Candlelighters
- Soloists
- Other

THE SEASON OF THE HOLY SPIRIT

ALL SAINTS' SUNDAY

(The First Sunday in November)

Liturgical Color: White

Gospel: Luke 6:20-36 (Common)
Matthew 5:1-12 (Lutheran)

Theme: Above all else, you must be happy — Another look at the Beatitudes.

Planning Notes

Pastoral Invitation to the Celebration

One pastor does this occasionally:

Invite the people to shout out a praise word or phrase. The pastor repeats the word; then, the congregation reverently repeats it. Let the process continue for a few moments; some people think more slowly than others.

Follow with this declaration of joy:

Pastor: Just who are you? Who are we?
Ministers: **A mixture — of joy and sorrow; of high and low moods; of hypocrisy and honesty; of hope and despair; of sadness and gladness; of hate and love.**
Pastor: You're right. We are all of those and more.
Ministers: **What do you mean, "more"?**
Pastor: I mean that whatever we are, in whatever situation, in whatever mood we find ourselves; God is there first. God beat us to the draw and because of that, we can know for a fact that God cares, that God has compassion, that God has concern for each of us, for all of us.
Ministers: **Great news! God loves us! God loves the church! God loves the world!**
Pastor: Rejoice and be glad about that!
All: **We shall. We are.**

(author unknown)

Confession and Forgiveness

One pastor did this:

Make certain that the people know the Beatitude's definition of "happiness," that it differs from the standards of the American people. One good definition is "how complete, how satisfied, how fulfilled are . . ."

Give the people an opportunity to spend some quiet time with the following sheet of paper. *(Be sure that everyone gets a copy.)*

Conclude the time with prayers from the congregation; or before the prayers, ask the people to share one thought from their meditation. Be certain that all worshipers will hear the statements.

Rank Yourself on Your Response to These Beatitudes

	Very Weak	Very Weak Improving	Moderately Strong	Very Strong
Happy are those who know they are SPIRITUALLY POOR. Have you come to the place where you can admit to others that you don't have all the answers? That you have needs? That you need God and others? Are you able to let others know where you are "Spiritually poor?" To "let it all hang out?"	1	2	3	4
Happy are those who MOURN. Are you able to show your emotions? To express your feelings? To feel deeply your own and others' needs? Do you "release" others to show their emotions? Are you really free of "graveclothes" in your emotional life?	1	2	3	4
Happy are the MEEK. Are you the kind of person who enables other persons to come forth because of your gentle spirit? Are you able to lead from weakness? To affirm others' strengths?	1	2	3	4
Happy are those whose GREATEST DESIRE is to do what God requires. Are you excited about God's leading in the daily decision of your life as you ought to be? What really motivates you? In the hard-nosed decisions of your professional life, where does God come in? Do you really put *people* above *things*?	1	2	3	4
Happy are those who show MERCY to others. Are you a "caring" kind of person? Sensitive to others needs? Giving yourself without thought of return? A "grace" giver — like Christ?	1	2	3	4
Happy are the PURE IN HEART. Have you come to terms with yourself to the extent that you are able to be yourself? The same person in church that you are in the world? The same language? Are you transparent? Open? Honest? Willing to let others know you deeply?	1	2	3	4
Happy are those who work for PEACE among people. Are you able to reconcile differences without destroying their uniqueness? Is your own manner disarming? Do you bridge differences? Can you accept genuinely and sincerely those who do not agree with you?	1	2	3	4
Happy are those who SUFFER PERSECUTION because they do what God requires. Are you able to take criticism from those nearest to you without reacting defensively? How about from your children? Do personal attacks tend to destroy your own self-image? Are you able to "Take the heat" in your home or place of business?	1	2	3	4

Used by permission from Serendipity House
Littleton, Colorado. Copyright 1980.
All rights reserved.

Planning Notes

Message to the Children of All Ages

Try this: Ask, "What makes you children happy, joyful, pleased, more than anything in the world?" Be aware how much the children's values reflect those of their parents. You might want to suggest an idea from *Peanuts*. "Happiness is a thoughtful friend," said Snoopy, after receiving turkey in his food dish. For Jesus to call us his friends can bring the greatest joy of all. For us to be friends with others is the greatest gift we can give.

Proclamation of the Word

Consider this: Begin by asking the people to fantasize about happiness, in relation to self, home, job, relationships.

Raquel Welch was quoted in *Look Magazine* many years ago with these words: "You know I'm perpetually unhappy . . . always worried about my work. Everything must be perfect or I'm unhappy . . . I want to do one thing perfectly."

True joy, happiness comes, however, not from having so much to live *on*, but from having much to live *for*.

Stewardship Challenge

Try this: A poster reads: "No deed of kindness or gratitude ever goes unheeded." We receive the good news in order to share the good news. True joy is a willingness to share what we have received. Think about how we will do that this coming week.

Charge to the Congregation

Suggested: Build around this statement by Storm Jameson: "Happiness (true joy) comes from the capacity to feel deeply, to enjoy simply, to think freely, to risk openly, to be needed daily." We can add one more: Happiness means to share graciously, yet confrontively.

Planning for Your Congregation

Suggestions	Your Situation

I. Other Scriptures

- Psalm 149
- Psalm 34:1-10
- Daniel 7:1-3, 15-18
- Isaiah 26: 1-4, 8-9, 12-13, 19-21
- Ephesians 1:11-23
- Revelation 21:9-11, 22-27 (22:1-5)

Lay readers:

II. Hymn Possibilities

"Open Now the Gates of Beauty"
   Benjamin Schmolck, 1732
   Translated by Catherine Winkworth, 1863;
   altered, 1972
Response to the Children's Message
   "Clap Your Hands"   Ray Repp
   (Text and music Copyright 1966 by F.E.L. Church Publications, Ltd. from *New Wine*, Copyright 1969 by Board of Education of the Southern California — Arizona Conference of the United Methodist Church.) *Text has been revised to eliminate sexist language.*
"Rejoice, O Pure in Heart"
   Edward H. Plumptre, 1865; altered
   Refrain added, 1883

Hymn selections:

III. Other Music Possibilities

Music for Preparation
   "Toccata"   Frescobaldi
Response to the Proclamation
   "Prayer of Supplication and Thanksgiving"
   Locklair
Offertory
   "Prayer"   Humperdinck
Doxology
   Consider using the tune, Duke Street L.M.
Music for Dismissal
   "For All the Saints"
   William Walsham How, 1864; altered
   (If you have people who play the trumpet, invite them to participate.)

Music selections:

IV. Bulletin Cover

Bulletin design ideas:

V. Bulletin Symbols

VI. Miscellaneous Details *(Assignments):* _____

- Ushers
- Banners
- Flowers
- Assistant(s) at Holy Communion

- Greeters
- Candlelighters
- Soloists
- Other

THE SEASON OF THE HOLY SPIRIT

THANKSGIVING EVE/DAY

Liturgical Color: White

Gospel: Luke 16:1-15

Theme: Thanksgiving

Planning Notes

Pastoral Invitation to the Celebration

Consider this: A poster says, "For all that has been, thanks; for all that will be, yes!"

Follow this with a litany based on Psalm 100. Have your choir director line it out to include a soloist, choir, and congregation.

Act of Recognizing our Humanness and Act of Receiving New Life

Suggested: Ahead of time, ask three lay people to prepare brief prayers of confession. Perhaps you will want to assign themes, perhaps not. Following their prayers, give the congregation the opportunity to offer sentence prayers of confession.

Then, do the same for the prayers of pardon.

Conclude by having the people offering a verbal thanks to God, and greetings of acceptance to one another.

Proclamation of the Word

Try this: Topic — *Thanks for the Memories (Bob Hope's theme).*

    I. Recalling our Heritage and Keeping it in Perspective
      1. Heritage of our birth
      2. Heritage of our friends
      3. Heritage of our Christianity
      4. Heritage of our congregation

Some of this we want to forget; some we appreciate. Yet, all of it comprises our lives.

    II. Responding to our Heritage
      1. Rejecting the bad stuff
      2. Recalling the "gold old days" which were not nearly as good as our fantasies about the good old days.
      3. Learning from the past. Someone said, concerning Dante, that he stood with one foot firmly planted in the middle ages and the other in the Renaissance.

Give the people an opportunity to share names or events in their own history, which are significant for our religious history and freedom and opportunities.

Stewardship Challenge

One pastor did this:

Compare what we spend on ourselves with what we share with others.

Charge to the Congregation

Try this: A. H. Glasow has said, "If we can't be thankful for what we receive, we should be thankful for what we escape." I invite you, encourage you, urge you, in the name of the living God to live lives of thanks, to be lives of thanks, even when you don't feel like it, for Christ's sake, for the world's sake, for your sake.

Planning Notes

Planning for Your Congregation

Suggestions	Your Situation

I. **Other Scriptures**   *Lay readers:*

- Psalm 100
- 1 Corinthians 1:4-9

II. **Hymn Possibilities**   *Hymn selections:*

"Blessing and Honor and Glory and Power"
    Horatius Bonar, 1866; altered, 1972
"Before the Lord Jehovah's Throne"
    Based on Psalm 100
    Isaac Watts, 1719
    Altered by John Wesley, 1737, and others.
"Now Thank We All Our God"
    Martin Rinkart, 1636
    Translated by Catherine Winkworth, 1858; altered, 1972

III. **Other Music Possibilities**   *Music selections:*

Music for Preparation
    "Now Thank We All Our God"   Bach
Response to the Act of Receiving New Life
    Congregation and Choir
"Put Your Hand In the Hand"
    Words/Music, Gene MacLellan
    (from *The Genesis Songbook,* compiled by Carlton R. Young, published by Agape, Main Place, Carol Stream, Illinois 60187)
Response to the Psalm
    "Thanks for the Memories"   Soloist
Offertory
    "Thanks Be to Thee"   Handel
Response to the Benediction
    "Bless Be the Tie That Binds"
Music for Dismissal
    Medley of Thanksgiving Hymns

IV. **Bulletin Cover**   *Bulletin design ideas:*

V. **Bulletin Symbols**

VI. **Miscellaneous Details** *(Assignments):* _____

- Ushers
- Banners
- Flowers
- Assistant(s) at Holy Communion
- Greeters
- Candlelighters
- Soloists
- Other

Appendix

How to Make Worship Banners and Visuals

Warren S. Satterlee II

Foreword

The appendix was written primarily as a "how to" resource for the altar guild, banner fabricators group, church school worker, and others who might find themselves responsible for visuals as part of the worship setting.

The banners and visuals that will be explained on the following pages can be completed by one person or by many working together in a cooperative effort. Children as well as adults with limited or advanced experience in art and related areas, can accomplish the examples with work and encouragement. A great deal of patience will be needed for some of the visuals. However, within the Body of Christ, there are many temperaments. All will be needed to accomplish these proclamations to God.

The appendix is divided into two sections:

1. banner fabrication;
2. visuals.

All of the banners and visuals mentioned in the text have been fabricated by the author and groups with whom he has worked. All are presently the property of several churches in the Central Texas Conference of the United Methodist Church and Presbyterian Church, of Crowley, Texas.

There are several questions which I would like to invite you, the readers, to ask yourselves as you are reading this appendix:

1. What catches the eyes of the members of the congregation as they enter the worship area?
2. What do we see as we look around the sanctuary of our own church building or the church building where we are visiting?
3. How do we, the members of the congregation, feel? What are our first impressions of members and visitors as they prepare to commune with God?
4. What can we as members of the altar guild, banner fabricators group or church school leaders do to enhance our surroundings so that we and others feel that we are one with God?
5. Could not well-conceived visuals and banners enhance our feeling of God's presence as we worship in our churches and other settings?

I hope that your experience with visuals in the church will be enhanced by your use of this appendix.

Barbara Meador-Carter
Chairperson, Board of Discipleship
Central Texas Conference
United Methodist Church
August 1988

List of Illustrations

Illustration 1	Lenten Banner Layout and Dimensions	Page 284
Illustration 2	Layout of the Progressive Lenten Banner	Page 287
Illustration 3	Dimensions and Physical Characteristics of the Progressive Lenten Banner	Page 288
Illustration 4	Metal Loop Layout	Page 289
Illustration 5	Cross Construction	Page 289
Illustration 6	Palm Sunday/Maundy Thursday Banner Layout	Page 290
Illustration 7	Affixing Large Cross to Banner	Page 290
Illustration 8	Jesse Tree Banner Felt Layout	Page 292
Illustration 9	Full Size Illustration of Apple and Serpent	Page 294
Illustration 10	Full Size Illustration of Mary and Manger	Page 295
Illustration 11	Construction of Banner Pole	Page 297
Illustration 12	Placement of Curtain Rod On Banner Pole	Page 297
Illustration 13	Lenten Hoop Visual	Page 298
Illustration 14	Wrapping the Hoop	Page 299
Illustration 15	Cross Supports for Hoop Visual	Page 300
Illustration 16	Placement of the Cross	Page 301
Illustration 17	Installing the Butterfly Symbol	Page 301

Banner Fabrication

In Section 1, seasonal, multipurpose and progressive banners and various terms will be explained in a simple how-to style. The themes, inspiration, description of construction, art terms, materials and other information will be given necessary for fabricating each type of banner.

Seasonal Banners

A Banner for Lent

The first banner will deal with the Season of Lent. This season begins on Ash Wednesday and ends with the Eve of Easter Sunday. There are many symbols that can be used to express ourselves and there are many resources available to be used as inspiration to develop a banner that is not only meaningful to ourselves, but can be interpreted for our congregations in a way that they can understand.

Much of the inspiration for the banners, visuals, and logos to be discussed has come from God. Some of the inspiration for the Lenten Banners came from a record album entitled *Gregorian Chant I — Paschale Mysterium: Holy Week* (produced by Document & Masterwork, ABC Records, Inc., Los Angeles, California). The notes accompanying the record give the Latin as well as English translation of each chant. Two chants were used to develop the following banner examples.

Ecce Lignum Crucis

Ecce lignum crucis, in quo salus mundi pependit.	Behold the wood of the Cross on which was hung the Salvation of the world.
Venite, adoremus.	Come, let us adore.

Crucem Tuam

Crucem tuam adoramus Domine: et sanctam resurrectionem tuam laudamus et glorificamus: ecce enim, propter lignum venit guadium in universo mundo.	We adore Thy cross, O Lord; We praise and glorify Thy holy resurrection. For behold, by reason of that wood, joy hath come in all the world.

Scriptures, Sunday church school lessons and texts of different kinds can also add support and give insight into the period or Season of Lent. For example, in *The Methodist Hymnal* on page 674 of the Commerative Edition 1784-1984 there appears a breakdown of *Seasons of the Church*. Following this page are *Aids For the Ordering of Worship* which indicate the season, color, and other information useful to the development of banners. In the case of the first banner, black was used as a background color and in the second, purple.

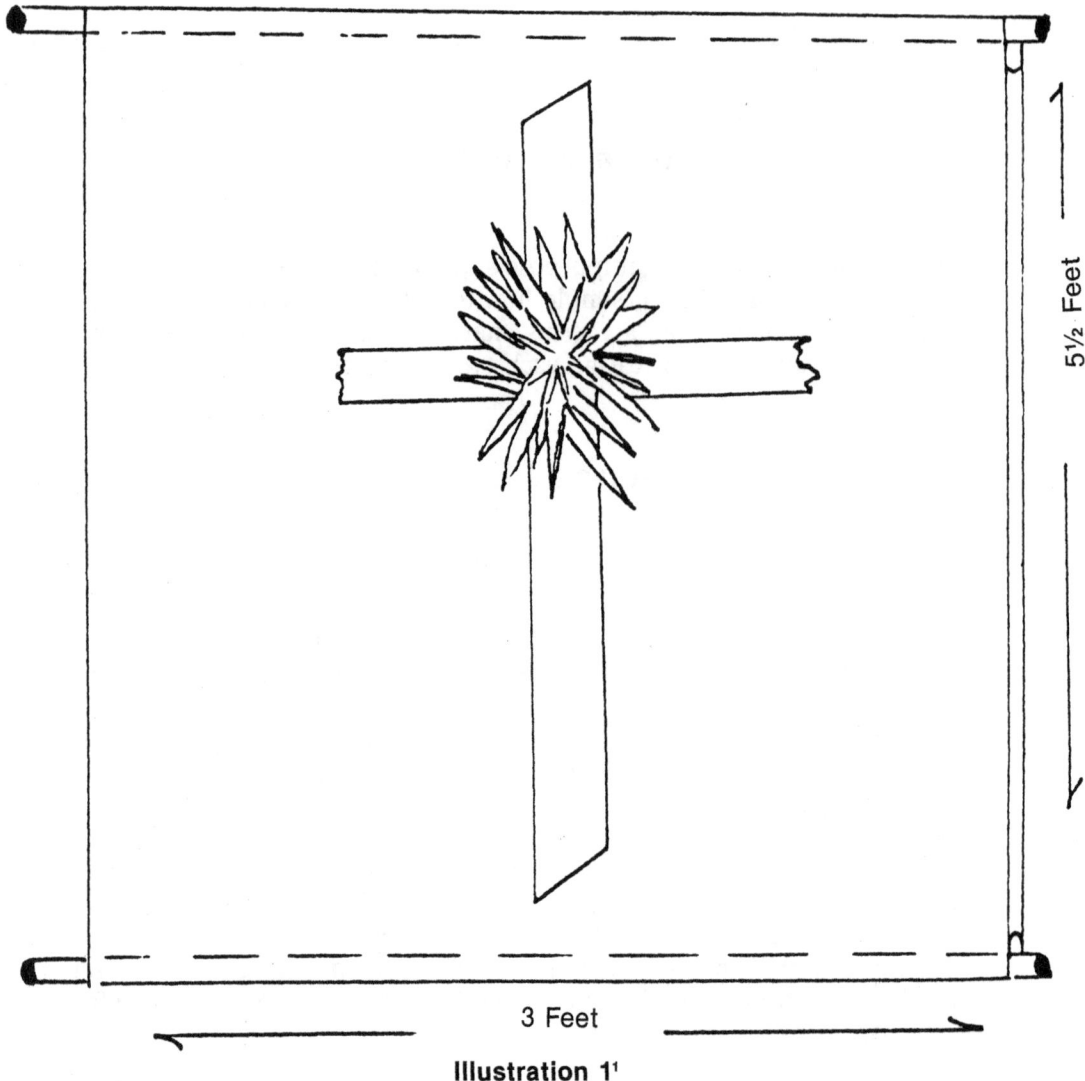

Illustration 1¹

¹ Banner is the property of First Presbyterian Church, Crowley, Texas.

This Lenten Banner is five and one-half feet long and three feet wide. The background material is a heavy, black cotton linen. The cross is made of wood, and the starburst is made of yellowgold watercolor paper. The banner was hung by a large cafe curtain rod from the wall of the Chancel. Another cafe curtain rod was used at the bottom to keep the banner flush with the wall.

The black background depicts the darkness before the Resurrection. The Cross reminds us of the way in which Christ died for us, and the gold Starburst symbolizes the Resurrection and the light of joy that has come into the World.

If your group decides to construct this banner, the following materials will be needed:

• A large, black piece of cotton linen (or a lighter weight material like polyester may be used). Material size (when folded) is 5½ feet long by 3 feet wide.
• Thin pieces of weathered wood, six inches wide and lengths three feet long for the vertical piece and two feet long for the horizontal piece. Weathered plywood left in one's yard for one year will give one the color and grade needed.

By allowing the plywood access to the elements of nature for one year, one will find that it is easy to peel off as much wood as needed for the following projects. The wood should be left rough so the cross will appear as realistic as possible.

- Several sheets of yellowgold watercolor paper or like material, 12" x 18" (available at art supply stores). Colored construction paper will not work because it is too thin.
- Velcro
- Staples and stapler
- White glue or access to a hot glue gun
- Two cafe curtain rods and hangers
- Yellow felt pen or hi-lighter
- Black thread
- Access to a sewing machine

Open the fabric out full, then fold it in half, right sides together. Sew up each side, to within three inches of the top and bottom. This leaves room for the curtain rods. Turn the banner right side out and sew along the top of it, about three inches down from the top and three inches up from the bottom edges of the banner *(see illustration 1)*. This will give the curtain rods easy access. After sewing is complete, lay out the cross on the material to be sure that it is centered and that the wood pieces are not too long. After the cross is in place the starburst should be cut from the paper. A paper pattern may be made to be certain that the burst will be large enough to cover the center of the cross, where it will be affixed to the material. The starburst will hide this area, yet let enough of the center wood show to let even the most inquisitive congregational member wonder how the banner was completed.

Now that all of the pieces have been laid out and all of them appear pleasing to the eye in their placement, it is time to join them to the material.

The cross can be put on the banner using one of two methods. One way is to sew Velcro on the material in the areas where the cross will be placed. The remaining side of the Velcro can be put on the back of the cross with hot glue or by using white glue. This will enable the altar guild to remove the cross and clean the material. The second way to fasten the wood is by a direct method. This method may prove frustrating, whereas Velcro is easier and more practical.

Now that the cross is in place, it will be necessary to put the starburst directly on the wood. After the starburst has been cut out, position it on the cross to be certain that it is pointing out in all directions, showing bits of wood and material between the rays *(see illustration 1)*. The starburst, if in several sections, needs to be glued together to make one large burst. The rear sections can be stapled directly to the wood. In other areas, white glue can be applied. When dry, this glue is transparent and will not be seen from a distance of ten feet or more. (***Note:*** *if too much glue is applied, the paper has a tendency to turn red, especially if you use Strathmore Brand Watercolor Paper. In this case, it will be necessary to use a yellow felt pen or hi-lighter to cover up any red that may appear on the paper.*)

After all the glue has dried, the curtain rods can be inserted and the banner is ready to hang. Allowing the cross and sunburst to become one unit allows for easier cleaning/storage.

As one steps back to look at the work hanging in the sanctuary, one should note that the light-colored wood and starburst stand out from the background. A three-dimensional quality should be evident.

On Ash Wednesday, as the congregation enters the church, they will see a new banner. What does it mean? There is a cross, so it clearly has something to do with Lent. Conveying the meaning of the banner can be done in several ways. One way is by incorporating the information into the Order of Worship. An example of this follows:

Prayer of Adoration

Leader: Look down, O Lord, upon this your household, for it is for men and women like ourselves that our Savior Jesus Christ did not hesitate to be delivered into the hands of wicked men and women, and to suffer the torment of the cross.

Women: Behold the wood of the cross, on which was hung the salvation of the world.

Men: Behold the radiance, for by reason of that wooden cross the light of joy has come into all the world.

[On Easter Sunday the same prayer may be expanded with the following]:

Unison: We adore your cross, O Lord, for here we have reason to praise and glorify your Holy Resurrection.

Leader: This is the day which the Lord has made! Christ is risen!

Unison: Thanks be to God!

The content for this prayer was drawn from the Gregorian Chants. The information was incorporated into the message and prayer giving the congregation a reference to the banner. Prior to the beginning of the service, the congregation was told the symbolism, as seen by the artist.

Several meetings with the minister of this church not only led to the development of the Prayer of Adoration, but also allowed the author to share feelings and thoughts with the minister on the ideas and progress of the banner itself. It was through this cooperative effort that these things were accomplished. In a large church setting, it would be advantageous to involve the following people:

1. The minister
2. Worship Coordinator/Chairperson
3. Church secretary or communications coordinator, who will type your information for the bulletin inserts and/or bulletins.

The ideas the designers will develop will need the cooperation and input from the several individuals mentioned. There may be other interpretations that need to be considered other than those arrived at by the original designer or the banner committee. It is wise to remember that the minister has the last word on whether a banner is acceptable. Be sure that all persons concerned are contacted.

A Progressive Lenten Banner

The second seasonal banner is Progressive and Multipurpose. The advantage of progressive banners is that they can be used for a whole season rather than for just one service. In other words, the Progressive Lenten Banner can be used from Ash Wednesday through Easter Sunday, its appearance changing week by week. This gives the congregation more awareness of the season and allows them to develop deeper feelings, as well, for the events that take place during this particular season.

The inspiration for the following banner is not only from the Gregorian Chants, listed previously, but also from God's Word in the Gospels of Mark, Luke and John.

Layout of the Progressive Lenten Banner

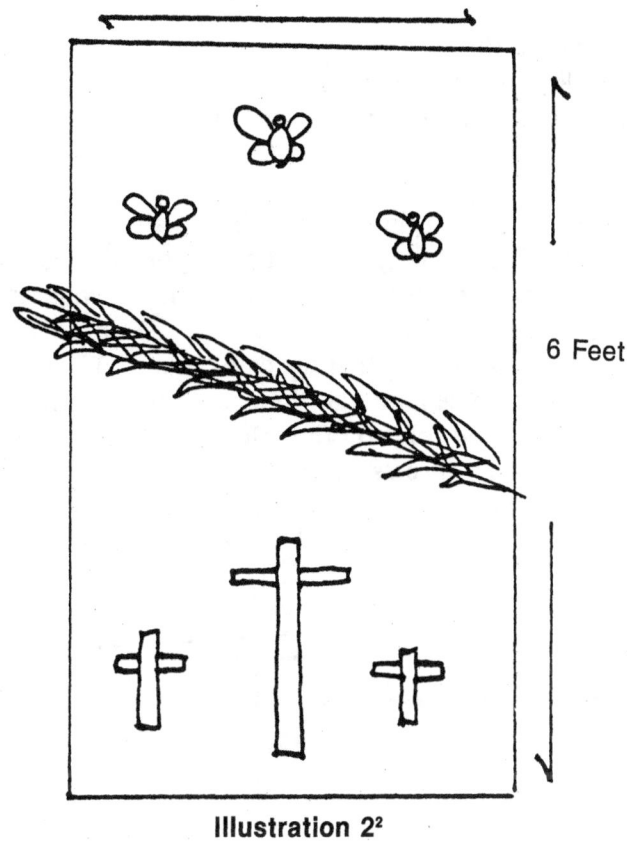

Illustration 2[2]

[2] Banner is the property of Grace United Methodist Church, Arlington, Texas.

The banner is six feet long, doubled from a piece of material twelve feet long. A purple polyester material was used, as purple is a traditional color for Lent. There are three white butterflies at the top, two Commodore Palms cutting diagonally across the middle of the banner, and three crosses.

The materials and symbols should be collected and laid out on the banner to see how they relate to each other spatially. Negative Space plays an important role in the overall development of the banner. Negative Space is that space which surrounds a positive object. For example, the three crosses at the bottom of the banner must not be placed too near the palm branches, yet must not be placed too far from them. Balance is necessary to tie the banner together as a whole, but the symbols must be able to stand alone as well. The banner is "read" from the middle, to the bottom, to the top. On Easter, when it is filled out, it will be "read" as a whole.

This is not a complicated banner to construct, and can be a very dramatic tool for helping develop the theme of Lent.

Materials required for this banner are:

• Twelve feet of purple polyester or other washable material, 22 inches wide when folded lengthwise

• Thin pieces of weathered wood (obtained from the "yard" supply), ½" wide by approximately 7" long

- Two Commodore Palms or other variety available at a local flower shop
- Four metal belt loops or buckles (semicircle in shape); these can be found at most fabric shops
- Magnetic Strips. Fourteen are needed, more if the banner will be carried in procession
- Three white butterflies, 4" x 4" wing tip to wing tip and body length of at least 2"
- Black sewing thread
- Availability of a sewing machine
- White glue or an adhesive of your choice
- One telescoping cafe curtain rod, at least 24" long

When selecting the purple material, choose a piece 12 feet long 22 inches wide (when folded in half lengthwise). Leaving one side completely open and the long fold on one side of the work table, fold the material in half so that it is now six feet long and 22 inches wide. At the top fold, move down two inches and sew along a line so that the cafe curtain rod can be inserted at the top of the banner. Please note that there are four distinct edges on one side of the material and two folds on the other side. *Please do not sew the four edges together.* It will be necessary to affix the symbols inside the banner during Lent. It will be necessary to sew the *bottom* edges. Move up from the bottom two inches on each section and sew *(see diagram)*.

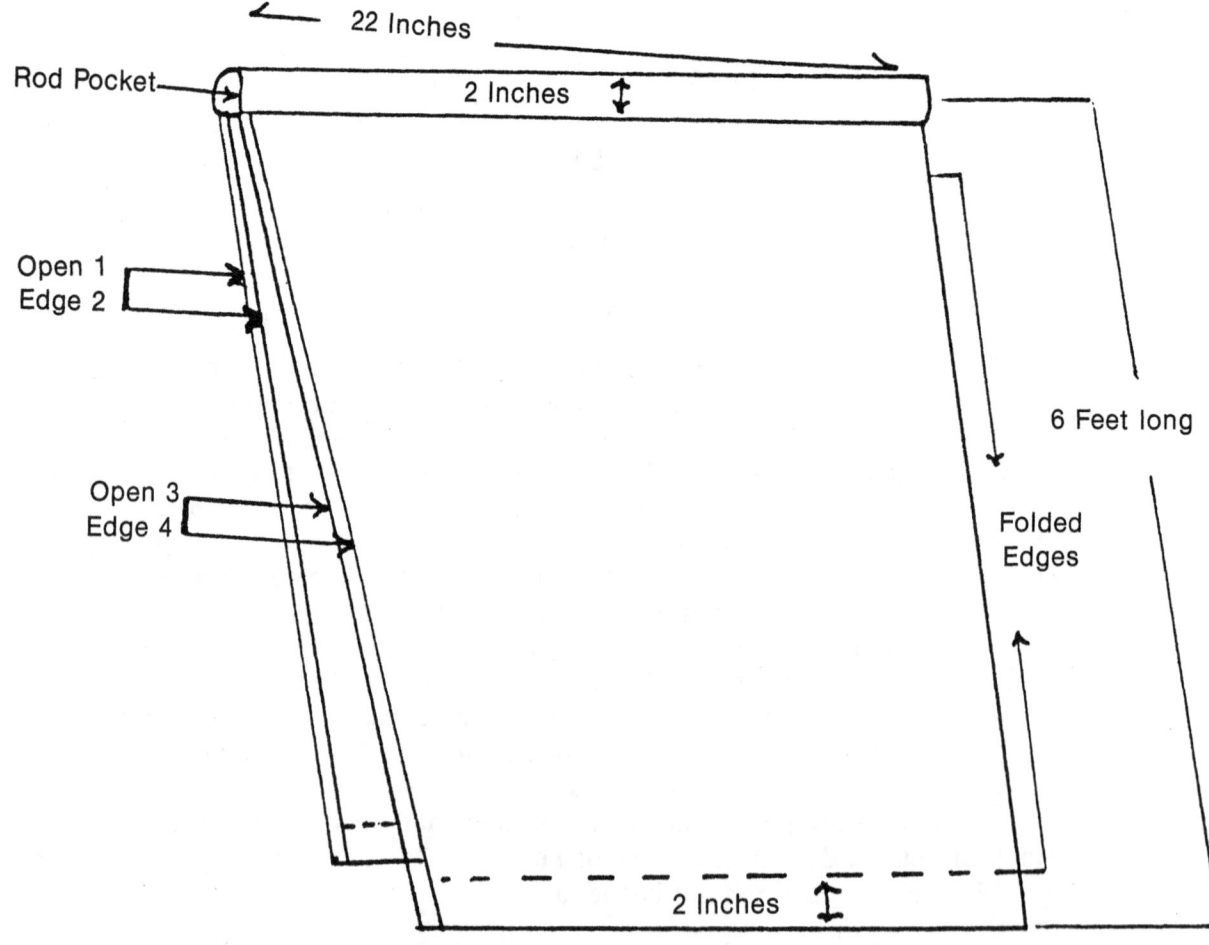

Illustration 3

The banner is now ready for the Ash Wednesday Service. Your congregation may question the fabricators as to why nothing is displayed on the banner. Encourage them to be patient. As Lent progresses the banner will change dramatically.

Prior to Palm Sunday, it will be necessary to remove the banner from the sanctuary and add two small metal belt loops or buckles, angled upward, in the center of the banner and two loops at the bottom. Lay out the small crosses so that the position of the loops is correct. (*Note: be sure, when the Altar Guild personnel arrive with the palms, that someone from your group gets two palms and positions them through the middle loops before anyone enters the sanctuary. See illustration 4.*)

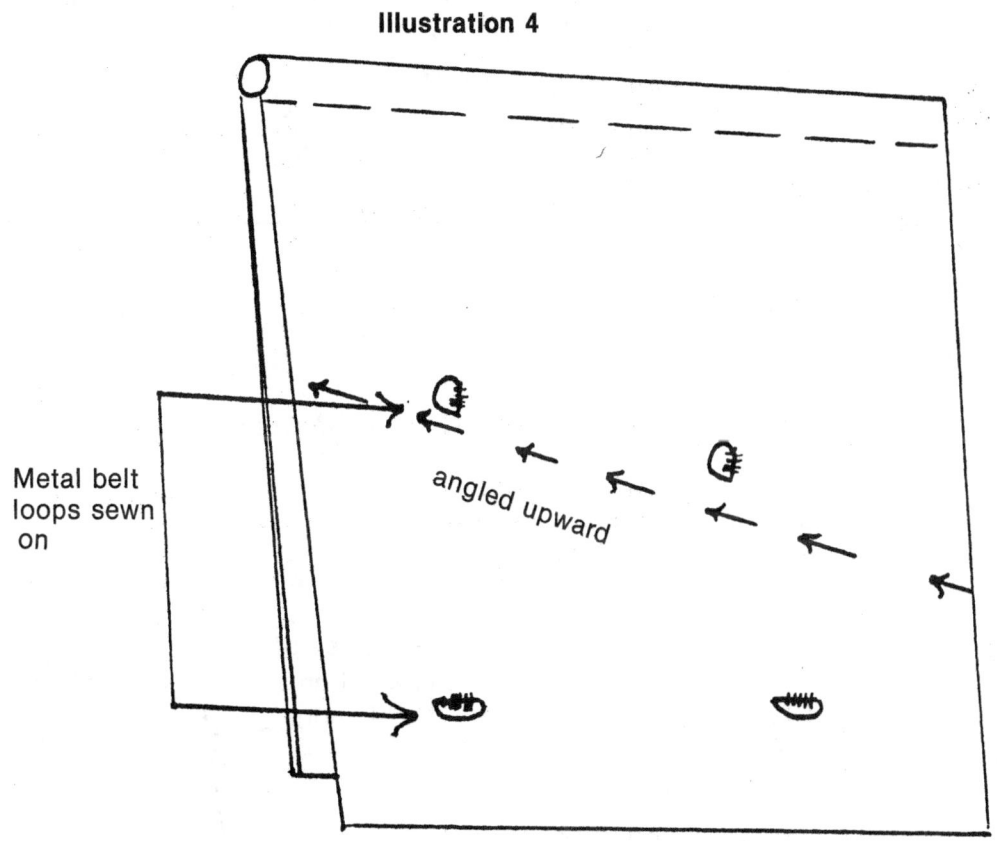

Illustration 4

When constructing crosses, black sewing thread can be used to wrap around the vertical and horizontal pieces of wood. *(See illustration 5.)*

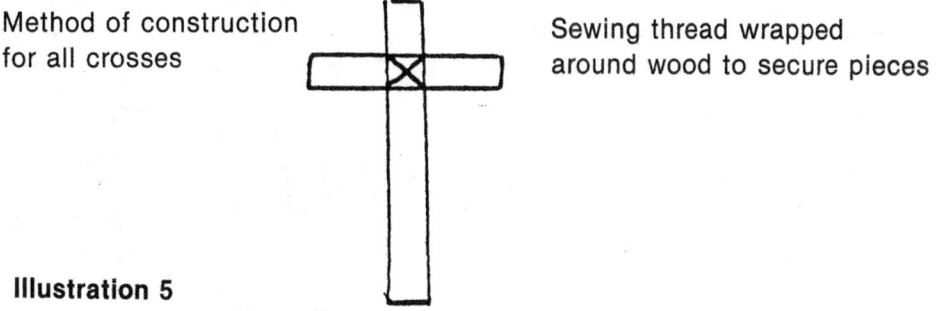

Illustration 5

On Maundy Thursday (or Palm Sunday if your church does not have a Maundy Thursday Service) the small crosses should be added to the right and left hand sides of the banner. The large cross should also be added, equidistant between the smaller crosses. *(See illustration 6.)*

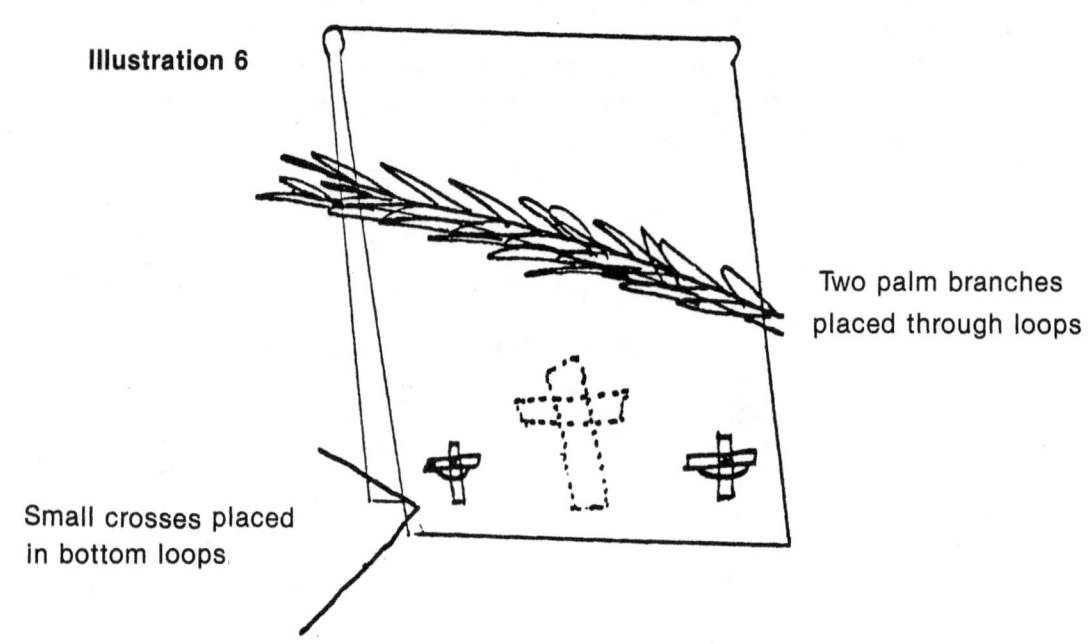

Illustration 6

Two palm branches placed through loops

Small crosses placed in bottom loops

Affixing Large Cross to Banner

Illustration 7

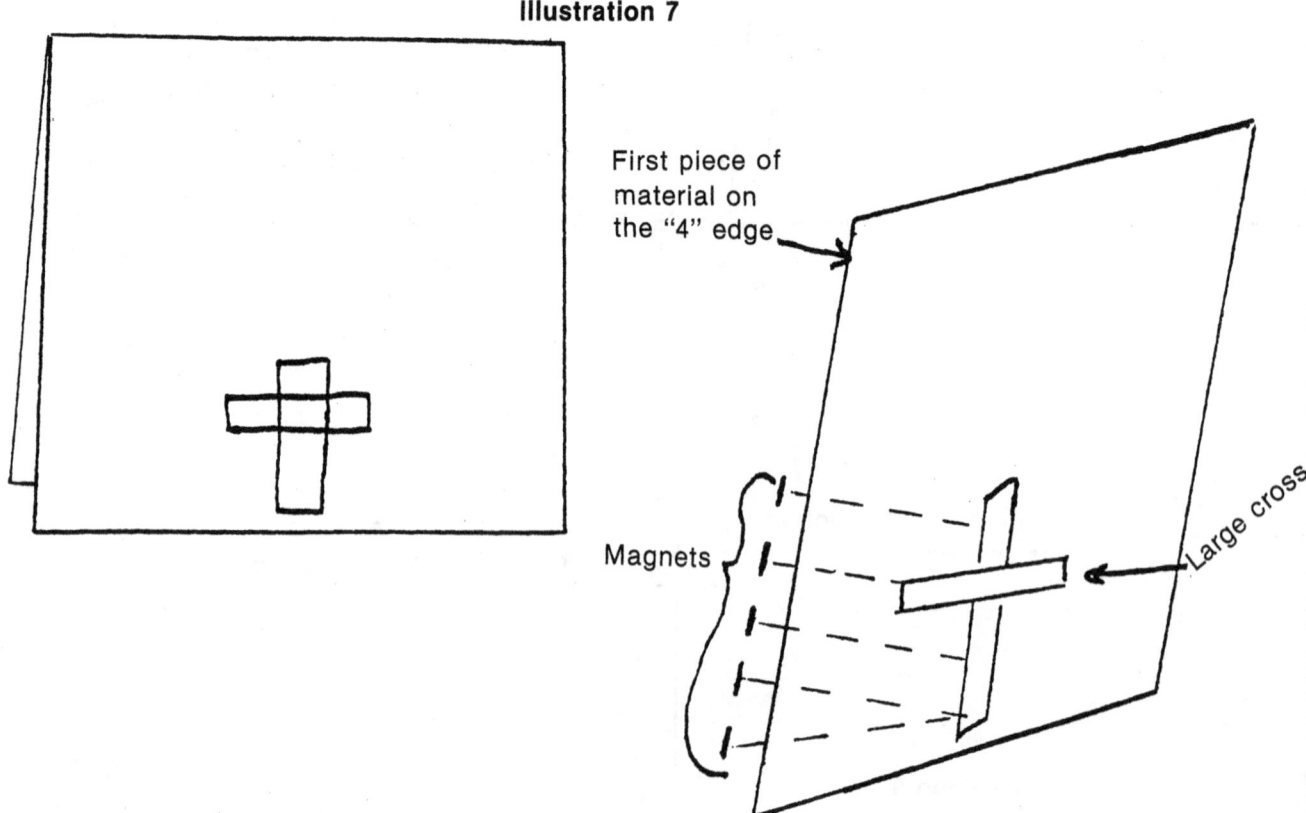

First piece of material on the "4" edge

Magnets

Large cross

The large cross is put on the banner by using magnetic strips — flexible magnetic tape with adhesive backing, ½" wide x 4" long. It can be purchased from hobby supply stores in your area and used as follows. Remove the white paper from the back of the strip and place glue on this sticky substance. (It is not strong enough to adhere to the wood.) It will take four strips (more if you feel necessary) on the vertical piece and two (or more) on the horizontal piece of wood. Someone can hold the cross in place while someone else takes the magnets and applies them to the material directly behind the cross. (See illustration 7.) Reaching into the first section, one can feel the cross magnets and the adhesion of magnet, cloth, magnet, is enough to keep the cross in place. Rather than trying to carry it during worship, this banner does well already in place at the front of the sanctuary. (Processing with the banner would mean additional magnets would be needed to keep the cross in place.)

On Easter Sunday, three white butterflies are added to the top of the banner, forming a triangle. Each butterfly has a magnet strip on its reverse side. As the large cross is put in place, so are the butterflies, with one strip each. The progression is complete and the banner has been used successfully for an entire season.

When ready for storage or cleaning, the magnets are removed as are the symbols that held them in place. The only permanent objects remaining on the banner will be the metal loops.

It will be necessary to use bulletin inserts to allow your congregation to fully understand the symbolism used in the progressive banner. Sample bulletin inserts, used at Grace United Methodist Church, Arlington, Texas, follow. When printing, it is helpful to use the season's liturgical color, as it helps your congregation become more aware of its significance.

Palm Sunday Additions to the Banner

The progressive banner became part of our Sanctuary decor on [Date]. Until this time the banner has remained plain, with the purple symbolizing mourning, fasting, suffering, and the color that Christ wore when he was mocked.

Today we see additions; symbolic additions: The palm represents the triumphant entry of Jesus into the city of Jerusalem and marks the beginning of Holy Week.

Beneath this statement one could add some Scriptures for Holy Week or other information pertaining to Lent. Another insert example that could be used for Easter Sunday is:

The Easter Banner

Three white butterflies are positioned at the top of the banner in the shape of a triangle.

The Color: White symbolizes purity, glory and joy.

Triangle: symbolizes the Holy Trinity; the butterflies are positioned to represent the Father, Son and Holy Spirit. The topmost butterfly is a symbol of Christ risen from the dead and the promise of eternal life.

Butterfly: symbolizes the resurrection and eternal life as it emerges with a glorified body, able to fly into the sky.

The three crosses and palm branches are still on the banner. The progressive banner is interpreted from the middle, to the bottom, then to the top. The total banner reflects the essence of the Easter Story.

Your group's banners will receive many comments from your congregation because they will be innovative, creative and original. They will help enhance your services and begin to allow your groups to think about other ways to design and fabricate for other occasions. New and different materials will have been used for these banners, and the results of hard work, patience and cooperation will reap many unspoken rewards.

A Banner for Advent

The Advent Banner will require patience and a good amount of time. It is also progressive and will allow one week "lead time" between symbols that are selected for the banner. The inspiration for this third example banner came from a book called *The Jesse Tree,* by Raymond and Georgene Anderson; Stories and Symbols for Advent. It is published by Fortress Press and is also available from Cokesbury. This banner is progressive and multipurpose, since it will be fabricated on the back of the Lenten Banner. *(Note: for churches on small or limited budgets, this multipurpose progressive banner is very practical.)*

A tree trunk of felt sections stretches from the top of the banner to the bottom. Four branches "grow" from specific points on the tree and from these branches will come the symbols used during Advent. It will be necessary to remove all of the symbols from the Progressive Lenten Banner and turn it over to its unused sides. Since the Advent Banner may be used for only four Sundays, your group will have to select five symbols to use on your Jesse Tree. *(This will give you the opportunity to use two symbols on Christmas Sunday. Note: the Lenten banner will actually be inside rather than just turned to the backside.)*

Materials needed for the Jesse Tree Banner:

• Reverse side of the Progressive Lenten Banner, or length of material described in Lenten Banner example
• Dark brown felt, two 12" x 12" squares
• Light brown felt, five 12" x 12" squares
• Cardboard squares, approximately six inches by six inches
• Velcro. Enough for all applications, approximately 6 feet long
• White Glue or adhesive of your preference
• A variety of yarn scraps of many colors
• The book, *The Jesse Tree*
• Scissors

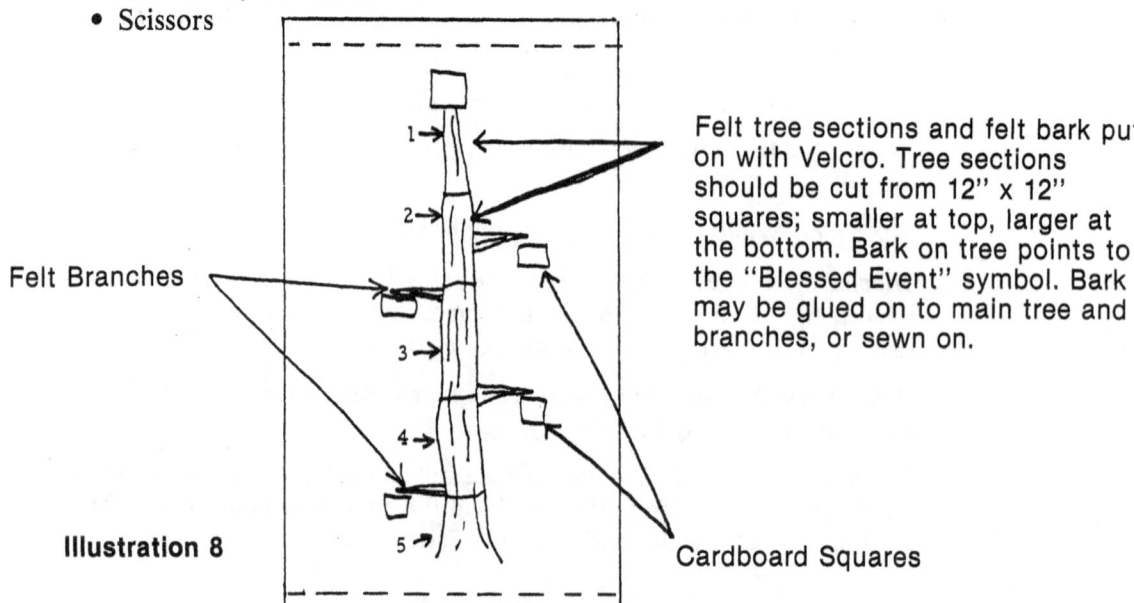

Illustration 8

Turn the Lenten Banner completely over so that it is inside now and two completely unused sides are exposed. The first items needed will be the felt pieces. They may be applied to the banner fabric with any type of adhesive, or they may be sewn on. Velcro was used on the original, so using the Velcro again would simplify cleaning. See the example of the "tree" on page 292 for layout.

Symbols used from the first through the fourth Sundays in Advent were, from the bottom to the top of the tree: Apple and Serpent, Advent Rose, Angel, Mary and Manger, and (at the top) Chi Rho.

The process used to fabricate the symbols is called Yarn Painting. The yarn paintings can be attached to the banner by gluing a piece of Velcro on the reverse side of the cardboard symbol and also putting a piece of Velcro under each branch so that when the symbol is attached, it will appear to be hanging on the given branch.

To begin the first symbol, select a given symbol from the book. For this example the Serpent and Apple will be explained. Take a piece of cardboard and the symbol and decide what colors of yarn will be needed. Yellow, green, browns, and red are the suggested colors. (*Note: it is important, when fabricating symbols, that they appear to be what you wish them to be at a distance of ten feet from the congregation.* Up close they will appear very basic). It is best to start from the outside of the cardboard and work toward the center. Drawing an outline of the subject on the cardboard is helpful, since it will be the guide and this process is slow and time consuming. The next illustration is a full size drawing of the Apple and Serpent, to give one an idea of how basic the finished design should be. Colors have been suggested for each area of the symbol. When beginning a yarn painting, it will be necessary to lay a "bead" or line of glue or adhesive, around the edge of the cardboard, this will begin the boarder of the design. Select a long piece of brown yarn and press it into the glue with your finger(s). It will be necessary to follow around the edge completely; then move in to form a new line which will continue around the cardboard and butt up against the first piece glued in place. *(See illustration.)* Continue around until the center symbol has been reached. Since the symbol has been drawn in, the lines can be followed until the background has been completed. It may be necessary to let the first three rows of yarn dry before going on to the next step. (Each symbol may take from ten to eighteen hours to complete.)

After the background is complete, begin working on the leaves of the apple. Green yarn can be curved around the leaf outline and gently held in place as the glue firms up. As one works with yarn painting, one will develop methods of one's own for executing this technique. If necessary, refer to Illustration 9 for "helps" while working on the first symbol.

One of the most unique and innovative symbols that can be chosen from the book is that of Mary and the Manger. The cardboard shape that is needed for this symbol will be different from the original squares. In the original symbol created for the banner displayed at Grace United Methodist Church, Arlington, Texas, eight different types of yarn and threads were used to create the feeling at the ten foot distance. On close observation one would note a star shape used to outline the top of the cardboard bringing together the bottom of the symbol. The book drawing gives the designer the opportunity to be creative with this symbol *(See illustration 10.)* We need to caution at this point that the backing Velcro should not be allowed to touch the completed paintings. It will literally destroy given sections of your hard work and make one wish that Velcro had never been invented!

Illustration 9

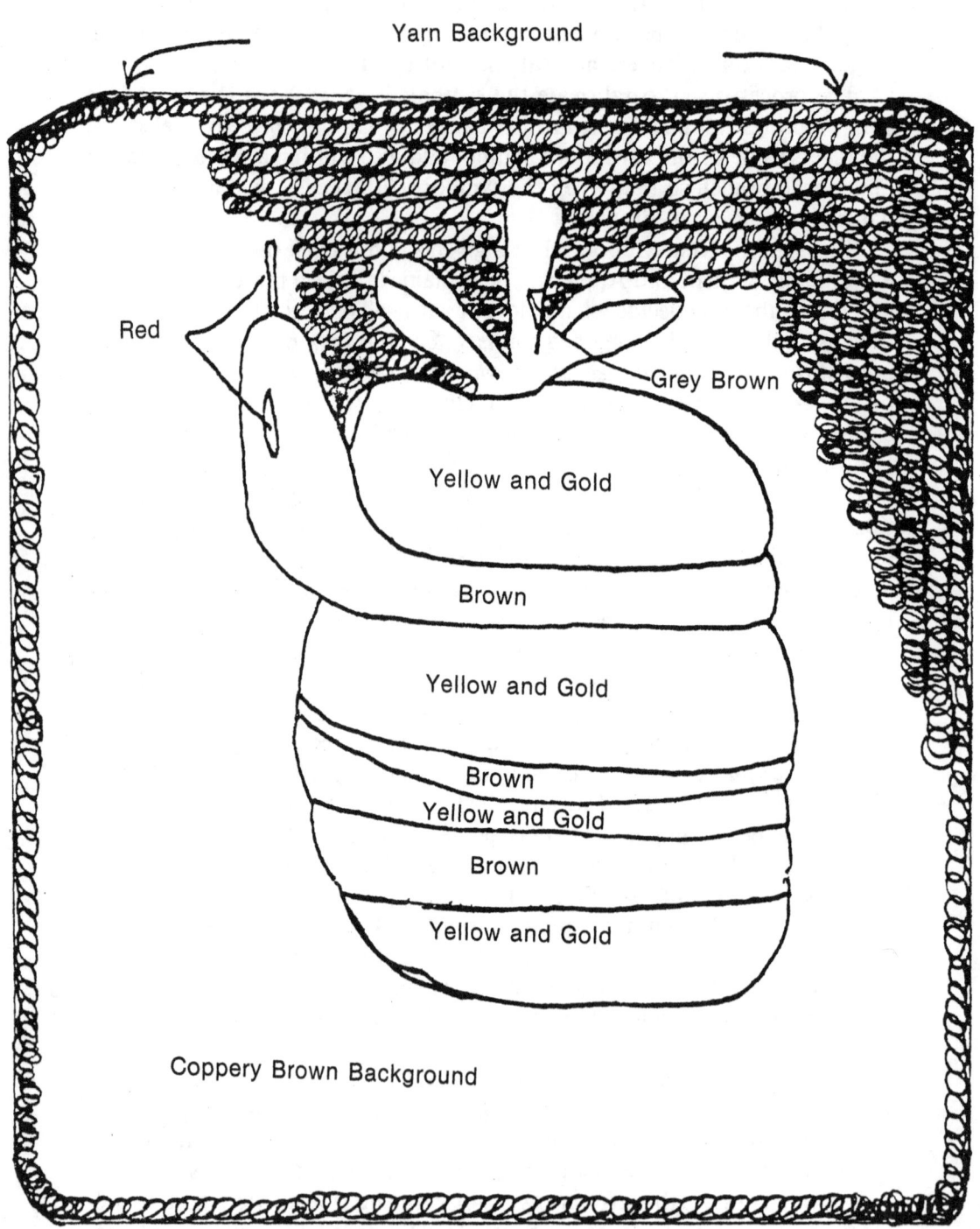

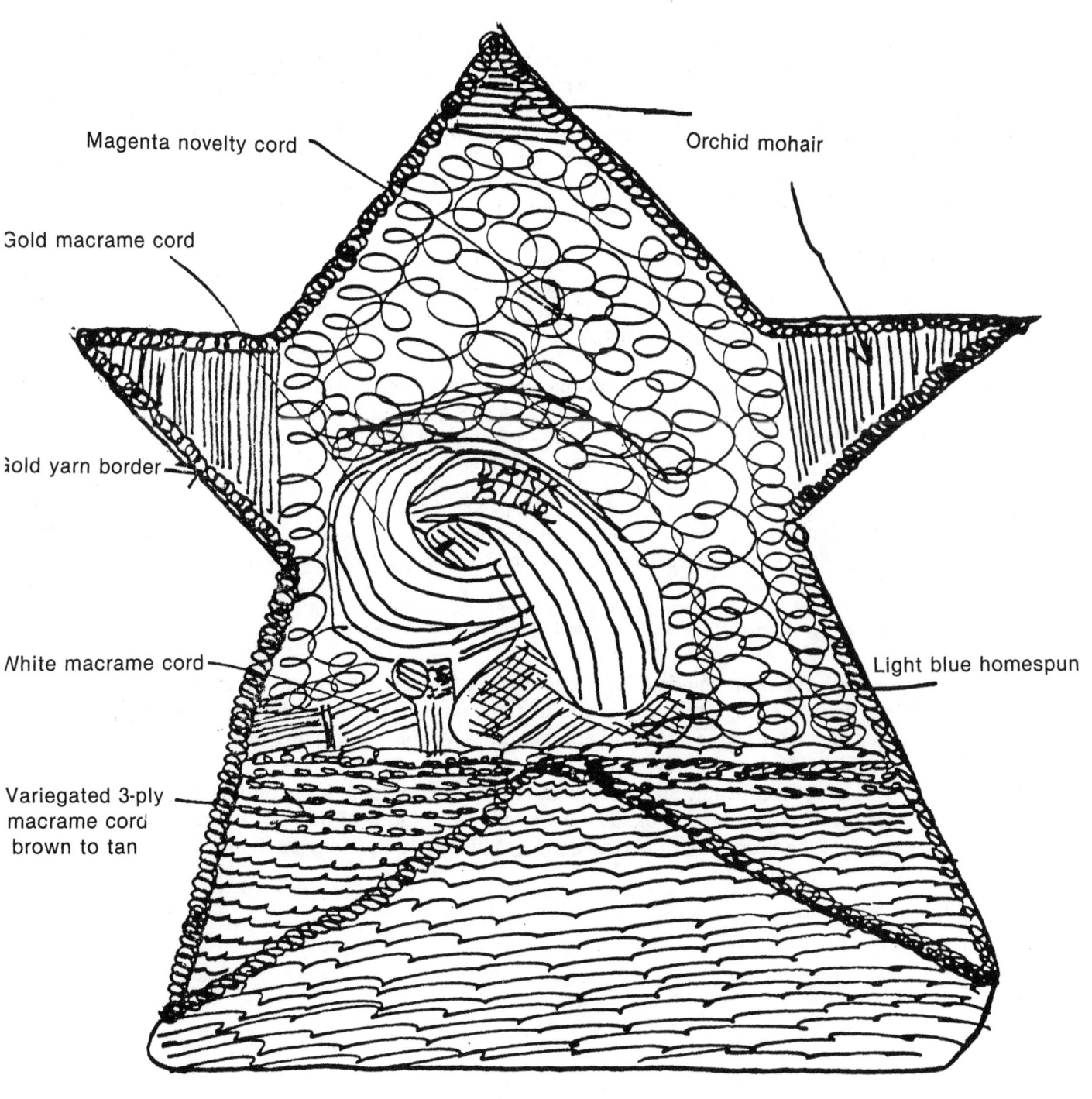

Illustration 10

It will be necessary to explain to the congregation what the Jesse Tree is and what each symbol represents. Below is a sample bulletin insert, originally printed on paper of the season's color, purple (if you don't reverse the Lent banner for this one, your Advent banner and bulletin could be blue, a recently more popular Advent color).

Advent Banner

For the next four Sundays, we will be celebrating the season of Advent with the sights and sounds which will, we hope, focus our hearts and minds on the coming of the Christ Child.

Symbolic Expression

During the Advent season, the banner theme will be that of *The Jesse Tree*. The idea of the Jesse Tree is derived from Samuel 16:1-13. Jesse was the father of David, who was anointed by the prophet Samuel to establish a royal family.

One-thousand years later, Jesus was born into the royal line, in Bethlehem, the ancient city of David. Because of this family tree, the names of Jesse and David are often linked, in poetry and song, with Jesus, "anointed one" (this is the literal meaning of Messiah or Christ).

The Old Testament tells us, for example, "There shall come forth a shoot from the stump of Jesse and a branch shall grow out of his roots." (Isaiah 11:1) In Advent, we link this prophecy with Jesus: "O come, thou Rod of Jesse, free thine own from Satan's tyranny."

Today, the first symbol represents the first week in Advent. Adam and Eve, symbolized by the apple and the serpent. A person must live, goes a popular dodge by which we often try to justify our worst actions. Call it what you will — self-centeredness, self-defense, self-preservation — these are the roots of sin in all its forms. From the beginning of human existence this was so, causing humankind to exalt its own will above God's will. Sin makes us more beast-like than God-like. It binds us to earth when we are capable of heaven. Yet, like a haunting dream, the voice of God is eternally calling us upward . . .

Selected excerpts, illustrations, and ideas are adapted from *The Jesse Tree* by Raymond and Georgene Anderson, Copyright © 1966 by Fortress Press. Used by permission.

Each following Sunday, for the remaining Sundays in Advent, an insert was used to explain the progression of the banner. Sometimes the text was used directly from the book and at other times paraphrased, giving the credit line at the bottom of the insert.

The contact people at your church may have additional ideas on how to use the material in the book. These are only suggestions of how one church handled the problem of disseminating symbology to the congregation.

Banner Display

Since Grace United Methodist Church, Arlington, Texas, was a "beginning church," our budget was such that inexpensive, temporary methods of banner display were necessary. Materials for the first banner pole were as follows:

- Six-foot long broom handle with screw end
- One foot long piece of broom handle with screw end intact
- One piece of PVC pipe connector with screw-in capability for broom handle (the reducing end takes plain end of the short piece)
- One PVC "T" of the same diameter as the short broom handle. Short piece screws into "T" and is glued in place as are the other connections
- Remainder of broom handle sawed into two equal pieces
- Remaining pieces glued into "T"
- Two cup hooks (screwed into end pieces and bent outward)
- Cafe curtain rod (fits into cup hooks to hold banner to pole)

The base was made from four right triangles cut from a sheet of ¾" plywood and nailed together. For added strength, it would be necessary to glue these pieces together. (*See illustration 11.*)

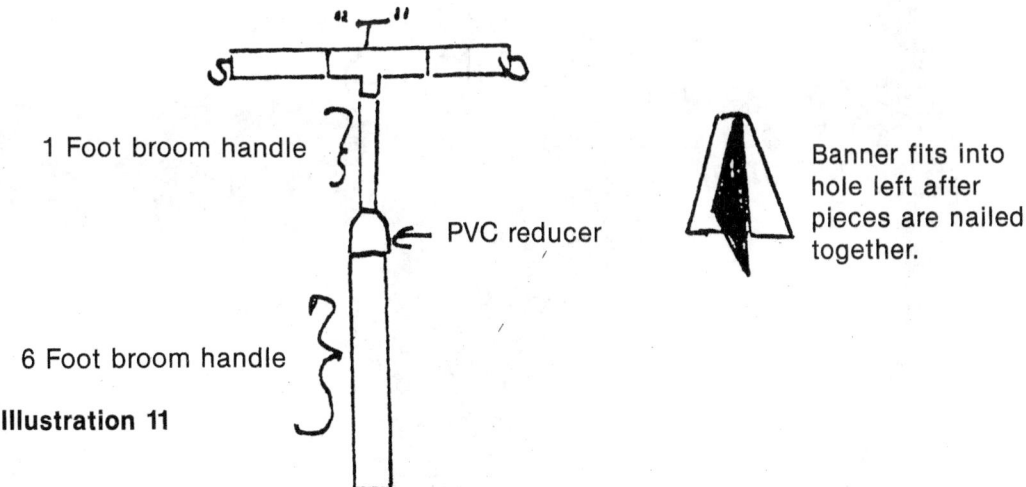

Illustration 11

The cafe curtain rod is placed through the top of the sewn piece of the banner and is fastened to the cup hooks. The hooks are turned up, holding the rod and banner in place (***Note:*** *the cafe curtain rod should have a small hole in either end to hook onto the cup hooks.*)

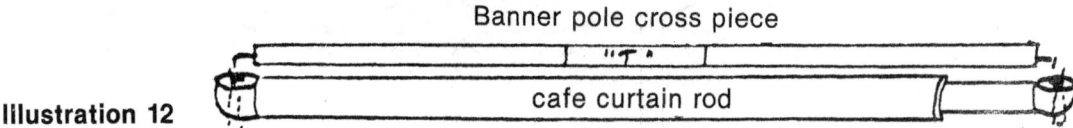

Illustration 12

Visuals

Visuals can play an important role in the church. They can be hung above or at eye level to describe a total season or special event. They may be sculptural, two- or three-dimensional, and used to reinforce an idea one may have for a banner theme.

One Visual will be described in this section. It is distinct and fairly easy to fabricate.

Lenten Visual

A Visual that can be used throughout the Season of Lent can be fabricated from simple materials. The basic symbols used for this Visual are a butterfly, cross, crown of thorns, encompassed in a hoop. (*See illustration 13.*)

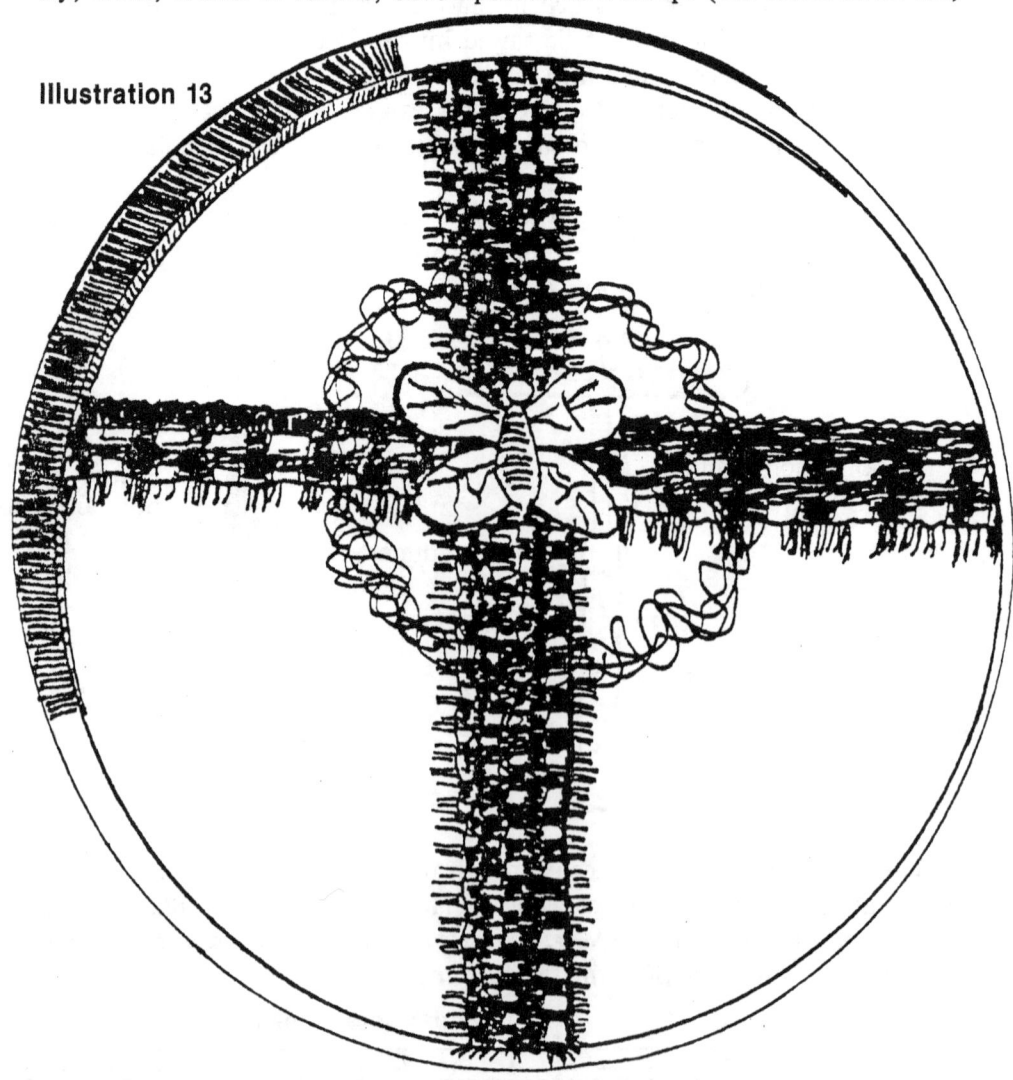

Illustration 13

Materials required for the Visual:

• Wooden hoop, 22 inches in diameter or smaller, one inch wide and ¼" thick. (*Note: Hoops may be purchased from hobby stores or from the following Mail Order House: Grey Owl Indian Craft Company, Incorporated, 113-15 Springfield Boulevard, P.O. Box 507, Queens Village, New York, 11429. Catalog available at $1.00.*)
• Purple or lavender yarn
• Macrame cord (2 or 3 ply, thin cord or dark colored rug yarn)
• Butterfly, 12" long red (pipecleaner type) chenille (available from hobby or specialty shops). This would be the same size butterfly as used in the Progressive Lenten Banner — 4" x 4"
• Red open weave upholstery trim (available from fabric shops), 70" in length
• Tapestry needle
• Scissors
• Vine for Crown of Thorns. You can use Virginia Creeper, grapevine, or any vine with or without thorns. Secure enough to make a circle eight inches in diameter
• Thin wire or clear monofilament fishing line to use as a hanger

Construction

Begin construction by wrapping the hoop with lavender or purple yarn *(See illustration.)* Wrapping may be done with long, continuous pieces of yarn or many shorter pieces. It is preferable to use several shorter pieces of yarn, since beginners sometimes find that this method is easier to handle.

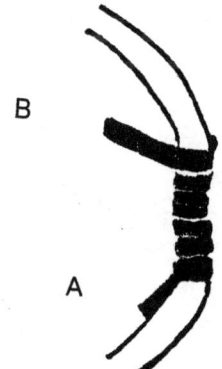

Illustration 14

To wrap the hoop, take a piece of yarn and tape end A to the hoop. Wrap the hoop so that no wood shows through. When end B is about three inches long, thread a tapestry needle and work end B back into the previously wound section at least four wraps and pull through. Snip off excess yarn and begin the process again, until the complete hoop has been wrapped. It is *very important* to keep wraps close and tight or it will not remain flush with the hoop. When the first piece of yarn has been wrapped on and end B has been pulled through, untape end A, thread the tapestry needle, and pull this end through four wraps. Cut off the excess and start with the next piece of yarn. Wraps can sometimes be pushed down to meet the last wrapped area.

When the hoop wrapping has been completed, it will be necessary to thread the hoop vertically. With the dark colored yarn or cord, thread the tapestry needle and catch one, inside wrap, near the top of the hoop and pull the cord through. Knot the end so that all of the cord does not pull out. Go to the bottom of the hoop and run the tapestry needle through a loop of wrap. Pull tight (but not so tight that the hoop becomes an oval). It must be taut but not rigid. Continue this up and down looping until an area one inch wide by 21 inches (or other hoop diameter) has been done. This will support the vertical piece of the cross. The horizontal support should be the same length and width as the vertical support. Using your eye as a measuring device, move down about a quarter of the way from the top of the hoop. Begin stringing the horizontal support. When it has been finished there will be a cross in the hoop (*see illustration*).

Illustration 15

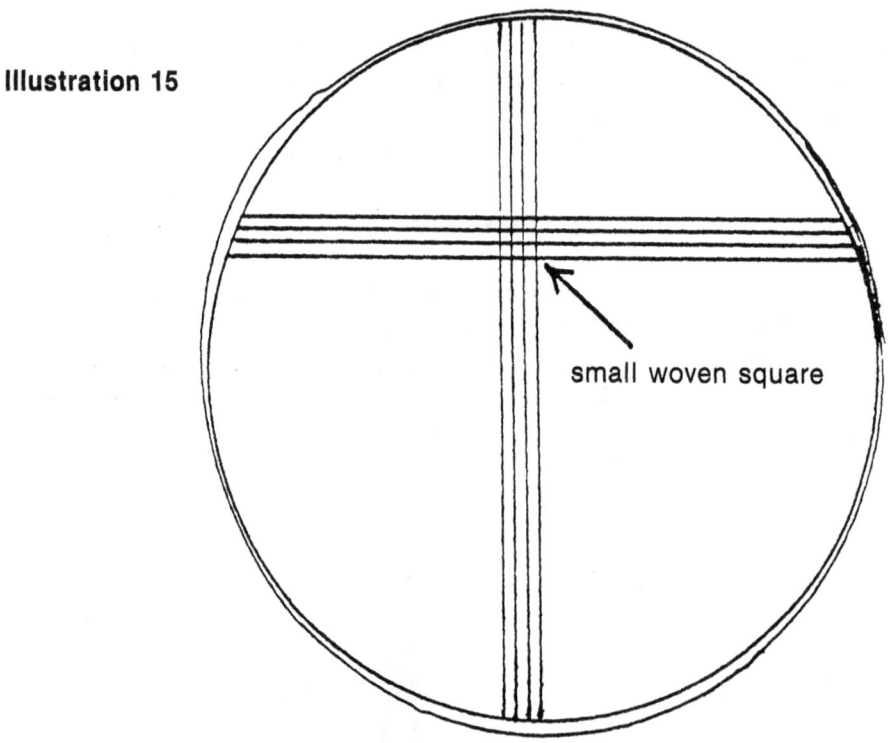

When the horizontal support is added, the support yarn should be woven over and under the vertical support strands so that a small woven square appears in the middle of the hoop. Cut three pieces of upholstery trim the same length as the cross supports and lay them on the work table. Two of the pieces should be sewn together, straight edge to straight edge, with the "frilly" sides facing out. This will be the vertical section of the cross. Sew the upholstery trim to the support with needle and thread. The third piece of trim will be used as the horizontal piece of the cross. This should be sewn on the horizontal support with the frilly edge facing down, and the straight edge lined up evenly with the top of the support (*see illustration 16*).

Illustration 16

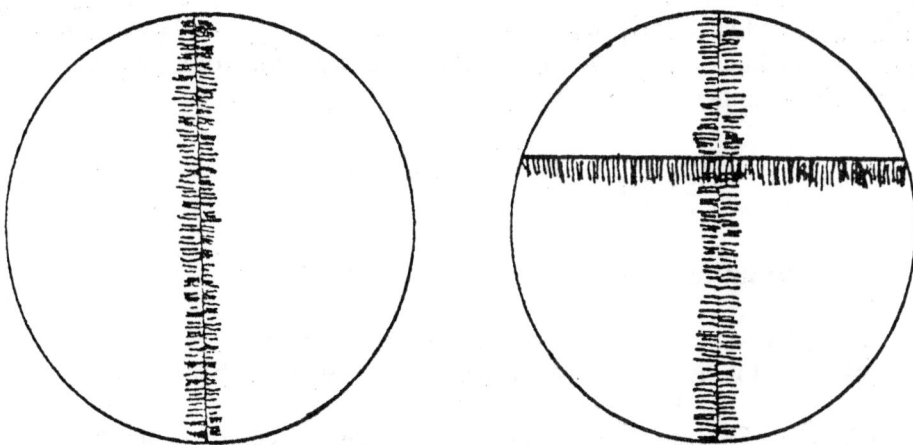

Illustration 16 has been simplified for easier interpretation of this step.

The Crown of Thorns, when wrapped around the cross, should form equal quarters at the center, letting the background color show through. The last step is the fabrication of the butterfly symbol for the center of the Visual. Using a butterfly that measures 4" x 4" from wing tip to wing tip, and a body measurement of two inches, glue two each together for stiffness. The design side should face outward. Using a red chenille, one foot long, glue to the back of the butterflies so that it (chenille) can be bent 90 degrees just above the point of gluing. Run the chenille through the upholstery material and bend it down in back of the Visual and secure it to the cross support. At the top of the Visual, one will need to connect a piece of wire or monofilament line so that the Visual can be suspended from a wall.

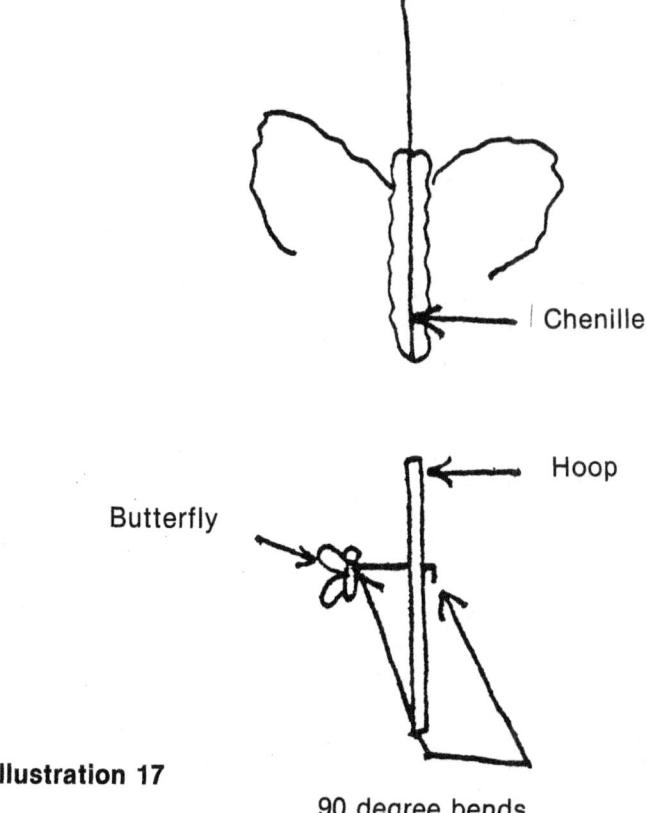

Illustration 17

90 degree bends

In order to inform the congregation of the meaning of this Lenten Visual, the following could be used. On the front of the bulletin, at the beginning of Lent, a drawing of the likeness of the Visual could be used *(see illustration 13)*. On the back of the bulletin a symbolic description could be given in the following manner:

A Visual for Lent

Symbolic Interpretation:

Latin Cross: the form of the cross upon which our Lord was crucified. The oldest and most basic in design used as a Christian symbol.

Crown of Thorns, the Cross, the colors red and purple: symbolize Christ's suffering.

White Butterfly: white is for purity, glory and joy. The butterfly symbolizes the resurrection and eternal life.

Your own interpretation should be added to make the visual more meaningful to you.

This sample bulletin could be printed on the liturgical color for the season — purple. This visual could be used in addition to a banner in the sanctuary or in the narthex. It could also be used in place of a banner.

A hoop Visual might be used at different times during the church year to enhance or emphasize a given idea or theme. The above illustration was used by Bethel United Methodist Church in Fort Worth, Texas while the Visual was on loan during Lent 1985.

www.ingramcontent.com/pod-product-compliance
Lightning Source LLC
Chambersburg PA
CBHW060509300426
44112CB00017B/2596